True love

2 CORINTHIANS 8–13

by James Hughes

thegoodbook
COMPANY

True love
The Good Book Guide to 2 Corinthians 8–13
© James Hughes/The Good Book Company, 2018.
Series Consultants: Tim Chester, Tim Thornborough,
                    Anne Woodcock, Carl Laferton

The Good Book Company
Tel (UK): 0333 123 0880
Tel: (US): 866 244 2165
Email (UK): info@thegoodbook.co.uk
Email (US): info@thegoodbook.com

Websites
UK: www.thegoodbook.co.uk
North America: www.thegoodbook.com
Australia: www.thegoodbook.com.au
New Zealand: www.thegoodbook.co.nz

ISBN: 9781784981266

Printed in Turkey

CONTENTS

Introduction: Good Book Guides

Every Bible-study group is different—yours may take place in a church building, in a home or in a cafe, on a train, over a leisurely mid-morning coffee or squashed into a 30-minute lunch break. Your group may include new Christians, mature Christians, non-Christians, mums and tots, students, businessmen or teens. That's why we've designed these *Good Book Guides* to be flexible for use in many different situations.

Our aim in each session is to uncover the meaning of a passage, and see how it fits into the "big picture" of the Bible. But that can never be the end. We also need to appropriately apply what we have discovered to our lives. Let's take a look at what is included:

⊕ **Talkabout:** Most groups need to "break the ice" at the beginning of a session, and here's the question that will do that. It's designed to get people talking around a subject that will be covered in the course of the Bible study.

⊕ **Investigate:** The Bible text for each session is broken up into manageable chunks, with questions that aim to help you understand what the passage is about. The **Leader's Guide** contains **guidance for questions**, and sometimes ⊗ additional "follow-up" questions.

⊙ **Explore more (optional):** These questions will help you connect what you have learned to other parts of the Bible, so you can begin to fit it all together like a jig-saw; or occasionally look at a part of the passage that's not dealt with in detail in the main study.

→ **Apply:** As you go through a Bible study, you'll keep coming across **apply** sections. These are questions to get the group discussing what the Bible teaching means in practice for you and your church. ⊡ **Getting personal** is an opportunity for you to think, plan and pray about the changes that you personally may need to make as a result of what you have learned.

⊙ **Pray:** We want to encourage prayer that is rooted in God's word—in line with his concerns, purposes and promises. So each session ends with an opportunity to review the truths and challenges highlighted by the Bible study, and turn them into prayers of request and thanksgiving.

The **Leader's Guide** and introduction provide historical background information, explanations of the Bible texts for each session, ideas for **optional extra** activities, and guidance on how best to help people uncover the truths of God's word.

Why study 2 Corinthians 8 – 13?

"We have spoken freely to you, Corinthians, and opened wide our hearts to you ... I speak as to my children—open wide your hearts also ... I will not be a burden to you, because what I want is not your possessions but you ... So I will very gladly spend for you everything I have and expend myself as well."

(2 Corinthians 6 v 11, 12 and 12 v 14, 15)

Welcome to one of Paul's most deeply personal letters.

Many think of 2 Corinthians as a "difficult" letter of the apostle Paul, and we need to read it carefully to understand his relationship with the Corinthian church. But it reveals a great deal about Paul himself, showing us his passion both for God's truth and for Christ's people, and a heart filled with true love—Christ-like love—for this church.

And the church in Corinth desperately needed such love. These Christians struggled to accept struggle, prioritising prosperity over faithfulness. They eagerly followed those offering fame and fortune rather than loyalty to God's word. Their problems were, essentially, with failing to understand and appreciate how Jesus loves us, and how we are to love each other. They were heading for spiritual danger, and needed to hear sometimes hard truths. Paul loved them enough to set out those truths in the second half of this letter.

We Christians now are really not so different from those in first-century Corinth. We too need to hear Paul speak to us today, encouraging us, challenging us, warning us—loving us. We study this letter then because it speaks to us as it spoke to them.

In these seven studies, covering the last six chapters of this letter, you'll see Paul's zeal, faith, grief, sacrifice and humility—the fruit of his devotion to Christ and the gospel—and you'll be changed by true love.

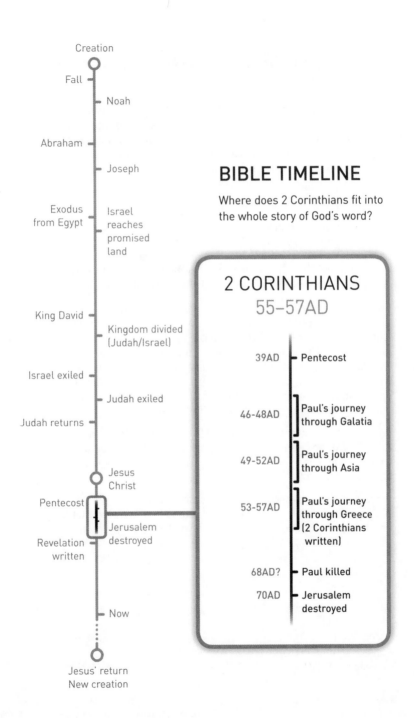

Creation

Fall

Noah

Abraham

Joseph

Exodus from Egypt

Israel reaches promised land

King David

Kingdom divided (Judah/Israel)

Israel exiled

Judah exiled

Judah returns

Jesus Christ

Pentecost

Jerusalem destroyed

Revelation written

Now

Jesus' return
New creation

BIBLE TIMELINE

Where does 2 Corinthians fit into the whole story of God's word?

2 CORINTHIANS
55–57AD

39AD	Pentecost
46-48AD	Paul's journey through Galatia
49-52AD	Paul's journey through Asia
53-57AD	Paul's journey through Greece (2 Corinthians written)
68AD?	Paul killed
70AD	Jerusalem destroyed

1

2 Corinthians 8 v 1-24

GIVING AND RECEIVING I: FOLLOWING GOOD EXAMPLES

The first seven chapters of 2 Corinthians are perhaps some of the most personal in all of Paul's letters: they deal with his understanding of what ministry is, in the face of challenges from the church in Corinth. It is full of memorable phrases and ideas: how we have the light of the gospel as "treasure in jars of clay" (4 v 7), how Paul is Christ's ambassador (5 v 20), and how, facing opposition and persecution, Paul has "nothing", yet possesses "everything" (6 v 10).

The subject matter changes a bit as we reach chapters 8 – 9, which focus on giving; but then in chapters 10 – 13 Paul is forced to give a "boasting" defence of his gospel and ministry against "false apostles". But although this is a very personal lesson, it is full of insight into what it means to live for Christ day by day, and the reality of living in a fallen world.

⊕ talkabout

1. What's been your experience of hearing the subject of money and giving mentioned or discussed in church?

• What's your reaction, and why do you think you react like that?

⊕ investigate

2 Corinthians 8 and 9 form a distinct part of Paul's letter, dealing with one of the topics we often don't like to talk about in church—money. In the first two studies, we'll look at what Paul says about a collection for the Christians in Jerusalem, to see how it helps us have the right perspective on giving, and receiving; and to discover and reflect upon some important principles of giving.

❯ Read 2 Corinthians 8 v 1-8

There are two examples to learn from in this passage. This first is that of the Macedonian churches, which would include the Thessalonians, Philippians and Bereans.

2. What does the "grace" that the Macedonian churches have been given look like (v 1-3)?

3. How did the Macedonians view their giving (v 3-5)?

4. What does Paul want the Corinthians to do (v 6-8)?

• What should their motivation be (v 8)?

5. To help summarise this section, make a list of the words used in verses 1-8 to describe giving.

⮕ apply

6. How does the giving of the Macedonians compare with your experiences of money and giving in church?

• What difference should the Macedonian example make to us?

⊡ getting personal

Think over what you have learned about the Macedonians.

• They were richly generous.
• They gave as much as they could and more.
• They were eager to help.

Which of these things would you like people to be able to say of you?

What do you need to do now to make that possible?

⬇ investigate

▶ **Read 2 Corinthians 8 v 9-15**

7. How does Paul want the Corinthians to follow the example of Christ (v 9-11)?

8. What makes the gift acceptable (v 12)?

9. What are the principles of giving and receiving set out in verses 13-15?

- What would the family of God's people look like if we were to follow Paul's instructions?

⊡ explore more

optional

> **Read 2 Corinthians 8 v 16-24**

Why is Titus coming to see the Corinthians (v 16-17, v 23)?
What are the qualifications of the two "brothers" (the first mentioned in v 18-19; the second in v 22)?
What is Paul's concern here (v 19-21)?
What should the Corinthians do, and why (v 24)?
What does these brothers' example tell us about dealing with money?

⊟ apply

10. What principles of giving have we learned today?

• How are you going to apply these principles to your own giving?

⊡ getting personal

"You know the grace of our Lord Jesus Christ, that though he was rich, yet for your sake he became poor, so that you through his poverty might become rich."

Do you feel rich?

If not, why not, do you think? And how can you come to appreciate your true wealth in Christ?

If yes, is that seen by others? How can your life display the riches that Christ has given to you?

⬆ pray

Spend some time praying for anything that has come up in the study—but particularly:

• for generous hearts that desire to give to the Lord's work.

• for wisdom in knowing how and what to give.

• for a fuller understanding of all that we have received in Jesus Christ.

2

2 Corinthians 9 v 1-15

GIVING AND RECEIVING II:
TRUSTING, SOWING, REAPING

The story so far

Generosity is a natural outworking of giving ourselves to the Lord, as we imitate the examples of Jesus and those who sincerely love him and his people.

⊕ talkabout

1. What might make people—and you too, perhaps—reluctant to give generously?

⊥ investigate

In this study we conclude our look at Paul's teaching about money and giving in 2 Corinthians 8 and 9. Look out for principles that help us grow the right attitude to money and giving, while keeping in mind the principles we learned last time.

❯ Read 2 Corinthians 9 v 1-5

Here we see how Paul wants the Corinthians to respond, and what we can learn from their example—both positively and negatively.

DICTIONARY
Achaia (v 2): the region around Corinth.

2. Why does Paul say he has "no need to write" (v 1-2)?

3. Why are the brothers being sent (v 3-5)?

4. Why do you think that Paul writes as he does in these verses (look back at 8 v 8 and 12)?

⇥ apply

5. How might these verses help us to keep going in our commitments—in giving, and in church life more generally?

⊡ getting personal

"I know your eagerness to help, and I have been boasting about it."

Would Paul be able to say this about you if he were here today? Would he also be concerned that his confidence might be misplaced?

In what area could you make an eager commitment to help others? How can you make sure that you carry out that commitment?

▶ Read 2 Corinthians 9 v 6-15

6. What is the principle set out in verse 6?

DICTIONARY

Sows (v 6): plants seed.
Reap (v 6): harvest.
Under compulsion (v 7): feeling you have to.
Abound (v 8): overflow; thrive.

- What does "reap generously" actually mean (see Proverbs 11 v 24-27 and 1 Timothy 6 v 17-19)?

- How do people get this wrong?

7. How does God help us to be generous, cheerful givers (2 Corinthians 9 v 7-10)?

optional

⊡ explore more

> **Read Psalm 112**

What kind of people are described in this psalm (v 1, 6)?
What do these people do (see especially verse 9)?
How does this passage help us to understand what Paul is saying in 2 Corinthians 9?

8. Why does God enrich his people (v 11)?

9. What effect will the Corinthians have on the world when they give generously (v 12-15)?

10. What principles of giving do you see here?

- Now make a "master list" of the principles of giving found in 2 Corinthians 8 and 9.

⤷ apply

11. Which of these principles of giving have you been most struck by, and why?

- What will help you become a more cheerful and more generous giver?

⊡ **getting personal**

"Thanks be to God for his indescribable gift."

Paul wants us to reflect on all that we have received in Christ Jesus. How will reflecting on this gift help you to use the gifts God has given you?

⬆ **pray**

Spend some time praying for anything that has come up in the study—but particularly:

• for faithfulness to carry out your promises.

• for complete trust in God's abundant grace to supply all that you need to be generous.

• for increasing love between fellow Christians, and that your own giving would result in increasing praise of God.

3
2 Corinthians 10 v 1-18
BOLDNESS AND BOASTING:
SERVANT-HEARTED LEADERSHIP

The story so far

Generosity is a natural outworking of giving ourselves to the Lord, as we imitate the examples of Jesus and those who sincerely love him and his people.

Our faithful, cheerful, generous giving doesn't just help others, but also enriches us; and it brings glory to God, causing people to praise him.

⊕ talkabout

1. How do you respond when someone tells you what you should do?

⊕ investigate

Paul has just challenged the Corinthians about giving. Now, in a very personal and quite difficult section of the letter, he reveals his deep love and concern for them, and how he might need to behave when he visits them again. Here in chapter 10 Paul writes about appropriate boldness, and appropriate boasting. He challenges us all to think about how we respond to those in authority over us.

▶ Read 2 Corinthians 10 v 1-11

2. What do the Corinthians think about Paul, and what are they saying about him (v 1, 7-11)?

DICTIONARY

Pretension (v 5): claim.

• What does Paul understand about his own ministry (v 7-8)?

3. What is Paul's plea to the Corinthians (v 1-2)?

4. What is the "warfare" that Paul is waging (v 3-6)?

⊡ **explore more**

optional

❯ **Read Ephesians 6 v 10-18**

Can you summarise what it means in practice to be fully armoured as a Christian?
What is the weapon of attack mentioned here?
What does the Christian's "armour" mean in practice for the task of winning people's hearts, minds and souls, to bring them into obedience to Christ—as we've seen Paul labouring to do with the Corinthians?

5. How does Paul see the relationship between his visits and his letters (v 1, 9-11)?

6. Why do you think Paul writes so strongly here?

⊕ apply

7. How might Paul's example help us in those situations where we need to be bold in speaking to our brothers and sisters in Christ?

⊕ investigate

❯ **Read 2 Corinthians 10 v 12-18**

8. Why won't Paul compare himself with those who are commending themselves (v 12)?

> **DICTIONARY**
>
> **Classify (v 12):** identify; group with.
> **Commend (v 12):** promote.
> **Sphere (v 13):** area.

• What will Paul boast in, and what won't he boast about (v 13-15)?

9. What is Paul's plan and how does it involve the Corinthians (v 15-16)?

10. What is the ultimate antidote to inappropriate boasting (v 18)?

11. How would you describe Paul's attitude in verses 12-18?

→ **apply**

12. Think about how Paul wants the Corinthians to respond to what he says in this passage. What can we learn from that desired response?

⊡ getting personal

"For it is not the one who commends himself who is approved, but the one whom the Lord commends."

In what ways do you need to modify your behaviour in the light of 2 Corinthians 10, so that it is commendable to your Lord?

⊤ pray

- Pray for wisdom in discerning who we should listen to.
- Pray for your leaders, and for help in following them.
- Pray for the strength and courage to follow Paul's example of humble boldness.

4 2 Corinthians 11 v 1-15
TRUTH AND DECEPTION:
TRUE GOSPEL MINISTRY

The story so far

Generosity is a natural outworking of giving ourselves to the Lord, as we imitate the examples of Jesus and those who sincerely love him and his people.

Our faithful, cheerful, generous giving doesn't just help others, but also enriches us; and it brings glory to God, causing people to praise him.

True servant-hearted leaders of God's people sometimes need to speak boldly to correct error, and look to the Lord alone for commendation.

⊕ talkabout

1. What kind of qualities do you look for in a preacher or Bible teacher?

⬇ investigate

In chapter 10 Paul began to defend his ministry, by talking about how he might have to be "bold" if the Corinthians refuse to listen to him, and how he only boasts in what the Lord does through him. In chapter 11 he starts to take on the problem of some other teachers whom the Corinthians liked to listen to, contrasting his approach with theirs.

❯ Read 2 Corinthians 11 v 1-7

2. What is Paul's attitude towards the Corinthians (v 1-2)?

> **DICTIONARY**
>
> **Snake (v 3):** the devil (see Genesis 3 v 1-5; Revelation 12 v 9).
> **Sincere (v 3):** real, rather than faked.

3. What does he fear (v 3-4)?

4. Who is leading the Corinthians astray (v 4-5)?

5. Why do the Corinthians find the teaching of the "super-apostles" more attractive than Paul's (v 5-6)?

⊡ explore more

optional

❯ **Read Genesis 3 v 1-7**

What does the snake say about God in these verses?
Why does Eve decide to eat the fruit (v 6)?

⊟ apply

6. Why are Christians deceived by false teaching today? Why do they "put up with it"?

⊡ **getting personal**

"But I am afraid that … your minds may somehow be led astray from your sincere and pure devotion to Christ."

What do you need to watch out for so that you are not led astray?

⊥ investigate

> ❯ **Read 2 Corinthians 11 v 7-15**

7. How was Paul supported while in Corinth (v 7-9)?

> **DICTIONARY**
>
> **Masquerading (v 13):** pretending to be; acting as.

8. What is Paul's boast (v 10; see also 10 v 13 and 17)?

• Why will Paul keep on boasting (v 10-12)?

9. How have the Corinthians misinterpreted Paul's approach in bringing the gospel to them?

10. How would you characterise the false apostles from this chapter?

11. What qualities of Paul come through from this chapter?

🠒 **apply**

12. How can we make sure we're not deceived by "deceitful workers"?

⬆ **pray**

Pray for all those who preach in your church, that God will give them the character, knowledge and skills that they need.

Pray that your church will be a place that honours godly wisdom and teaching, supremely in the true gospel of the real Jesus.

5 2 Corinthians 11 v 16-33
SUFFERING AND SUCCESS:
THE CHRISTIAN LIFE

The story so far

Our faithful, cheerful, generous giving doesn't just help others, but also enriches us; and it brings glory to God, causing people to praise him.

True servant-hearted leaders of God's people sometimes need to speak boldly to correct error, and look to the Lord alone for commendation.

We need to be able to distinguish genuine servant-hearted gospel teachers from outwardly impressive but manipulative and money-grabbing counterfeits.

⊕ talkabout

1. How do we measure success? What makes something or someone successful?

⊥ investigate

In this section we find some clear indications of the problems in Corinth, including that of false teachers (11 v 13)—the so-called "super-apostles" (v 5). Paul wants his readers to understand what makes a good apostle, and therefore what it takes to follow Christ.

> **▶ Read 2 Corinthians 11 v 16-33**

2. Why should the Corinthians "put up with" Paul's boasting (v 16-19)?

DICTIONARY

Puts on airs (v 20): pretends to be better than they are.
Abraham (v 22): the ancestor of Israel.
Gentiles (v 26): here, Paul is referring to non-Christian non-Jews.

3. What was Paul too "weak" to do (v 20-21)?

• So how is Paul different from those the Corinthians were listening to?

⊕ apply

4. What kinds of things will gospel-hearted people boast in, that the world would probably try to keep hidden?

⊡ getting personal

What do you "boast" in? Should anything change so that you boast less in the wrong things and more in the right thing?

⊕ investigate

5. What does Paul "boast" about first (v 21-22)?

6. How does Paul show that he is a servant of Christ (v 23-27)?

7. How does Paul relate to all the churches (v 28-29)?

8. Why does Paul boast in his weakness (v 30-31)?

9. Why might Paul's boasting have offended or surprised the Corinthians?

Paul wants the Corinthians to see what being a servant of Christ is really about. Some in Corinth seemed to think that serving Christ was about success, power and prestige, and Paul wants to set them straight.

10. How does this passage help us understand "success", and what is of value?

• v 23-27

• v 28-29

• v 31

☺ **explore more**

optional

❯ **Read Matthew 16 v 24-25**

What do you think Jesus himself might have said to the super-apostles?

→ **apply**

11. How should we adjust our priorities in life to follow Paul's example?

☺ **getting personal**

What is going to be different about your week next week as a result of what you've seen in this passage? Be specific!

⊡ pray

- Pray for a heart that is concerned for other Christians.
- Pray for the courage to face challenging situations and suffering.

6
2 Corinthians 12 v 1-21
STRENGTH IN WEAKNESS:
AN APOSTLE'S HEART

The story so far

True servant-hearted leaders of God's people sometimes need to speak boldly to correct error, and look to the Lord alone for commendation.

We need to be able to distinguish genuine servant-hearted gospel teachers from outwardly impressive but manipulative and money-grabbing counterfeits.

In genuine gospel ministry we don't avoid suffering, but instead we suffer for Christ.

⊕ talkabout

1. How do you deal with situations where everything you do seems to be wrong?

⊕ investigate

Having been very "foolish" for the last two chapters, Paul now wants the Corinthians to see that he has spoken like that out of concern for their welfare; and he wants them to respond to his warnings before he has to come and see them. Now he has one final lesson about strength and weakness to give them.

> **▶ Read 2 Corinthians 12 v 1-10**

2. What is Paul "boasting" about (v 1-4)?

DICTIONARY

I know a man (v 2): the "man" is almost certainly Paul!
Warranted (v 6): fair; justified.
Conceited (v 7): proud.
Sufficient (v 9): enough.

3. Paul had a great spiritual experience. But how does he want the Corinthians to respond to him (v 5-6)?

4. Why was Paul given a thorn in the flesh that wasn't taken away (v 7-9)?

• What does this reveal about the purpose of weakness?

5. What is Paul's attitude to strength, suffering and weakness (v 10, see also v 5)?

⮕ apply

Paul experienced spiritual highs—and physical lows. Yet throughout, his focus was not on his experiences, but on the Lord Jesus Christ.

6. How can Paul's attitude to suffering and weakness help us in our walk with Christ?

⊡ getting personal

"My grace is sufficient for you, for my power is made perfect in weakness."

What is God seeking to teach you right now about your weakness and the way his power can be at work in and through you? Are you willing to learn those lessons?

⊡ explore more

❯ Read Acts 5 v 40-42 and 12 v 1-5; 1 Peter 4 v 1-2

What does the apostle Peter teach us about suffering?

⊡ investigate

❯ Read 2 Corinthians 12 v 11-21

7. Why should the Corinthians have commended Paul (v 11-12)?

> **DICTIONARY**
>
> **Discord (v 20):** arguing; tension.
> **Slander (v 20):** deliberate and damaging false statements about other people.
> **Debauchery (v 21):** indulging in sexual sin.

8. Why was Paul never a burden to the Corinthians (v 13-15)?

9. What else shows that Paul hasn't wronged the Corinthians (v 16-18)?

10. Why has Paul written about his ministry (v 19-21)?

11. What does this passage tell us about Paul's heart for the Corinthians?

→ **apply**

12. What have we learned from Paul about following the right priorities in dealing with people?

↑ **pray**

- Pray for wisdom in dealing with people who you find difficult.
- Pray for a willingness to embrace weakness in the service of Christ.

7
2 Corinthians 13 v 1-14
WEAKNESS AND STRENGTH:
GOD'S WORK IN US

The story so far

We need to be able to distinguish genuine servant-hearted gospel teachers from outwardly impressive but manipulative and money-grabbing counterfeits.

In genuine gospel ministry we don't avoid suffering, but instead we suffer for Christ.

Weakness doesn't invalidate true gospel ministry and spectacular-sounding experiences don't validate it; both show Christ's power at work in us.

⊕ talkabout

1. Think back to the last time you filled in a resumé or a job application, or had a job interview, or something similar. What did you find hard about it?

⊥ investigate

In this final section of 2 Corinthians, Paul is encouraging the Corinthians to be ready for his next visit. However, there are some things they need to do to make sure that they are ready.

▶ **Read 2 Corinthians 13 v 1-14**

2. What will Paul's purpose be when he visits (v 1-2)?

> **DICTIONARY**
> **Testimony (v 1):** evidence.

• What does the quotation in verse 1 (from Deuteronomy 19 v 15) show us about how he will do this?

3. How should the example of Christ change the way the Corinthians view Paul (2 Corinthians 13 v 3-4)?

4. Given what Paul has said so far in this letter, how do the Corinthians need to test themselves (v 5)?

5. What is Paul's primary concern in verses 6 and 7?

6. Why might Paul sometimes seem to be a failure (v 7-8)?

7. What has motivated Paul's letter to the Corinthians (v 9-10)?

• What do the Corinthians need to do to be ready for Paul's visit?

optional

⊡ explore more

> ▶ **Read 1 Corinthians 13 v 8-13**

What is Paul looking forward to in this passage?
How does this passage help us to understand the supremacy of love?
How does this help us to understand Paul's concerns in 2 Corinthians 10 – 13?

⊖ apply

8. How can we help each other to examine ourselves about our faith?

⊡ getting personal

"Do you not realise that Christ Jesus is in you?"

How are you going to allow the truth that Christ lives in you by his Spirit help you in weakness and suffering?

investigate

9. How does Paul encourage and challenge the Corinthians in verses 11-14?

apply

Paul wants the Corinthians to examine themselves, in light of all he has taught them, to be ready when he comes. Though not expecting an imminent visit from an apostle, we too can learn from Paul's teaching.

10. Think back over what we have learned from 2 Corinthians 8 – 13. Where do we need to examine ourselves in the light of this letter? How will this help us to rely on Christ?

getting personal

Write down one particular thing that has struck you in 2 Corinthians 8 – 13, which, with the Lord's help, you want to work on changing.

pray

Pray through your responses to Question 10 and the Getting Personal section.

True love
LEADER'S GUIDE

Leader's Guide

INTRODUCTION

Leading a Bible study can be a bit like herding cats—everyone has a different idea of what the passage could be about, and a different line of enquiry that they want to pursue. But a good group leader is more than someone who just referees this kind of discussion. You will want to:

- correctly understand and handle the Bible passage. But also…

- encourage and train the people in your group to do this for themselves. Don't fall into the trap of spoon-feeding people by simply passing on the information in the Leader's Guide. Then…

- make sure that no Bible study is finished without everyone knowing how the passage is relevant for them. What changes do you all need to make in the light of the things you have been learning? And finally…

- encourage the group to turn all that has been learned and discussed into prayer.

Your Bible-study group is unique, and you are likely to know better than anyone the capabilities, backgrounds and circumstances of the people you are leading. That's why we've designed these guides with a number of optional features. If they're a quiet bunch, you might want to spend longer on *talkabout*. If your time is limited, you can choose to skip *explore more*, or get people to look at these questions at home. Can't get enough of Bible study? Well, some studies have optional extra homework projects. As leader, you can adapt and select the material to the needs of your particular group.

So what's in the Leader's Guide? The main thing that this Leader's Guide will help you to do is to understand the major teaching points in the passage you are studying, and how to apply them. As well as guidance for the questions, the Leader's Guide for each session contains the following important sections:

THE BIG IDEA

One or two key sentences will give you the main point of the session. This is what you should be aiming to have fixed in people's minds as they leave the Bible study. And it's the point you need to head back toward when the discussion goes off at a tangent.

SUMMARY

An overview of the passage, including plenty of useful historical background information.

OPTIONAL EXTRA

Usually this is an introductory activity that ties in with the main theme of the Bible study, and is designed to "break the ice" at the beginning of a session. Or it may be a "homework project" that people can tackle during the week.

So let's take a look at the various different features of a Good Book Guide:

talkabout

Each session kicks off with a discussion question, based on the group's opinions or experiences. It's designed to get people talking and thinking in a general way about the main subject of the Bible study.

⊌ investigate

The first thing you and your group need to know is what the Bible passage is about, which is the purpose of these questions. But watch out—people may come up with answers based on their experiences or teaching they have heard in the past, without referring to the passage at all. It's amazing how often we can get through a Bible study without actually looking at the Bible! If you're stuck for an answer, the Leader's Guide contains guidance for questions. These are the answers to direct your group to. This information isn't meant to be read out to people—ideally, you want them to discover these answers from the Bible for themselves. Sometimes there are optional follow-up questions (see ✅ in guidance for questions) to help you help your group get to the answer.

⊡ explore more

These questions generally point people to other relevant parts of the Bible. They are useful for helping your group to see how the passage fits into the "big picture" of the whole Bible. These sections are OPTIONAL—only use them if you have time. Remember that it's better to finish in good time having really grasped one big thing from the passage, than to try and cram everything in.

➔ apply

We want to encourage you to spend more time working at application—too often, it is simply tacked on at the end. In the Good Book Guides, apply sections are mixed in with the investigate sections of the study. We hope that people will realize that application is not just an optional extra, but rather, the whole purpose of studying the

Bible. We do Bible study so that our lives can be changed by what we hear from God's word. If you skip the application, the Bible study hasn't achieved its purpose.

These questions draw out practical lessons that we can all learn from the Bible passage. You can review what has been learned so far, and think about practical differences that this should make in our churches and our lives. The group gets the opportunity to talk about what they personally have learned.

⊡ getting personal

These can be done at home, but it is well worth allowing a few moments of quiet reflection during the study for each person to think and pray about specific changes they need to make in their own lives. Why not have a time for reporting back at the beginning of the following session, so that everyone can be encouraged and challenged by one another to make application a priority?

⬆ pray

In Acts 4 v 25-30 the first Christians quoted Psalm 2 as they prayed in response to the persecution of the apostles by the Jewish religious leaders. Today however, it's not as common for Christians to base prayers on the truths of God's word as it once was. As a result, our prayers tend to be weak, superficial and self-centred rather than bold, visionary and God-centred.

The prayer section is based on what has been learned from the Bible passage. How different our prayer times would be if we were genuinely responding to what God has said to us through his word.

1

2 Corinthians 8 v 1-24
GIVING AND RECEIVING I

THE BIG IDEA
We need to be generous with our resources, following the example of God's people (the Macedonians) and of Christ himself.

SUMMARY
2 Corinthians chapters 8 – 9 form a distinct section in Paul's letter, dealing with a collection for the Christians in Jerusalem—i.e. dealing with money. If you are following straight on from looking at 2 Corinthians 1 – 7 (see True discipleship: The Good Book Guide to 2 Corinthians 1 – 7), this can feel like quite a change of gear.

The new direction here is indicated by 8 v 1, as Paul introduces the example of the Macedonians. He mentions various things about how the Macedonians have given, which should be imitated by the Corinthians. Titus has come to urge them (v 6), and now Paul urges them (v 7), to be as good at giving as they feel themselves to be at other things.

Paul is clear that he is not commanding the Corinthians (v 8), but he does want them to look at their own love compared to that of others: the Macedonians (v 1-5), and also Jesus Christ (v 9). And so they are to finish the work which they started, and to give what they can willingly (v 10-12).

Paul adds some general comments on giving and receiving (v 13-15). Note the principle here: that those who have plenty supply those who don't, confident that the Lord himself will supply.

For an outline of verses 16-24, see the Explore More section.

Note: Before you begin this study, decide

how you are going to use the "Explore More" section (after Question 9). It helps us think about the importance of being trustworthy with money, and gives additional material for reflection on what makes good giving and receiving.

OPTIONAL EXTRA
If people know each other: Each person selects or is given the name of another person in the group, and writes down a gift they would give that person. Ask what each will give and why. Suggested gifts will probably vary widely for different reasons, including: someone's need, what can be afforded, what the giver likes, what the giver thinks they can get away with, etc. When asking the reason for the gift, listen out for answers like, "Because you told me to". This should be a light-hearted activity, but the point is to see how our attitudes to giving might need to match up better with Paul's instructions to the Corinthians.
If people don't know each other well: Do the same activity but use pictures of people taken from magazines or the internet. (Refer back to people's reasons for giving when you come to apply Questions 6 or 10.)

GUIDANCE FOR QUESTIONS
1. What's been your experience of hearing the subject of money and giving mentioned or discussed in church?
• **What's your reaction, and why do you think you react like that?**
These questions are designed to get people thinking about money and giving. Churches don't generally talk about money without mentioning giving, and people may offer a

number of responses. A flipchart or similar might be useful here.

If your group are slow to answer, try playing a game of word association: everybody gives one word to do with "church and money". If you want to spend more time on this question, you could draw up two lists of positive and negative responses. If helpful, tease out why people feel negative about giving. If lack of trust is the issue, reflecting on 8 v 16-24 may be particularly helpful (see Explore More). (You could refer back to these answers in Question 6.)

2. What does the "grace" that the Macedonian churches have been given look like (v 1-3)? It's the grace to give generously and joyfully. (Here "grace" is used as we might use the word "gift".) It results in generosity: giving as much as they are able (v 3), based on their overflowing joy (v 2). The amount they give is not set but varies according to what people have.

3. How did the Macedonians view their giving (v 3-5)? Clearly they viewed it as a privilege (v 4): something that they wanted to do for others, and as a natural part of giving themselves to the Lord (v 5). This is an important principle: giving generously is a natural outworking of being part of God's people, and not an added extra just for some.

4. What does Paul want the Corinthians to do (v 6-8)? The Corinthians are to follow the example of the Macedonians, and excel in the grace of giving.

• **What should their motivation be (v 8)?** Paul is testing the sincerity of their love. Do the Corinthians mean it when they say they love fellow Christians or the Lord? For Paul, giving to help other Christians in need is about far more than doing the

right thing or being a good witness. It's a matter of whether we truly love Jesus and his people—and, more widely, humans created by God.

5. To help summarise this section, make a list of the words used in verses 1-8 to describe giving. It may be helpful to write up answers. Among them will be giving as:
• grace (v 1, 6, 7).
• the privilege of sharing (v 4).
• service to the Lord's people (v 4).

6. APPLY: How does the giving of the Macedonians compare with your experiences of money and giving in church? Refer back to the answers given in Question 1. Contrast what people have seen of giving in churches, or how they have approached it themselves, with the following characteristics of the Macedonians:
• Their giving wasn't hindered by severe trials or extreme poverty (v 2).
• It was accompanied by overflowing joy (v 2).
• They gave as much as they were able to, and even beyond (v 3).
• They took the initiative in giving (v 3).
• They viewed it as a privilege and begged to do it (v 4).
• They exceeded Paul's expectations in their giving (v 5).
• Their giving flowed out of their relationship with the Lord—seeing themselves in submission to and service of him. In other words, it was part of their worship (v 5).

• **What difference should the Macedonian example make to us?** It should move us as it was intended to move the Corinthians—to encourage us to be generous, and to see giving as a natural part of our life in Christ. Do spend some time teasing this out, but remember the study is not over, and that there is an opportunity to revisit these issues in Question 10.

7. How does Paul want the Corinthians to follow the example of Christ (v 9-11)?
The Corinthians should follow Christ's example because he sacrificed what he had for the sake of others who were in need. We are to respond to the LOVE of Christ. (If some are not familiar with the gospel, take them through what verse 9 means: that Christ became poor—in coming to earth and dying on a cross for us—so that we might be rich—having a restored relationship with God through Christ's death, which we did not earn and do not deserve.) Paul's advice is simple: *Get on with it! You started well; now finish well. Don't worry about the final amount, as long as you have given what you can.*

8. What makes the gift acceptable (v 12)?
The gift is acceptable based on ability to give, not absolute amounts. This is an important principle that crops up a number of times in the passage: give what you can. It should encourage everyone to give.

9. What are the principles of giving and receiving set out in verses 13-15?
The principle here can be summarised as: give not to make your life difficult, but for you to give out of abundance to others that don't have enough, so that at some future time they might do the same for you.

- **What would the family of God's people look like if we were to follow Paul's instructions?** We'll be a family where no one lacks what they need just because they are weaker or going through hard times. No one need be anxious about providing for themselves in the future. No one has to be in debt, or a workaholic,

or feel guilty that they can't give much, or feel shamed by poverty. In fact, when God's people live in God's way, we form the kind of community that the whole world would like to be part of.

EXPLORE MORE
Read 2 Corinthians 8 v 16-24
We read here that Titus is coming to see the Corinthians (v 17), to help them make good on their promises. There will be two other people with Titus: a brother mentioned in verse 18, and "our brother" mentioned in verse 22. Their job isn't so much to help Titus gather the offering, but to make sure that everyone knows that the offering is being properly administered. Therefore, Paul makes a lot of their qualifications: how they are chosen by the churches, how they are servants of the gospel, and so on. It seems that he wants the Corinthians to have confidence that everything is being done properly.

Why is Titus coming to see the Corinthians (v 16-17, v 23)? He is concerned for the Corinthians (v 16); Paul has asked him to come, and he wants to (v 17). He is also well qualified to be Paul's representative as a fellow worker (v 23).

What are the qualifications of the two "brothers" (the first mentioned in v 18-19; the second in v 22)? We don't know why the two brothers aren't named. It may be because they are not well known to the Corinthians, or because the Corinthians already know who they are! Or perhaps Paul wants to focus on their qualities, rather than who they are.

So what are the first brother's qualifications? First, he is praised by all the churches for his service to the gospel—that is, for being a gospel worker, sharing the good news of Jesus Christ. Second, he is praised, and has been chosen, by the churches—probably those in Macedonia and Achaia (modern-day Greece). Third, he has been chosen to accompany Paul in carrying the offering—not because the churches didn't trust Paul, but so that everything can be seen to be done properly.

The qualifications for the second brother are similar: he is eager and zealous (v 22) and represents the churches (v 23).

What is Paul's concern here (v 19-21)? That he honours the Lord and that people know he is eager to help with the offering (v 19); and also that no one can criticise how the gift is administered (v 20). He is concerned that everything is being done right before the Lord, but also before men (v 21); he doesn't want there to be any accusations of "financial irregularity". We might be surprised by this statement, because Paul often says that he is concerned not about what men think, but what the Lord thinks: he fears the Lord, not men (e.g. 5 v 11). But here he is concerned about how people view the offering, probably because the willingness of the Corinthians to give will be related to whether they trust those who handle the money., but certainly because financial irregularity, or even what only appears to be such, will dishonour the Lord.

What should the Corinthians do, and why (v 24)? The Corinthians should give generously—showing all the churches the proof of their love and the reason for Paul's pride in them, by their generosity. They can give generously because of all that has been said so far in chapter 8, but particularly—from what is suggested in verses 16-24—because they can have confidence in those administering the gift.

What does these brothers' example tell us about dealing with money? The answer to this question will depend on the perspective of your group. If you have

people serving in administrative roles in the church, they might focus on seeking to have the qualities Paul has talked about here. Others might discuss how to recognise those qualities in administrators, and therefore be willing themselves to give generously.

10. APPLY: What principles of giving have we learned today? Before you reach this question with the group, you could write up each principle of giving as it occurs in the study.

I would summarise them as follows:
- Give generously and joyfully.
- Give what you can.
- Giving is a grace and a service—it is an opportunity, not a burden.
- Giving is part of our natural response to Christ as our Lord and Saviour.

- **How are you going to apply these principles to your own giving?** Spend time teasing out the principles, and then spend time applying them! It might be a good idea to read through each of the principles you have agreed together (again, make use of a flipchart or pieces of paper or sticky notes), to see how they apply to your group.

2 Corinthians 9 v 1-15
2 GIVING AND RECEIVING II

THE BIG IDEA
Our giving doesn't just help others, but also enriches us, and brings glory to God, causing people to praise him; so we should give faithfully, cheerfully and generously.

SUMMARY
In chapter 8 Paul encouraged the Corinthians to follow the example of the Macedonians and of Christ, and to give generously (v 1-15). They had already promised to—now he wanted them to follow through. We saw that the Corinthians could have confidence in those administering the collection (v 16-24).

2 Corinthians 9 v 1-5 contains a number of rhetorical devices—that is, ways of speaking—to help the Corinthians give. So, in verse 1 Paul says there is no need to write about this service (their promise to give) to the Lord's people—but then he writes anyway. He praises them in verse 2 for their eagerness but still sends the brothers to make sure they follow through. In verse 4, he suggests that their failure to give would shame him. All these rhetorical devices are here to encourage the Corinthians, as verse 5 indicates, to give generously.

In verse 6 we come to a key principle: those who sow generously will reap generously. Proverbs 11 v 24 appears to lie behind this passage; in the context of Proverbs, that means this is a general life principle—that generosity to others will, over a lifetime, generally be reciprocated. Verse 7 contains another related principle: give cheerfully what is in the heart.

Then in verses 8-10, we see how God will work in the hearts of his people to enable them to be generous and cheerful givers. They will be like the people of Psalm 112 (see Explore More), giving gifts because God will enlarge their harvest of righteousness.

It is important to notice here a slight shift of emphasis in these verses; once Paul begins to talk about a harvest of righteousness, it is clear that he is not just thinking of riches, or generosity, or reaping in purely financial terms. This isn't just about money as riches, but about God's grace at work in the believer bringing all kinds of riches which can be shared generously. So, in verse 11, they will be generous in every way, and this will bring thanksgiving to God

Finally, in verses 12-15, we return to the language of service (see also 8 v 4), as Paul puts giving in the context of thanksgiving to God. Others will see the generosity of the Corinthians and praise God, and pray for them—even as they express their thanksgiving with generosity.

All this takes place in the context of the indescribable gift of 9 v 15: what God has done in Jesus Christ, and all the consequences of what he has done.

OPTIONAL EXTRA
To illustrate "whoever sows generously will also reap generously" (v 6), give each person 10 units of a "currency" (e.g. M&Ms). Tell them that before they get to enjoy their wealth, you would like them to give some to a worthy cause (e.g. missionaries that you know or a poor church in another country). As people give their chosen number of units, note down the quantity. Then give each person double the amount they've given

(so those who have been more generous will now be better off). Perhaps change the currency at this point (e.g. grapes), since financial giving may result in greater riches but not necessarily money. Ask people to give a second time, and see if the principle of verse 6 has encouraged greater generosity. Again, give people double the amount they've given and explain the point of the exercise. (This activity links with Question 6.)

GUIDANCE FOR QUESTIONS

1. What might make people—and you too, perhaps—reluctant to give generously? There will be all sorts of reasons why people struggle to be generous, including the issues of trust we talked about last time, lack of certainty about what to give to, etc. However, in terms of leading into this study, it would be helpful at least to mention reluctance due to worry about the consequences: "If I give generously, won't that just leave me with less money?" being the (usually unspoken) question here.

2. Why does Paul say he has "no need to write" (v 1-2)? Paul truly does have no need to write because the Corinthians have already expressed their eagerness to help. However, he does write—to remind them that he has told others of their enthusiasm, as an extra encouragement to them to follow through on their promises.

3. Why are the brothers being sent (v 3-5)? To receive the collection and as a final encouragement to the Corinthians to give generously. The brothers will serve as a physical encouragement to give rather than putting it off, as the Corinthians seem to be doing.

4. Why do you think that Paul writes as he does in these verses (look back at 8 v 8 and 12)? Paul wants to encourage the Corinthians to give, and does not want to command them in this matter (8 v 8). He wants to teach them about giving—but then he wants to make the connection with their own actions and give generously, and not grudgingly (9 v 5). If they give just because he commands them, then they will not have given willingly, and that is crucial (8 v 12).

5. APPLY: How might these verses help us to keep going in our commitments—in giving, and in church life more generally? There are a number of possible answers here, which will probably include:
- We need to keep our promises (v 3-4).
- We take seriously our responsibility to others (v 4).
- We look at and learn from the example of others (v 1-2).
- We understand our giving and our commitment as a response to Christ, who loved us so much he died for us (8 v 9).

6. What is the principle set out in verse 6? Those who sow (or give) generously will reap (or benefit) generously, but those who sow (or give) sparingly will reap (or benefit) sparingly.

- **What does "reap generously" actually mean (see Proverbs 11 v 24-27 and 1 Timothy 6 v 17-19)?** Naturally a verse like 2 Corinthians 9 v 6 throws up questions: specifically, what kind of reaping is it that takes place? Proverbs 11 v 24-27 shows us that "reaping" here is what we might call the general benefits of being a generous person. 1 Timothy 6 v 17-19 goes further and shows that Christians who are generous and willing to share store up the kind of treasure that is a firm foundation for their eternal future—"treasure in heaven" as Jesus called it.

- **How do people get this wrong?** The so-called "prosperity gospel", popular in some churches and parts of the world, teaches that if people give generously (especially to the prosperity-gospel teacher's ministry), God will increase their financial wealth. The New Testament, however, does not lead us to expect this automatically, or even usually. Paul didn't promise this to the Macedonians (8 v 1-5); nor did he experience great financial wealth himself as a result of giving to the work of the gospel and fellow Christians (e.g. 11 v 27). Neither did Jesus—our perfect example in every way, including in generosity—ever enjoy great financial wealth (e.g. Matthew 8 v 20).

7. How does God help us to be generous, cheerful givers (2 Corinthians 9 v 7-10)? Notice that God loves a cheerful giver! Make sure people understand that in the context of verse 7, this means someone who has made up his or her own mind about what to give, not under compulsion from others, and not reluctantly—the giver has understood why we should give generously.

(1) God helps us to be generous through his grace at work in us (v 8)—his abundant generosity that we in no way deserve—so we have everything we need to be generous.

(2) Paul then quotes Psalm 112, which is a description of the righteous man and his actions: by God's grace, this is the kind of person we will become.

(3) Finally, in verse 10, we see that we can have confidence in God's provision (at this point, you can link Paul's words here back to the unspoken worry that was

raised in Question 1), and that through being generous we will reap a harvest of righteousness.

EXPLORE MORE
What kind of people are described in this psalm (v 1, 6)? Those who fear the LORD, and so are righteous.
What do these people do (see especially verse 9)? They are marked by justice, mercy, generosity and righteousness—they are godly people. Notice how they give "freely" in verse 9 (also v 5). Godly people show this kind of generosity because they understand that everything they have received from God is a gift of grace.
How does this passage help us to understand what Paul is saying in 2 Corinthians 9? We see here the kind of conduct which Paul wants us to imitate in 2 Corinthians 9—the same attitude to giving and life in general that these people who fear the LORD have.
We also see again that what generous people reap is so much more than merely financial wealth e.g. benefit to their children (v 2), enduring righteousness (v 3), light in darkness (v 4), "good" (v 5), security and strength (v 6) and that they will be remembered, no fear of bad news (v 7), triumph over their foes (v 8), and honour (v 9).

8. Why does God enrich his people (2 Corinthians 9 v 11)? We are made rich by God—and in the context of verse 10 this is clearly not primarily about wealth (God enlarges "the harvest of [our] righteousness"). And for what purpose? So that "[we] can be generous on every occasion". In other words, generosity not only enriches us (we reap generously because we sowed generously), but also means we can be more generous. It's a virtuous circle. Our own personal harvest of righteousness should lead us, and others, to praise God.

9. What effect will the Corinthians have on the world when they give generously (v 12-15)?
We see that in verse 12 their giving overflows in much thankfulness to God. In verses 13-14 others will see their generosity and praise God, and pray for the Corinthians. I also think it is implicit in verse 15 that the Corinthians will recognise that the ability to give is itself a gift from God, and so will give thanks, as Paul does here. It is noticeable here that the gift of generosity will strengthen the bonds of fellowship between brothers and sisters in Christ in different churches and places.

10. What principles of giving do you see here?
• **Now make a "master list" of the principles of giving found in 2 Corinthians 8 and 9.**
Here is another opportunity for members of the group to summarise what we've seen in the study so far. Bear in mind that this question is answered best not when people exactly match up with an approved list, but when they are able to articulate the principles at work here.
Among the principles mentioned from 9 v 1-15 will be the following:
• Keep your promises about giving.
• Give generously and cheerfully.
• What we give—whether generous or otherwise—will have an impact on our own Christian growth (i.e. we will reap in accordance with how we have sown).
• God will supply what we need, and specifically what we need in order to be generous.
• As we give, we and others will be moved to give thanks to God.

11. APPLY: Which of these principles of giving have you been most struck by, and why?
• **What will help you become a more cheerful and more generous giver?**
Both these questions are deliberately quite personal. Encourage people to write something down, but reassure them that they don't have to share it with the group, unless they would like to. Again, the answer to Question 11 will very much depend on each person in your group—just make sure that everyone who wants to gets a chance to contribute.

3
2 Corinthians 10 v 1-18
BOLDNESS AND BOASTING

THE BIG IDEA
We need to understand why leaders sometimes have to say the things they say; and that true servant-hearted leadership looks to the Lord alone for commendation.

SUMMARY
2 Corinthians 10 – 13 is one of the hardest sections of 2 Corinthians to understand, as we need to grasp Paul's relationship with the Corinthian church in order to understand it properly. In addition, Paul's argument here is quite complex, because he knows that he needs to confront the Corinthians in a certain way for them to hear what he has to say, as one of the key problems is that they are listening not to him but to false apostles ("super-apostles", which we will read about in chapter 11). In fact, Paul's problem can be summarised as this: how do you persuade people to listen to you when they are listening to other people who say, "Don't listen to Paul"?

But if we can get to grips with this section of the letter, then it will give us a real insight into apostolic ministry—and into serving Christ wholeheartedly. So, here in chapter 10, we begin examining Paul's defence of his ministry by looking at boldness and boasting.

Paul begins in verses 1-2 with an appeal. When he comes to the Corinthians, he doesn't want to have to be bold —that is, he doesn't want to have to speak strongly to them. He hopes that this letter will deal with the outstanding issues so that when he comes he can be (in their words) "timid". The problem appears to be that Paul is

being accused of living "by the standards of this world"—which leads him to make it clear in verses 3-5 that he does not "wage war" like the world. He says this to help the Corinthians see that they shouldn't either— they shouldn't think in a worldly way; nor should they, by implication, follow leaders who act in this way. They need to listen to Paul because otherwise there will be a reckoning (v 6).

He continues with this theme in verses 7-11. Verse 7 isn't just a statement that Paul is saved; in the context, it is about apostleship. If Paul belongs to Christ, which he does, then they should listen to what he has said to them as the one who brought the gospel to Corinth. This then makes sense of what is said in verses 8-11—Paul will be forceful in letters or in person, if that is what is necessary to build the Corinthians up.

Verse 12 then begins a new section, although it builds on what has come before. Here, Paul begins to talk about those who will in chapter 11 be classified as false apostles. First, in 10 v 12, he advises against the kind of self-commendation they are engaged in. Then Paul himself turns to "boasting"—presumably because that is what the false apostles are doing. But Paul will not boast beyond proper limits: though he can boast that he did bring the gospel to Corinth (v 14), and he hopes to extend the work beyond Corinth (v 15-16), he does not boast about work done by others (v 15). He does then have a proper field of "boasting", but he boasts in the Lord, and the approval he looks for is not from himself or from men but from the Lord (v 17-18).

Paul has explained why he speaks with boldness when necessary, and has related this to proper boasting in the Lord. The question we're left with is: how would the Corinthians respond, and how will we?

OPTIONAL EXTRA

Blindfold a volunteer to carry out a task like putting three dry ingredients (e.g. flour, rice, porridge oats) into 3 labelled bottles or jars. Divide everyone else into two groups. One group gives instructions to help the volunteer complete the task; the other gives incorrect instructions to sabotage the task. Start by seeing if the volunteer can work out which group they should listen to. Partway through, tell the volunteer who to listen to. The opposing group should try to drown out or distract the volunteer from the correct instructions. This illustrates Paul's problem in this passage: he needs to persuade people to listen to him when other influential leaders are saying, "Don't listen to Paul". (You could link back to this activity when you discuss apply Question 12.)

GUIDANCE FOR QUESTIONS

1. How do you respond when someone tells you what you should do? In simple terms, the answer to this question depends on who it is who is giving the instruction! It will also depend on what is being asked, and how. Try and get the group to think of different scenarios and times when they would find it easy to obey, as well as times when it would be difficult. Feel free to relate this to the church. This study is about how the Corinthians respond to Paul, particularly when he has hard things to say to them; how would we respond to Paul?

2. What do the Corinthians think about Paul, and what are they saying about him (v 1, v 7-11)? The Corinthians are accusing Paul of being timid in person and bold in his letters (v 1, 10). They are saying that he is inconsistent—bold when he is absent, and weak when he is present. They are saying that he boasts of his authority (v 8) and tries to hurt them with letters (v 9). Because they judge him by appearance (v 7), they are also not impressed with his physical presence, and how he speaks (v 10).

• **What does Paul understand about his own ministry (v 7-8)?** His authority over the Corinthians has been given to him by the Lord, and its purpose is not to tear them down but to build them up. Verse 7 isn't just a statement that Paul is saved; in the context, it is about apostleship. If Paul belongs to Christ, which he does, then they should listen to what he has said to them.

3. What is Paul's plea to the Corinthians (v 1-2)? That the Corinthians would listen to what he has to say in this letter, so that he won't have to be bold when he comes.

4. What is the "warfare" that Paul is waging (v 3-6)? The warfare is not worldly; rather it is godly warfare: demolishing arguments against the knowledge of God—a warfare designed to take every thought captive. You might call it spiritual warfare—warfare for the hearts, minds and souls of the Corinthians, with the end result of bringing them into obedience to Christ.

EXPLORE MORE

Can you summarise what it means in practice to be fully armoured as a Christian? Truth (Ephesians 6 v 14), righteousness (v 14—both Christ's righteousness given to us by God and the work of the Spirit growing righteousness in us), readiness to take the gospel of peace out to others (v 15), faith (v 16) in the God who can conquer all the schemes of the evil one, salvation, and the word of God (v 17)—all these items of armour are found only in the gospel of Jesus Christ. We are fully armoured when we know for ourselves and live out the gospel.

What is the weapon of attack mentioned here? "The sword of the Spirit, which is the word of God" (v 17).

What does the Christian's "armour" mean in practice for the task of winning people's hearts, minds and souls, to bring them into obedience to Christ—as we've seen Paul labouring to do with the Corinthians? We cannot take the route of the false apostles, trying to gain influence through the "right" appearance; or through manipulation—appearing to be one thing at one point and something different at another; or through saying what people want to hear or find impressive. We can only speak and live consistently with the truth of the gospel, as found in God's word, regardless of whether that finds favour or is despised.

5. How does Paul see the relationship between his visits and his letters (v 1, 9-11)? He will be bold in person if necessary because he and his letters are the same.

6. Why do you think Paul writes so strongly here? He writes out of his deep concern for the Corinthians, and because they are endangering themselves so much by rejecting Paul's words, which, because he is Christ's apostle, are words from God.

7. APPLY: How might Paul's example help us in those situations where we need to be bold in speaking to our brothers and sisters in Christ? The answer here will depend on issues that individuals struggle with. Some possible answers may include:

- There are times when it is appropriate to be bold, even if that is hard and causes others pain.
- Being bold is not incompatible with being humble.
- Being accused of inconsistency does not mean we have been inconsistent.

8. Why won't Paul compare himself with those who are commending themselves (v 12)? Because to enter into the comparison is to lower himself to their level. When Paul says "we do not dare" in verse 12, he may be being sarcastic—these are "super-apostles" after all. He may also be highlighting again the folly of human comparisons, in the light of what he will say in verse 18. Their self-commendation is pure folly (v 12).

- **What will Paul boast in, and what won't he boast about (v 13-15)?** Paul boasts in the work God has given him to do. However, he refuses to boast in the work done by others. (The implication here is that the self-commenders are boasting in what Paul has done.)

9. What is Paul's plan and how does it involve the Corinthians (v 15-16)? Paul's plan is to extend the work beyond Corinth. The Corinthians can be involved in this as their faith grows—presumably at least in prayer and financial support.

10. What is the ultimate antidote to inappropriate boasting (v 18)? To recognise that we do all things before the Lord, and it is his approval we seek. There is no need to tell God what we have done, and there is no point in exaggerating achievements. Instead, we seek to serve the Lord, and seek his commendation.

11. How would you describe Paul's attitude in verses 12-18? This question is designed to help your group work through the feel of this passage. Some may find Paul harsh; if so, it is worth exploring again why he says what he says.

Hopefully, by the time you've discussed this question, people will be able to see two key points: that Paul's confidence is in the Lord—and that he speaks as he needs to speak for the sake of the Corinthians.

12. APPLY: Think about how Paul wants the Corinthians to respond to what he says in this passage. What can we learn from that desired response? Paul wants the Corinthians to respond to correction! Draw out what that would mean for them; for example, it means listening to what Paul says, accepting that they have been wrong, and then seeking to change their attitudes and behaviour.

Do take the opportunity to discuss what that might mean for your group in the context of the church family. For example, when someone corrects us, can we be grateful for that or do we only respond badly? (Note: This should include correction from all brothers and sisters in Christ, and not just from church leaders.)

4 2 Corinthians 11 v 1-15
TRUTH AND DECEPTION

THE BIG IDEA
Paul starts to take on the false apostles ("super-apostles"), who are deceiving the Corinthians; he wants the Christians to see the difference between genuine and counterfeit gospel ministry.

SUMMARY
Again, as in the last session, this is a complex section of 2 Corinthians, and so it takes some teasing out to get to the heart of this passage.

Paul starts with a bit of irony in asking the Corinthians to put up with more of his foolishness (v 1). The irony here is that they think Paul is foolish anyway, because he is not like the super-apostles they so revere. And so what is Paul's foolishness here? He is jealous for them (in a godly way) (v 2), because he fears that, although they have been promised as a bride to Christ, they will

be led astray. He uses the imagery of the church as the bride of Christ here (see also Ephesians 5 v 31-32), and also references Eve being deceived in the Garden of Eden (2 Corinthians 11 v 3; see Genesis 3 v 1-13). They have been prepared as a bride for Christ but they are in danger of going their own way because they are willing to put up with false teaching (2 Corinthians 11 v 4).

Notice how the false teaching is described: as another Jesus, another Spirit, and another gospel. Why do they give a hearing to such blatant false teaching?

Apparently because of who is teaching it—these super-apostles (v 5). Again, notice the irony in that description. The super-apostles think they are superior to Paul, presumably because they are trained speakers (v 6), but Paul doesn't feel inferior; in fact, he also has knowledge.

Verses 5-6 are crucial for understanding what the super-apostles are like. Notice what Paul is and isn't saying here.

First, knowledge seems to be a key word, as if the super-apostles come with a special knowledge that Paul doesn't have, to supplement what the Corinthians have already been taught. The problem is that anything which adds to the gospel takes something away, resulting in another Jesus, Spirit and gospel.

Second, these men are trained speakers, unlike Paul. Paul is not deriding speaking gifts, or attacking rhetoric (the art of persuasive speaking); after all, 2 Corinthians is full of rhetoric. But it seems that the super-apostles' impressive speech covers up the false content of their message (see v 13-15).

Another problem that the Corinthians have with Paul is that he preaches the gospel free of charge (v 7-9), relying on support from elsewhere and his own resources, not because he thinks his message isn't worth anything, but so he won't burden them. But they have misinterpreted his intentions; they seem to feel insulted. But Paul defends his practice, which simply means he isn't burdening them as he preaches the gospel to them.

In fact, Paul will continue to boast (v 10)—probably a reference to his "boasting" of chapter 10, as well as his defence of the way he organises his financial support—to show how the way he operates contrasts with that of the super-apostles, who clearly don't preach for free (v 11-12).

And as this section draws to a close, we get some home truths about these super-apostles, who are now exposed as false apostles (v 13). They are really serving Satan (v 13-14). These are strong words

and explain Paul's anxious concern. These false teachers look, however, like servants of righteousness, so Paul must help the Corinthians see through them and where they are leading. He is confident that the super-apostles will be exposed (v 15); he just doesn't want the Corinthians to follow them to destruction.

OPTIONAL EXTRA

In this session we will see Paul contrasting his own ministry with the fake ministry of the so-called "super-apostles"—this will highlight some of the characteristics that distinguish real from false teachers. By way of introduction, you could do a "Spot the fake" activity with your group. Select from news, art, designer clothes, photos, etc. and google "Spot the fake [insert your chosen category] quiz" to find a suitable image-based quiz. (Refer back to the importance of distinguishing the fake from the genuine when you discuss apply Question 12.)

GUIDANCE FOR QUESTIONS

1. What kind of qualities do you look for in a preacher or Bible teacher?
This question focuses particularly on the preacher because the issue in this section is the contradiction between how the false apostles present themselves and what they teach. You don't need to point out correct or incorrect answers at this stage, but it will be interesting to see whether people focus on content or style. You could return to this after Questions 3-5.

2. What is Paul's attitude towards the Corinthians (v 1-2)? Paul is jealous for the Corinthians with a godly jealousy for their salvation in Christ. In the Bible jealousy is not always a negative quality. Paul's jealousy is jealousy for God's honour and glory, and is therefore a positive jealousy.

3. What does he fear (v 3-4)? Paul is jealous for the Corinthians because he fears they are going astray, and believing a different gospel. He cares for them and he is very concerned at how easily they seem to be led astray. The comparison with Eve is instructive. Like Adam and Eve, they are deciding to listen to something other than God's word.

4. Who is leading the Corinthians astray (v 4-5)? Preachers that Paul labels as "super-apostles" (highlighting their superior attitude), who present very different teaching from that of Paul and the other (true) apostles. He singles out three crucial areas where they depart from the truth: in their views of Jesus, the Spirit and the gospel.

5. Why do the Corinthians finding the teaching of the "super-apostles" more attractive than Paul's (v 5-6)? The so-called super-apostles are leading the Corinthians astray because they seem to be superior to Paul, because they come with certain speaking abilities, and seem to offer a certain kind of knowledge—a "knowledge" Paul describes in verse 4.

EXPLORE MORE
What does the snake say about God in these verses [Genesis 3 v 1-7]? The snake seeks to imply that God has not been entirely truthful in saying that Adam and Eve will die (v 4), and is trying to keep something good from them (v 5). It paints God as selfish and overbearing rather than generous and benevolent.
Why does Eve decide to eat the fruit (v 6)? She sees that is good for food—that is, she makes a decision for herself, rather than trusting God's word.

6. APPLY: Why are Christians deceived by false teaching today? Why do they "put up with it"? In every age Christians are tempted to believe teaching which appeals to their desires—whether for wealth, power or pleasure, or as a way out of suffering and hardships. Like Eve, we like to see with our own eyes, and so the appeal to our own reason over God's word is a strong one. We put up with it, because we like it.

7. How was Paul supported while in Corinth (v 7-9)? He was not supported by the Corinthians; he preached free of charge. Instead, he received support from other churches, notably the Macedonian church (Paul has already used this church as an example of how to give in chapter 8). This seemed to be a problem for the Corinthians, because for them it meant that Paul's teaching wasn't really worth very much.

8. What is Paul's boast (v 10; see also 10 v 13 and 17)? Paul's boast seems to be in a number of things. First, he is probably boasting in not receiving financial support from them, but offering the gospel for free. At the same time, just as he has already been boasting in chapter 10, he will boast in his work in the Lord, but only in what God has given him to do.

• **Why will Paul keep on boasting (v 10-12)?** Because he wants to expose the super-apostles for what they are (v 12). As we have seen, Paul boasts in what he has done in the Lord. As the super-apostles don't seem to have actually done anything, this will expose them. Paul is clearly motivated by his love for the Corinthians (v 11).

9. How have the Corinthians misinterpreted Paul's approach in

bringing the gospel to them? The Corinthians have seen Paul's lack, not of all skill in speaking, but of what was probably a fairly manipulative kind of speaking. They have misinterpreted this as a demonstration of the weakness of his message, rather than the power of the gospel. They have seen his failure to charge them as a sign that he didn't think his message was worth charging for, and they have generally failed to appreciate what he has done for them in sharing the gospel.

10. How would you characterise the false apostles from this chapter? They seem to be impressive speakers who offer interesting new knowledge, and who charge for their skills, but they are really false teachers. Paul's concludes that they are servants of Satan (v 14-15).

11. What qualities of Paul come through

from this chapter? Paul loves these people who are turning away from him. He says what they need to hear, even though they don't want to hear it. He is confident in the job God has given him to do—and he is committed to the free offer of the gospel.

12. APPLY: How can we make sure we're not deceived by "deceitful workers"? To avoid being deceived, we need to understand what people are saying, and not just be impressed or moved by how it is said; and we need to measure what is said against the Scriptures, so that we know the real Jesus is being preached. We also need to look out for people's motivation: their attitude to money, to other church leaders, and their view of their own importance. Are these teachers willing to say what people need to hear, or will they only say what people want to hear?

5 2 Corinthians 11 v 16-33
SUFFERING AND SUCCESS

THE BIG IDEA
As Paul continues to contrast genuine and counterfeit gospel ministry, we see that in real gospel ministry we don't avoid suffering, but instead we suffer for Christ.

SUMMARY
If needed, look back over 10 v 1 – 11 v 15 to remind yourself of where we've come from: Paul is defending his apostolic status, and seeking to persuade the Corinthians that true gospel ministry involves suffering and hardship, rather than the "success" which the super-apostles are peddling. His

task is complicated because the Corinthians don't really want to listen to him. Paul has to use all his rhetorical skills to make his point.

We begin here with a brief section on foolishness and boasting. Paul is not a fool (v 16), but he is engaged in an activity which is foolish—boasting. He feels he has to boast, although he knows the limits of boasting (v 17-18). And the Corinthian Christians should listen to his foolish boasting, because, after all, they listen to the foolish boasting of others all the time, as Paul points out in verse 19. But Paul won't take advantage of them, unlike the false apostles (v 20-21).

And so Paul's boast begins, perhaps as the Corinthians expect it to, with Paul talking about his descent (v 21-22). And I do think there is a little irony here—after all, what could Paul do about his parentage? But then the twist comes in verse 23: Paul is a servant of Christ, but he shows his credentials not with a list of privileges and status, but with suffering, beginning in verses 23-25 with some specifics, and then a more generalised list in verses 26 and 27 showing the lifestyle of the missionary apostle. Some of the events here we can recognise from the book of Acts, while others remind us that Acts is not (nor does it claim to be) a complete record of Paul's life. In verses 28-29 we see another addition to Paul's suffering—his concern for the churches, and that includes the Corinthians. Paul is so concerned for them, that when they sin, he burns within.

And so we get to the punchline in verse 30: Paul is happy to stand before God and declare his weakness, because he knows it to be true (v 31). Paul boasts in a way that subverts the boasting of others. In the end, he has nothing to boast in except his weakness; but as we'll see in chapter 12, that weakness reveals God's power at work in Paul. And so this is a good chapter from which to think about success and the kinds of things we might think are worthy of boasting in.

OPTIONAL EXTRA

Find pictures of celebrities from a variety of walks of life: acting, music, media, sports, politics, fashion, etc, plus one or two who are simply famous for being famous. Get people to list the marks of their success—medals, awards, chart hits, money earned, positions held, number of Twitter followers,

etc. The point of this is that none of these things are what the apostle Paul lists as "signs of success", though some of them are things in which the super-apostles might well have boasted. (This is a longer version of Question 1. You could return to this list when you discuss Question 10.)

GUIDANCE FOR QUESTIONS

1. How do we measure success? What makes something or someone successful? There are a number of measures, not all of which are necessarily bad in themselves. So, we might think of wealth, power, getting qualifications or sporting achievements, having the "right" number of children, and so on. If possible, try and get everyone to think of a success measure that would apply to their lives.

2. Why should the Corinthians "put up with" Paul's boasting (v 16-19)? There are a couple of reasons why the Corinthians should be able to put up with Paul's boasting. First, if they want to, they can put up with him as a fool (v 16) because he's talking as a fool (v 17). And then second, they can cope with fools as they are so wise (v 19), so putting up with Paul shouldn't be a problem. Note the ironic flattery here: the Corinthians have a sense of wisdom and foolishness that is the inverse of Paul's. Paul seems to be flattering them, but he is about to turn the screw on their inverted sense of priorities.

3. What was Paul too "weak" to do (v 20-21)? To take advantage of the Corinthians. He makes it clear here that this is what he thinks the false apostles or super-apostles are doing. And he has good evidence that he is not like them as he hasn't been taking the Corinthians' money.

• **So how is Paul different from those**

the Corinthians were listening to?
Though they boast about a lot, the super-apostles are in fact enslaving, exploiting, looking down on and abusing the Corinthians. Paul can only "boast", with great reluctance, that he does none of those things in his interactions with the Corinthians.

4. APPLY: What kinds of things will gospel-hearted people boast in, that the world would probably try to keep hidden? Although Paul is going to go on to say much more on this matter in verses 21-33, this apply question is a good opportunity to reflect on what we've already read so far. Paul has already boasted of his "weakness" in not taking advantage of the Corinthians, and has in 10 v 1 – 11 v 15 focussed on self-sacrificial service of Christ, so that may shape people's reflections here.

5. What does Paul "boast" about first (v 21-22)? Paul boasts about his parentage, as he is a Israelite. There is some irony here, as what could Paul do about his parentage? In addition, if the Corinthians think this kind of status is important, then Paul has it.

6. How does Paul show that he is a servant of Christ (v 23-27)? Paul shows that he is a servant of Christ not by listing his achievements and accomplishments, but by listing his sufferings, and specifically his persecution for the sake of the gospel (v 23), which he then talks about at greater length (v 24-27). Note the ironic oratory here; this is a well-composed speech (e.g. v 26) but it doesn't talk about how "successful" Paul has been—quite the opposite.
Also, some members of your group may wish to talk about when these events took place. Some of them we can place in Paul's life from elsewhere in Scripture; some of

them are more difficult to identify. They all happened, even if we can't easily place when and where. Some examples of what Paul describes can be found in the following places: imprisoned, Acts 16 v 16-40; stoned, 14 v 19-20; beaten, 16 v 22-23; betrayed by false brothers, Galatians 2 v 1-5.

7. How does Paul relate to all the churches (v 28-29)? Paul feels the burdens and sorrows of the churches, because he is deeply concerned for them (v 28). See how this is the opposite of someone who lords it over the churches; Paul is concerned for the welfare of the churches, which causes him to suffer for their sake. The super- / false apostles are only concerned for their own self-promotion, and therefore they are happy to receive plaudits from the churches, without being concerned for them. The irony here is that it is precisely the conduct which the Corinthians despise which demonstrates Paul's genuine concern for them.

8. Why does Paul boast in his weakness (v 30-31)? Because he is weak! And to admit this is to expose the reality of the boasting of the super- / false apostles. In Damascus Paul escaped from his enemies in a basket—a final example of this weakness (see Acts 9 v 19-25).

• **What does 2 Corinthians 1 v 8-10 tell us about why Paul went through such times of weakness?** So that he and his fellow missionaries might not rely on themselves but on God, who has true power and strength.

9. Why might Paul's boasting have offended or surprised the Corinthians? The main point here is that Paul was doing the opposite of what the super-apostles did. They must have dazzled the Corinthians with their oratorical skills (2 Corinthians 11 v 6), since they were taking advantage of the Christians (v 20), and yet many of the Corinthians seem to have been such fans of the super-apostles.

By contrast, Paul was weak, unimpressive, and didn't take payment (v 7); instead, he served the churches. This is not the kind of boasting that the Corinthians would have been expecting.

10. How does this passage help us understand "success", and what is of value? What is of value? I think there are three key areas to draw out from this passage:

- **v 23-27:** faithfulness to Christ, even under persecution

- **v 28-29:** care for others

- **v 31:** having a clear conscience before God.

We are "successful" when we are faithful to God, and don't follow the pattern of the world. This doesn't mean totally rejecting the world, but it does mean not following the way the world does things, and not going along with worldly assumptions. We should avoid following a worldly way of doing things, and being too impressed by worldly success. Instead, we should look for faithfulness, compassion and godliness in those who serve the church.

EXPLORE MORE
[From Matthew 16 v 24-25] What do you think Jesus himself might have said to the super-apostles? Perhaps something like, *When you despise weakness and suffering, you show that you are not my disciples. You cannot be my disciples if you refuse to "lose your life".*

11. APPLY: How should we adjust our priorities in life to follow Paul's example? This is a big question, and you will probably only scratch the surface of it in this study. However, it is important to make sure this study questions our ideas of success and challenges our worldly assumptions. For example, you could get people to discuss how to come to decisions about matters such as where you live; what job you choose or whether you take a promotion or not; where you serve in church, evangelism or mission; what's important in the education of your children; who you invest your time in and seek friendship with, etc. Contrast how different these decisions would look if they were based on Paul's priorities or on those of the super-apostles and the Corinthians.

6 2 Corinthians 12 v 1-21
STRENGTH IN WEAKNESS

THE BIG IDEA

Paul wants the Corinthians to understand: (1) that his weakness doesn't invalidate his ministry, and nor does his spiritual experience validate it, but both show Christ's power at work in him; and (2) that his "defence" comes out of his concern for them, and they need to respond accordingly.

SUMMARY

Continuing from chapter 11, Paul will go on boasting (12 v 1) because he still has things he needs to say to the Corinthians. He has shown them that true gospel ministry doesn't avoid suffering, but is about faithfulness to Christ. He has shown them that the false super-apostles are leading them astray. Now, in a final reversal, he talks about a "strength" and a "weakness".

Paul's strength: first he describes a spiritual experience in verses 2-6. Notice that he refers to himself as "a man in Christ" (v 2) to draw the focus away from himself. Then there is some hesitation about how the vision happened (v 2-3). By contrast, we can imagine how the Corinthian "super-apostles" would have described their spiritual experiences in great detail, as can be seen in some first-century literature. Paul can't do that: he's not quite sure exactly what happened and anyway, he doesn't want to make too much of it. And then what wisdom can he bring to the Corinthians from heaven? Nothing—he is not permitted to tell (v 4). By mentioning this great spiritual experience, and then having nothing to tell, Paul neatly sets up what he wants to say next: *don't think more of me because of a spiritual experience (or, by* implication, less of me because I lack it), but look at what I do and say* (v 6). That is what is important.

Paul's weakness: He talks about this in verses 7-10. Interestingly, Paul connects the two in verse 7: the thorn seems to have been given as a consequence of the revelation. Despite much speculation as to what the thorn in the flesh was, we have to recognise that we simply do not know, and therefore its precise nature is not crucial. Of much greater importance is what we read in verses 8 and 9: it was not God's will to take the thorn away, but rather, for Paul to continue to experience the thorn so that God's power would be shown through Paul. This is why Paul can boast in his weaknesses, his sufferings and all the things the Corinthians think are unimpressive about him (v 9-10)—because they show his "strength" (v 10), which is God's strength working through him. We too need to look at our attitude to "strengths" and "weaknesses", and learn from Paul's example here.

Then Paul returns to the theme of foolishness (v 11-21, previously mentioned in 11 v 1, 16, 21) to summarise what he has told them so far. He is not inferior to the "super-apostles", and the Corinthians have seen him demonstrate the signs of a true apostle (v 11-12). Paul isn't trying to say that he is something: he is nothing, but God has been at work through him. In answer to the recurring charge that he should have received support from the Corinthians (v 13)—presumably because this would have shown that his message was worth hearing in their eyes—Paul compares himself to a parent, who won't burden their children and is willing to spend everything on their behalf (v 14-15). Rather than a sign of weakness, it is a sign of his love for them. Similarly, the people Paul has sent to the Corinthians have not exploited them but have also acted out of love for them (v 16-18).

In all of this Paul hasn't been defending his ministry (v 19), but speaking for the benefit of the Corinthians. Why? Because they need to listen to him, so that when he comes, he will not find the various problems listed in verse 20. If they deal with these issues now, he won't have to do that when he comes. In keeping with the tenor of this whole section, he focuses on how their continuing sin would grieve him before God (v 21). We can learn both from the problems evident among the Corinthians and from Paul's attitude to these people, whom he still loves.

OPTIONAL EXTRA

If you can bear the cheesiness, play a version of the country music song "No Charge" written by Harlan Howard (the song has been covered by both Johnny Cash and Tammy Wynette). Alternatively, pass round copies of the lyrics for people to read through. You might like to ask the parents in your group how accurately the song portrays parenthood. In this session, we will see Paul describe his attitude to the Corinthians as that of a parent towards their child—he has taken all steps possible to avoid being a burden to them and is willing to spend everything on their behalf. (You can refer back to this when you discuss Question 8.)

GUIDANCE FOR QUESTIONS

1. How do you deal with situations where everything you do seems to be wrong? Give an example of your own to encourage people to talk about those frustrating and upsetting situations, where,

try as you might, everything you do seems to be wrong. Whether it is a relative that can't be pleased, or someone at work who always reacts badly, or whatever, all of us face these situations in life.

Although this isn't exactly Paul's situation, it will help us to think about his perseverance for the sake of the Corinthians, despite their attitude and actions towards him.

2. What is Paul "boasting" about (v 1-4)? Paul is boasting about a vision and revelation from Christ, when he was caught up into heaven and saw inexpressible things. Note how vague Paul is about what exactly happened, and how he doesn't really have anything to report. He speaks of himself in the third person to draw attention away from the experience, and to focus attention on what Paul is now—weak. He might be able to boast about a man like that (v 5), but his boast for himself will focus on weakness. These are marks of his great reluctance to indulge in this sort of boasting.

3. Paul had a great spiritual experience. But how does he want the Corinthians to respond to him (v 5-6)? Paul doesn't want the Corinthians to focus on him—he doesn't want them to raise him up on a pedestal because he ticks all the boxes on their checklist of what makes someone worth listening to, e.g. great spiritual experiences. He will not boast in himself (v 5). The man in verse 5 is Paul, and so he *could* boast of his spiritual experiences. But he *won't* boast about his spiritual experience—he puts it in the third person—and instead, he *will* boast of his weakness. This is because he wants them to judge him by what he does and says (v 6).

4. Why was Paul given a thorn in the flesh that wasn't taken away (v 7-9)?

Paul was given a thorn in the flesh to keep him from becoming proud (v 7). It wasn't taken away because the Lord enabled him to bear it and learn from it.

• **What does this reveal about the purpose of weakness?** Paul's weakness shows the power and strength, and also the grace, of Christ (v 8-9).

5. What is Paul's attitude to strength, suffering and weakness (v 10, see also v 5)? Paul's attitude to strength, suffering and weakness is that weakness is good, because it shows Christ's strength and power. So Paul delights in the things that demonstrate the power of Christ (v 10). See also verse 5, where Paul boasts in weakness, but not in spiritual experiences.

6. APPLY: How can Paul's attitude to suffering and weakness help us in our walk with Christ? Like Paul, we need to recognise that it is not the highs of spiritual experience or the lows of personal difficulties that should define our walk with God. We should not be dependent on spiritual highs; rather, we should be working to see the big picture of what God is doing for the glory of Christ through us in our difficult situations.

EXPLORE MORE
[In Acts 5 v 40-42; 12 v 1-5; 1 Peter 4 v 1-2] What does the apostle Peter teach us about suffering? The passages in Acts indicate that Peter experienced suffering as an apostle of Christ, and that that included beatings and imprisonments. And yet, he views suffering for Christ in 1 Peter 4 as something which helps us follow the example of Christ, to stop sinning, and to focus our attention on God

7. Why should the Corinthians have commended Paul (v 11-12)? Paul's

actions amongst the Corinthians were commendable, as can be seen from reviewing chapters 10 and 11. In particular, Paul underlines that he is not inferior to the "super-apostles", and draws attention to the signs, wonders and miracles which accompanied his apostolic work. These signs and wonders are detailed in Acts; they appear to be have accompanied the gospel into new territory, like Greece.

8. Why was Paul never a burden to the Corinthians (v 13-15)? During his time in Corinth, he received support from other churches, because he wanted to focus on the Corinthians, not on their possessions. He describes his relationship with them as that of a parent towards their children: willing to love them sacrificially for their sake.

9. What else shows that Paul hasn't wronged the Corinthians (v 16-18)? The people Paul has sent to the Corinthians also show that he has not wronged them; they have conducted themselves properly, and also have shown their care and concern for the Corinthians.

10. Why has Paul written about his ministry (v 19-21)? For the sake of the Corinthians, and not for his benefit—so that when he comes, he won't find them as he fears. They need to listen to him, and take action now based on his word from God; that's why he needed to persuade them to listen. Notice that Paul is concerned for how he finds them—and how that might grieve him before God.

11. What does this passage tell us about Paul's heart for the Corinthians? Paul here shows his continued love and care for the Corinthians, despite their attitude to him. It can be seen in:

- his unwillingness to be a financial burden (v 13).
- his care as a parent (v 14-15).
- his self-sacrificial love (v 15).
- his expectation of grief if they do not change their ways (v 21).
- the fact of this letter—seeking to persuade them.

12. APPLY: What have we learned from Paul about following the right priorities in dealing with people? Paul continues to care for the Corinthians despite their attitude to him, and continues to act in their best interests—even if that means having to challenge them. We too need to do the same in our relationships with people, particularly with those we find difficult. This doesn't just mean giving them what they want, and it doesn't mean avoiding them at all costs.

Of course, we are not apostles like Paul, but nevertheless we seek to do what is right even if it is sometimes costly, recognising the call to all Christians to imitate Christ in serving others.

---

7 2 Corinthians 13 v 1-14
WEAKNESS AND STRENGTH

THE BIG IDEA
Paul wants the Corinthians to be ready and fully restored when he comes, so they must respond now to his letter by examining themselves.

SUMMARY
Note: The second part of this study is a little shorter than others, to allow time for reflection on 2 Corinthians 8 – 13 as a whole in the closing "Apply" and "Getting personal" sections.

In chapter 12, we saw a shift in focus from Paul's ministry to the spiritual state of the Corinthians. Paul's main focus throughout has been his concern for them (e.g. 12 v 19). Chapter 13 continues that focus, with Paul's final words before his third visit to them (13 v 1). The first visit is detailed in Acts 18 v 1-18. The second probably occurred during Paul's extended stay in Ephesus (Acts 19), and is the painful visit already referred to

(2 Corinthians 2 v 1). Paul doesn't want another painful visit; he wants them to be fully restored (13 v 9).

In 13 v 1 Paul quotes from Deuteronomy 17 v 6 and 19 v 15. Why does Paul say this here? Probably because he is going to investigate their conduct, and will deal with the "charges" against them fairly. Hence the warning in 2 Corinthians 13 v 2. The Corinthians have had enough time now to repent; he will not spare them when he comes, and will discipline those in the church who have not repented.

In verses 3 and 4 Paul returns to the familiar theme of his perceived weakness. He reminds the Corinthians that as Christ was crucified in weakness and yet rose again to glory, so although Paul may be weak, God's power also works through him. So, in preparation for Paul's visit, the Corinthians must test themselves (v 5)—to be sure that Christ is in them.

They do this by measuring themselves against what they have read so far in this letter, and checking if they are being obedient to Christ. Paul is motivated by his concern for the Corinthians (v 7, 9) and by his desire to always tell the truth (v 8). When he comes, he wants them to be ready for him—fully restored—so that he can spend time building them up, rather than having to tear them down (v 10).

He ends the letter with a final set of exhortations (v 11-14), summarising the message: they are to aim to be the people that God wants them to be, and to live in peace with one another (v 11), all in the context of verse 14—the work of God the Father, Son and Holy Spirit in their lives.

OPTIONAL EXTRA

Set a test on 2 Corinthians 8 – 13. Depending on your group, you could either take a gentle approach by calling it a quiz and allowing people to confer as they answer your questions; or you could give each person a sheet of questions to answer within a time limit and without conferring. (But do allow people to mark their own sheet and keep their score private to ensure that no one feels embarrassed.) This provides a review of what you have learned together, and also focuses on Paul's instruction to "examine yourselves" (v 5), highlighting how the Corinthians would do that: they needed to think about all that Paul had said and put it into practice. (It will be useful to refer back to this when you reach apply Question 10.)

GUIDANCE FOR QUESTIONS

1. Think back to the last time you filled in a resumé or a job application, or had a job interview, or something similar. What did you find hard about it? The purpose here is to get people thinking about how they would describe themselves. Whilst

this is always a somewhat uncomfortable process, it is more difficult if we don't know ourselves or know what is important. So, job interviews are particularly difficult when we don't know the answers to the questions we are being asked. Hopefully this question will set the scene for talking about self-examination a little later. As an alternative question (or additional question) you could ask: "Imagine you were asked to do a CV for your Christian life. What would you say?"

2. What will Paul's purpose be when he visits (v 1-2)? He will come to judge them if necessary, and he will not hold back.

- **What does the quotation in verse 1 (from Deuteronomy 19 v 15) show us about how he will do this?** The judgments he makes will be fair, based on appropriate testimony, and with plenty of warnings to provide sufficient opportunity for repentance.

3. How should the example of Christ change the way the Corinthians view Paul (2 Corinthians 13 v 3-4)? The Corinthians have been seeing Paul's weakness as a problem—as something which means they don't need to listen to him. He reminds them of how Christ was weak on the cross, and yet how he was raised through the power of God. Weakness is not a problem, but rather, an opportunity for God to work through Paul.

4. Given what Paul has said so far in this letter, how do the Corinthians need to test themselves (v 5)? By what Paul has taught them about true Christian ministry, and about the realities of the Christian life. They are not to look to their gifts and skills, but rather, to their relationship with Christ, and rely on him and his death for them.

5. What is Paul's primary concern in verses 6 and 7? Although Paul wants the Corinthians to recognise that Christ Jesus is in him and his associates, he is more concerned that the Corinthians do what is right; what they think of him is secondary to his concern that they should do the right thing.

6. Why might Paul sometimes seem to be a failure (v 7-8)? Paul can only work for the truth (v 8). He implies here that those who judge him as a failure, expecting him to act in line with their ideas of success, are working against the truth and pressuring him to do the same.

But Paul will:
- continue to do right (e.g. he refuses to preach a different gospel, as the super-apostles did, 11 v 4)...
- continue to speak the truth (e.g. he boasts about his sufferings, 11 v 23-33, rather than hiding them for fear that he would be seen as weak)...
- act according to the truth (e.g. he offers the gospel in Corinth for free, 11 v 7)...
... even if all that makes him appear a failure in some people's eyes.

7. What has motivated Paul's letter to the Corinthians (v 9-10)? Paul has written for the benefit of the Corinthians, so that when he comes, he will not need to be harsh with them, but will be able to encourage them. Again, he is not concerned about whether he appears weak or strong, but rather, about their restoration. Surely Paul's overriding concern is for their perfection or completion on the day Christ returns.

- **What do the Corinthians need to do to be ready for Paul's visit?** The Corinthians need to listen to what Paul has to say in this letter, and put it into practice.

EXPLORE MORE
What is Paul looking forward to in this passage [1 Corinthians 13 v 8-13]? He looks forward to a time when there will be no more need for hope or faith, a time when we will see God and Christ face to face—the new heavens and the new earth.
How does this passage help us to understand the supremacy of love? Because love continues into eternity. Love will continue to be shown when we are dwelling with Christ.
How does this help us to understand Paul's concerns in 2 Corinthians 10 – 13? Paul is motivated by love, and so he speaks strongly, boldly and forcibly. He is burdened by the Corinthians' sufferings, he cares for them—and so he will put himself out and bear much, for their sake.

8. APPLY: How can we help each other to examine ourselves about our faith? This is a difficult question to answer, because this is an area where we often struggle. We need to develop relationships where we know each other well enough to be able to speak honestly and accurately with each other. We need to avoid legalism and works-righteousness, but at the same time challenge one another's behaviours and call one another back to Christ.

9. How does Paul encourage and challenge the Corinthians in verses 11-14? Some encouragements:
- "Rejoice!" (v 11): in spite of all the hard things Paul has had to say, there is still much for true Christians to rejoice in.
- The presence of the God of love and peace (v 11).
- The greetings of Paul and the Christians with him (v 13).
- The grace, love and fellowship of the Trinity (v 14).

And some challenges:

- "Strive for full restoration, encourage one another" (v 11): aim for perfection and to be ready for Christ's return.
- "Be of one mind": be united on the truth of the gospel, and at peace with one another and with God.
- Show this harmony by greeting each other with a holy kiss—not a hypocritical one (v 12).

10. APPLY: Think back over what we have learned from 2 Corinthians 8 – 13. Where do we need to examine ourselves in the light of this letter? How will this help us to rely on Christ? Take the opportunity with these last two questions to summarise what your group members have each learned from the letter, to think about which areas of your lives you might need to look at, and to reflect on specific things that you as individuals might need to do.

thegoodbook
COMPANY

BIBLICAL | RELEVANT | ACCESSIBLE

At The Good Book Company, we are dedicated to helping Christians and local churches grow. We believe that God's growth process always starts with hearing clearly what he has said to us through his timeless word—the Bible.

Ever since we opened our doors in 1991, we have been striving to produce resources that honour God in the way the Bible is used. We have grown to become an international provider of user-friendly resources to the Christian community, with believers of all backgrounds and denominations using our Bible studies, books, evangelistic resources, DVD-based courses and training events.

We want to equip ordinary Christians to live for Christ day by day, and churches to grow in their knowledge of God, their love for one another, and the effectiveness of their outreach.

Call us for a discussion of your needs or visit one of our local websites for more information on the resources and services we provide.

Your friends at The Good Book Company

UK & EUROPE   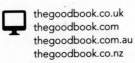 thegoodbook.co.uk   0333 123 0880
NORTH AMERICA   thegoodbook.com   866 244 2165
AUSTRALIA   thegoodbook.com.au   (02) 9564 3555
NEW ZEALAND   thegoodbook.co.nz   (+64) 3 343 2463

 WWW.CHRISTIANITYEXPLORED.ORG
Our partner site is a great place for those exploring the Christian faith, with a clear explanation of the good news, powerful testimonies and answers to difficult questions.

Good Book Guides
The full range

OH ... I AM A **LIVERPUDLIAN**
AND I COME FROM THE

SPION
KOP

OH ... I AM A **LIVERPUDLIAN**
AND I COME FROM THE

SPION
KOP

Sport Media

The first four verses are to the tune of 'The Red River Valley'. The rest is to the tune of 'The Sash'. Poor Scouser Tommy was originally penned in the 1960s and the popular version now has some subtle changes from the original. The line 'under the Arabian sun' was originally 'under the Libyan sun' and you'll hear Kopites standing side by side singing both versions, depending on which era they're from. The original didn't contain the 'I' in 'And I come from the Spion Kop', either. It was originally just 'And come from the Spion Kop'. The 'I get thrown out quite a lot' is often sung as 'I go there quite a lot' and there are various other words that have been exchanged for similar ones over time. And of course, the 'Rush scored one, Rush scored two, Rush scored three and Rush scored four' bit only appeared after a certain Merseyside derby at Goodison Park in 1982.

POOR SCOUSER TOMMY

Let me tell you the story of a poor boy,
Who was sent far away from his home,
To fight for his king and his country,
And also the old folks back home.

So they put him in a Highland division,
Sent him off to a far foreign land,
Where the flies swarm around in their thousands,
And there's nothing to see but the sand.

Now the battle it started next morning,
Under the Arabian sun,
I remember that poor Scouser Tommy,
He was shot by an old Nazi gun.

As he lay on the battlefield dying, dying, dying,
With the blood gushing out of his head, of his head,
As he lay on the battlefield dying, dying, dying,
These were the last words he said.

Oh I am a Liverpudlian and I come from the Spion Kop,
I like to sing, I like to shout,
I get thrown out quite a lot (every week!)
I support a team that's dressed in red,
It's a team that you all know.
It's a team that we call LIVERPOOL,
To glory we will go.

We've won the league, we've won the cup,
And we've been to Europe too.
We played the Toffees for a laugh and we left 'em feeling blue, 5-0.
One, two, one two three, one two three four, FIVE NIL!

Rush scored one, Rush scored two,
Rush scored three and Rush scored four,
nah nah nah nah nah nah nah nah nah . . .

Contents

'Oh ... I Am A Liverpudlian And I Come From The Spion Kop'
published in hardback in 2004. Compiled by Chris McLoughlin.
2010 revised and updated edition produced by Paul Dove.
Additional copy: liverpoolecho.co.uk, liverpoolfc.tv, The Irish Kop by John
Hynes, The Asian Liverbird by Mohammed Bhana.
Updated Kop mosaics article by John Pearman (www.redallovertheland.co.uk).
Photographs: Trinity Mirror (Liverpool Daily Post & Echo), Liverpool FC.
Scouser Tommy cartoon: Peter King.
Thanks to all the proud Kopites and others who contributed.
Printed by Bookmarque

Produced by Trinity Mirror Sport Media:
Business Development Director: Mark Dickinson. Executive Editor: Ken Rogers.
Editor: Steve Hanrahan. Production Editor: Paul Dove. Art Editor: Rick Cooke.
Sales and Marketing Manager: Elizabeth Morgan.
ISBN: 978-1-906802-42-4

Let me tell you a story

Spion Kop.

It's arguably the most famous suburb in Liverpool.

Never mind Edge Hill, Kensington, West Derby, Toxteth, Huyton, Walton, Aigburth, Anfield or anywhere else.

If you asked a Liverpudlian where he came from in the '60s, '70s or '80s then he'd tell you 'Spion Kop'.

Mind you, when you've got a messiah leading the club like Bill Shankly who once filled a form in and put his address down as 'Anfield' then it's no wonder that followers of Liverpool Football Club had an affinity with the Kop.

And that's what this book is all about – Kopites. The group of people who turned what was once just a pile of cinder into the most famous, most feared, most respected and most celebrated terracing in world football.

Man United had the Stretford End. Arsenal the North Bank. You'd find Evertonians on the Gwladys Street and Geordies in the Gallowgate End.

Famous? In their own rights. But not a patch on the Spion Kop.

Anfield has never needed a cheesy or tacky label like 'Theatre of Dreams' to sell itself.

It had the Kop. With dreams and songs to sing.

Even now, in the era of all-seater stadia, The Kop remains the most famous stand in any English football ground.

Liverpool and the Kop go hand in hand.

To the tabloid headline writers, the Kop IS Liverpool. How many other clubs do you see regularly referred to in the press by the name on one of their stands? None.

That's the impact, the lasting effect on the minds of those not associated with Liverpool, that the Kop has had. Anyone who stood on it will tell you that's not surprising.

The Kop was more than concrete and steel. More than an imposing structure that dominated the Anfield skyline. It was a church. A community centre. A way of life. All rolled into one.

Kopites didn't just attend Anfield for the football, they came for everything else that went with it too. They came, in droves, to stand on the Spion Kop. Their Kop. The laughs, the banter, the spirit. The status of being a Kopite.

Singing, shouting, chanting, celebrating, cat-calling, taking the piss or – if you had a copy of the Echo handy – taking a piss down the back of the fella in front of you. Those 25,000 Reds stood shoulder to shoulder, breathing down the visiting goalkeeper's neck.

Visiting goalies didn't just have what Liverpool put in front of them to contend with. They had an entire stand trying to suck the ball into the net behind them. They were intimidating without being nasty. They didn't need to be.

The noise and size of the support was enough in itself to have grown men trembling in their boots. Standing on the Kop wasn't a place to be for the faint-hearted either.

One banner, seen around the fields of Anfield Road in more recent times, says simply: 'Above Us, Only Sky'. The quote, from a John Lennon classic, didn't apply to the Kop. As well as the impressive and imposing steel roof, plumes of cigarette smoke would drift upwards into the air.

On some nights you could see steam rising off the Kop, like there was a cauldron on the boil behind the goal. Things would reach boiling point when Liverpool scored.

A crescendo of noise erupted as the Kop surged forward. It was bedlam. You'd find yourself carried forward and not be able to do anything about it.

Then, when the surge relented, you'd be carried back to

somewhere near to where you started. Finding your favourite spec on the Kop was one thing, staying in it for the full 90 minutes was another.

If Liverpool was the Capital of Culture in 2008 then the Kop was football's cultural capital for decades. It led the way in terms of noise, singing, colour, humour, chanting, ingenuity and even fashion. The rest have been playing catch-up ever since.

In 1994, the old Spion Kop was demolished to make way for a new all-seater stand and, a decade on, this book was first published to mark the 10th anniversary of its demolition.

2010 marks the 110th anniversary of the end of the Battle of Ladysmith on Spioenkop Hill, South Africa, after which The Kop was named. It is also five years since probably the greatest night of the seated Kop – the Champions League semi-final of 2005.

To commemorate those anniversaries, we have updated 'Oh I Am A Liverpudlian' so it not only looks back on the days of the old Kop, but tells the story of how it is now. Don't be expecting a chronological crawl through history, though.

When you stood on the Kop watching the mighty Reds you were never quite sure where you'd be carried to next and this book aims to reflect that. Expect the unexpected.

The highs, the lows. The heroes, the villains. The pain and the glory. You'll find it all here.

A unique crowd with a unique history deserves to have its story told and who better to tell the story than those who stood on, played in front of and even came up against the Kop?

'Oh . . . I Am A Liverpudlian And I Come From The Spion Kop' tells you the story of those who support a team that's dressed in red, a team that you all know.

Chris McLoughlin

Off To A Far Foreign Land

Defeat isn't a word that was particularly associated with the Spion Kop. However, it was defeat for a group of Liverpudlian soldiers that played a significant part in giving the famous old terrace its name.

In January 1900, scores of Scousers were part of the Lancashire Fusiliers that went to battle in the Boer War.

A fierce battle took place on a hill near Ladysmith, South Africa, that was known locally as Spioenkop Hill. The battle ended in defeat with more than 300 of the Lancashire Fusiliers losing their lives.

Six years later and that South African hill would become part of Merseyside folklore forever. The Kop itself was built as a reward for Liverpool supporters after the club lifted its second league championship in 1906. Anfield already had a small terraced area at the Walton Breck Road end but chairman John Houlding and club secretary 'Honest' John McKenna decided there was room for improvement.

A steep, cinder bank with wooden steps and no roof was designed by well-respected architect Archibald Leitch and constructed that summer. All they needed now was a name. At first they were, like a batsman out of his crease, well and truly stumped.

'Walton Breck Bank' sounded like something where you kept your shillings while they'd have never fitted 'The Walton Breck Road end' on match tickets.

The season kicked off and the new stand, which held around 20,000 spectators and gave some splendid views across Stanley Park, remained nameless.

It was Ernest Edwards, sports editor of the Liverpool Echo at the time, who had a moment of inspiration during that campaign.

Edwards said that Liverpool's new terracing reminded him of the hill where the battle of Ladysmith had taken place; so why not call the stand the Spion Kop?

There could have been a very different response if the battle had taken place on Mount Kilimanjaro but, as it was, the name stuck. However, Liverpool's wasn't the first Kop.

The same title had previously been given to terracing at Woolwich Arsenal but the name never caught on. The singing still hasn't at The Emirates, a modern day corporate hospitality venue that couldn't be further removed from everything Anfield stood for.

Arsenal's old North Bank gives you an idea of what could have been for Anfield if it wasn't for Edwards.

His suggestion was probably greeted with such enthusiasm because local men had lost their lives on Spioenkop Hill.

It was almost as if a belated memorial had been put up in Liverpool and everyone liked it.

A 1-0 win over Stoke on September 1, in blazing hot heat, was watched by 30,000 fans with many becoming the first to ever watch a game from the Kop.

Anfield may have initially been Everton's ground but their supporters never stood on the Kop as we know it.

For the eight years they played at Anfield – between 1884 and 1892 – their supporters had to make do with that unremarkable terracing on Walton Breck Road.

The Kop was entirely a Liverpool institution and the next major change came in 1928, largely thanks to the British weather.

Standing on the Kop with 20,000 other people was one thing. Standing on it in torrential rain, gale force winds or even through thunder and lightning was another.

The roofless Kop was an unpleasant place to be on a dreadful day, even for hardened dockers who'd regularly be battered by the elements down by the Mersey.

The prospect of soggy flat caps and wet ciggies all-round wasn't exactly going to attract people to Anfield, so the board of directors decided the time had come to build a roof.

Mr J Watson Cabre, an architect from Great Crosby, was put in charge of the new development and by the start of the 1928/29 season Anfield had the first roofed-in Kop in the country.

Part of the terracing was also redeveloped during the construction work so apart from the cinder hill beneath the terracing and three concrete staircases, Kopites had virtually a brand new home.

Up to 28,000 fans could now be accommodated, and the roof – 80 foot high, 425 feet long and 131 feet wide – dominated the Anfield skyline.

The outside walls and six internal stanchions of the Kop were said to carry a massive 45,500 square feet of roof space – into which 91 standard houses could be packed together in one layer.

It was a big roof for a big club who had big ambitions.

As the roof went up so did the entrance price. It now cost one shilling (five pence) to stand on the Kop.

You couldn't afford one of Fernando Torres' eyelashes for five pence these days but, nonetheless, that was still a hefty price for the majority to pay, particularly as unemployment was beginning to bite on Merseyside.

The new-look Kop was officially opened by the President of the Football League, and former secretary, director and chairman of the club, John McKenna on August 25.

Liverpool beat Bury 3-0 that day in front of 40,000 fans and McKenna was reportedly presented with a gold cigar to mark the occasion.

Far more significant for the 40,000 who weren't presented with gold cigars was the moment when Billy Millar opened the scoring for Liverpool.

With just 50 seconds on the clock Millar headed home and the new Kop erupted for the first time.

It was like a volcano had gone off. The acoustics were fantastic, the noise was something else.

The Kop had a wall like no other in football – a wall of noise.

Not only had putting a roof over the terracing stopped the rain from getting in, it had stopped the noise from getting out.

Liverpool Football Club had a 12th Man.

But it would be another 30 years or so, and the inspiration of one man, before they got the best out of him.

'The fans here are the greatest in the land.
They know the game and they know what they want to see.
The people on the Kop make you feel great – yet humble.
I'm just one of the people who stands on the Kop. They think the
same as I do, and I think the same as they do. It's a kind of
marriage of people who like each other'

– Bill Shankly

... And I come from the Spion Kop

A wild trip minus seatbelts or brakes
– Brian Reade, journalist

In the beginning I was never hard enough for the Kop.

Tales of drunken dockers, big lads who yockered in your hair and robbed your chip money sent me scuttling for the safety of the Anfield Road end. But it wasn't safe at all.

This was the late Sixties when no segregation meant nutters in Bakers, braces and boots flew past you knocking lumps out of shaven heads, while you soldered your hands to the crush barrier for fear of losing your life or, even worse, your spec.

They were the Alun Evans' seasons. Silverless years but golden days. Away from home Liverpool were Stoke City but at Anfield they were Real Madrid.

The players steamrollered opponents into submission, the manager's charisma set him apart from other mortals and the Kop was the greatest collective mass of passion, wit and song in any walk of British life.

I can still feel the surge of pride at ten to three as the teams were read out. The Wrigleys moving faster. The churn in the pit of the stomach, small at first, then spreading.

The sudden rush of adrenalin in the split second between Liverpool's substitute being announced and Gerry Marsden uttering "Whey–en," – the signal for that massive red and white shutter to rise and block everything else out on the horizon.

The faces on the away fans struck dumb by a vision, like George Best worth the admission fee alone, some of them raising kids above their shoulders to glimpse the eighth wonder of the world.

The men in the stands, standing. Faces riveted to the Kop. Watching grace being sung before the meal. There were few banners then: Europe had yet to be conquered. No adidas shirts or multi–coloured scarves. Money had yet to conquer. Just a wall of sound and a crashing sea of red and white.

I plunged into it on November 21, 1970. It was derby day, my second day as a teenager, and possibly the most delirious day of my life. Everton were champions and playing like it.

The Horse (Joe Royle) and the Rat (Alan Whittle) had put them two up with 20 minutes to go.

Misery stared me in the face as well as a surrounding knot of Evertonians on the outer edges of the Kop. (I never dared stand in the middle then. They were feudal plots handed down by fathers).

When Heighway scored, a huge wave that turned into a Blackpool rollercoaster lifted me and nearly unhinged my neck from my spine. When Toshack scored I flew a full 30 feet down the terrace and was thrown back like whiplash.

When Lawler scored the winner I went under like a dog tied to an old bed. I was sucked up, heaved back about 15 feet, tossed into the air and landed lodged between two men trying to make love.

For the remaining six minutes my feet didn't touch the deck and when they did I was minus one patent leather Chelsea boot and bus fare. I walked home to Huyton, a grin splitting my face and the concrete splitting my sole. It was the most lethal Ecstasy a teenager could taste.

In those days the Kop starred in its own movies and the players vied for best supporting actor. The film and sound crews turned up to record not a footballing phenomenon but a social one. Rock groups like Pink Floyd put us on best-selling albums. Kop albums were recorded. Foreign documentary teams sent their Dimblebys to record all this happening.

As the '70s turned into '80s and Liverpool went for world domination the players became stars.

They less and less needed a goal sucking in.

There were the breathless nights of emotion like St Etienne, but the Beatle–wigged Kopite had become Scouser Tommy, sent far away from his home to Paris, London and Rome.

That's where the big nights were. Domestic success had become like a rates bill – an annual demand paid in sobering instalments.

As the '90s approached, the Kop had changed.

Reduced capacity, success over-kill and increased traffic from York and Yeovil transforming its nature.

I headed for the stands when a mate moaned his wallet had grown but his body hadn't, but the eyes and the spirit were still there on big occasions.

The Kop really belonged to the '60s, '70s and part of the '80s when the mound was packed and you swayed with reckless abandon on a wild trip minus seatbelts or brakes.

We, more than any other set of fans, should appreciate why, sadly, the joyriding had to stop.

The Kopite wasn't wittier than the man on the Gwladys Street. He wasn't a better singer than a Stretford Ender.

But he was part of a collective voice, generosity, attitude, tradition and spirit that was unique.

'Which end is the Kop?'
– Steve Heighway, former Liverpool player

My first experience of the Kop was in May 1970.

I was still a student at Warwick University but had decided to sign professional for Liverpool on completing my degree in June.

As a student I was quite surprised to be called by Mr Bill Shankly who invited me to play in Gerry Byrne's testimonial for a Celebrity XI against a Liverpool side.

Not only was it my first visit to Anfield but at 22 it was my first ever visit to Liverpool itself. It was a filthy night with rain and sleet, but I recall that 50,000 people were there.

The two teams walked side by side to the centre of the pitch and

I stood next to an Everton full-back who was playing in the Celebrity team. With total honesty and complete naivety I quietly said to him: "Which end is the Kop?". He looked at me as if I had come from another planet and pointed to the bulging end rather than just the full end.

That was my first experience and, of course, there were many more opportunities to play in front of what was very obviously the fanatical end.

I had good games and bad games through my 11 years but I feel extremely fortunate that at no time did I ever feel any animosity from the Kop.

I would have found that very difficult to live with and I am eternally grateful that the Kop always seemed to recognise that I was doing my best.

The old Kop went back bloody miles!
– The late Sir Bobby Robson, football manager

I loved Liverpool. I just thought it was a great cathedral and a great place to play. I remember the old Kop, which went back bloody miles. I don't know how many it held – maybe 18-20,000 – everybody standing.

Those are the days that I remember; the swell of the Kop, the surge of the Kop, the singing of the Kop. Oh, it was a great place. I enjoyed going to Liverpool when I was with Ipswich. I never won. I remember getting a 3-3 draw one day. They were great days.

It always seems to be a cauldron there. The roar of the Kop; the enthusiasm within the public. It spills on to the pitch, I think.

There was always a smell of adrenalin at Liverpool, I tell you. I just think it's been one of the great stadiums of all time, for years and years and years. You have produced, over the years, fantastic teams.

Stars of a different kind
– Joe Fagan, former Liverpool manager

Kop support was above anything else and straight from the heart. Those supporters lifted players to undreamed of heights.

I have two personal memories from standing on the Kop as a lad before the war. Sunderland, in the days of Bobby Gurney and Raich Carter, were the smartest turned out team I had ever seen.

And I remember cracking my head on a barrier and seeing stars of a different kind!

Zico and Phil Eel
– Phil Neal, former Liverpool captain

I loved the night games at Anfield in the cool of the evening. With the steam coming off the Kop and the steam coming off my red jersey, we were together.

They nicknamed me 'Zico' one year. I was in the twilight of my career and I scored 11 goals. I think five of them were from outfield play and mostly scored at the Kop end. I was letting them fly left foot, right foot and amazingly, considering I was the number two, they nicknamed me Zico. I will always, always have that as my fondest memory.

To be given the name Zico, after that famous Brazilian, I must have been playing as a man possessed. I didn't want it to end. That was probably the most affection they gave me.

I used to be Liverpool's penalty taker and took quite a few in front of the Kop.

It was usually fine. Nine out of 10 went in and I just concentrated on striking the ball. I hated to miss them and I remember missing one on my birthday in the FA Cup.

That disappointed me more than anything else at the Kop end. It was Bob Paisley's last season, I think, and that miss led us to an exit in the FA Cup. That hurt me. I was very disappointed.

The Kop were great with me, though. They lifted me again and I look at it as a blip on the landscape. I carried on taking penalties after that and carried on knocking them in. They encouraged me and that helped a lot. There were some humorous nights that I remember well too.

We played Grimsby in the cup and were winning quite comfortably. The Kop decided to have some fun and with Grimsby being a fishing town they started to rename us with fish-related names. They were singing 'Jimmy Plaice' at Jimmy Case, 'Phil Eel' at me, 'Kenny Dogfish' at Kenny Dalglish and one or two others. It was fantastic. The humour was wonderful.

I wondered how they did it and how it could ring throughout that fantastic mass so quickly. The Kop had great tradition. I remember watching it on television before I even joined Liverpool and saw that somebody had fainted. They were passed down to the bottom over the top of the heads. I'd never seen that before.

I think it was a very happy, warm place, particularly on a chilly night. When we won the toss and kicked that way, second half we would bombard people.

I certainly learnt from the Scousers playing alongside me that it was a special place. It reminded me of when I went to the Nou Camp for the first time and on the way to the pitch there is a chapel. The Kop was my chapel, really, and the defining part of the ground. Anyone else who played there in a red shirt would probably say that too.

There's one thing I do rue about the Kop – never to have stood there and watched a game.

I've got a lad and it's something I should have done. But that's the way of the world and I've got some great memories of playing in front of it.

My mate's Kop cast-off
– Steve Devine, Kopite

What was better than a Saturday afternoon standing in the middle of the Spion Kop?

Jostling your way into the centre of the crowd – where the singing and chanting was; the songs, the swaying the atmosphere. It was second to none.

My memories of the Kop include the 3-3 draw with Man Utd and the 'parting of the red sea'. It was 3-2 to Man U at the time when suddenly I felt a little unwell! I shouted out to everyone around me that I was going to be sick and like the parting of the sea a space appeared as if from nowhere.

Seconds before we were all arm to arm, snuggled in, and then I was able to walk straight down the middle of the Kop to the St John Ambulance men at the front, where I was allowed to cool down before watching Razor Ruddock hammer an unstoppable header into the Anfield Road end past a helpless Peter Schmeichel.

Another memory was the victory against Auxerre when even though the Kop was only half-full the atmosphere was second to none. It was freezing but being in the middle of the Spion Kop generated enough heat to keep us warm. Mark Walters' goal, and his classic step-over, might not go down as one of the most explosive moments in LFC history but oh, what a memory.

And then, of course, there was the 'Kop's Last Stand' versus Norwich City. Four of us jostled our way into the Kop. One lad had a cast on his leg.

By the end everyone agreed that it will be missed forever, nearly as much as my mate's cast was. It had come off during the jostling of the match!

Nobody was hurt but this is surely one of the maddest things that has ever happened to someone.

'Come on, let's have a go!'
– Joey Jones, fromer Liverpool player

I did it on my home debut against West Ham when I ran out in front of the Kop for the first time. I heard them chanting my name so I put my fist up and it was something they could identify with because I had come off the Kop. Whenever the crowd chanted my name I felt like I was representing them so I acknowledged them with the clenched fist – 'come on, let's have a go'. It was never to cause trouble.

'I've never heard a roar like it'
– Harry Mooney, former club scout

I first went on the Kop when it opened. It was just a bank then with no roof on. I lived in Everton Valley back then and it was only a short walk to the ground. My uncle Bill would take me. He'd carry me on his shoulders. He took me into the ground, on to the Kop, and he put me on the barrier. He'd say: "This is where you belong, son" and I'd say "Yes, Uncle Bill."

I didn't realise that would be the start of all the wonderful years that I would be involved with the club because I ended up doing some scouting for them.

One game I'll always remember was in 1963 when we played Burnley in an FA Cup replay on a Wednesday night. The score was one each and it went into extra-time. Liverpool got a penalty in the last minute kicking towards the Kop. Dead silence. Nobody wanted to take it because it was so important. So Ronnie Moran picked the ball up and his attitude was 'let me take it'.

He didn't take penalties normally but he put it on the spot, walked back, ran up to the ball and cracked it. He scored and the Kop – well, I've never heard a roar like it. You see, the pubs and clubs used to close at ten o'clock then. It was quarter-to-ten and it meant we still had to rush down the Kop steps to get a pint.

The referee turned round and blew his whistle to signal the end of the game and we were straight off, running down the Kop steps.

There were some steps on the Kop in those days. There were so many I used to slide down the bannisters sometimes!

Anyway, we all went down as quick as we could, out of the gate and into the Walker's House next door. I think we had four pints and were in there to something like eleven o'clock. That was a great night.

I remember watching Wales play Scotland at Anfield. I was in the Paddock that night and even though it was strange watching a game there that didn't involve Liverpool, the atmosphere was still fantastic and still got to me. The Kop, as it was back then, used to act like an echo. The roar would go out of the ground and you could hear it down at the bottom of Utting Avenue by Broadway. You could hear the roar from there. Terrific.

It brought out our best
— Alan Kennedy, former Liverpool player

You never knew how many were in the old Kop. Allegedly, there were 25,000 but I think there could be more for really big games.

They affectionately nicknamed me 'Barney Rubble', maybe because I played like The Flintstones character; running through walls and giving everything.

The Kop was so vociferous. They used to really chant our names and get behind us. At times that ball used to be sucked into the back of the net. Maybe they came to expect us to win every game at Anfield but sometimes that wasn't the case. One of the good things about it was they always gave the opposing goalkeeper a round of applause. In 1981/82, when we won the league against

Tottenham, Ray Clemence came back and they gave him a great round of applause. I think that gees goalkeepers up.

Does anywhere else compare with the Kop? Not in this country. We played against Benfica in the Stadium of Light and that was a bit intimidating. It was a very high stadium, with 120,000 people. When people saw all those people on the Kop, the hair stood up on the back of the neck.

I'm sure some just froze at Anfield but it often also brought out the best in people.

Do you want gate receipts or cash from the empties?'
– Eric Doig, LFC statistician and lifelong fan

A match, which stands out in my mind, illustrates the difference between the old Kop and the present stand.

Liverpool met Glasgow Celtic in the second leg of the European Cup Winners Cup on April 19th, 1966. The first leg on the 14th in Glasgow was lost by 1-0 and the Celtic supporters were confident of a victory.

After all, no team had scored more than one goal against them in this competition. But we were sure of going through to the final.

Why? Because Shanks had said so.

The Celtic supporters started arriving in the morning for the evening game and were drifting around the ground carrying their 'liquid' refreshment. A few were so 'tired' that they missed the game, sleeping it off in the streets outside.

About two hours before kick-off I joined the crowd opting to use the turnstiles in the centre of the Kop as the queues were heavy up Kemlyn Road. There was no real attempt by the police at crowd control, only to keep the main road free for traffic.

There was a great press of humanity around the four gates, pushing and shoving to get near a gate. The crowd would surge and we would be swept past to start again from the other side.

Eventually getting in, a programme was bought from a man with a satchel, price four (old) pence.

The many steps up to the top were climbed (I never did count these), paused at the top to look back at the panoramic view of the city before turning again to see the best view in the world – Anfield from the very back of the Kop.

Down the terracing to the usual spec in the middle and soon joined by a small group of fans from Hull who travelled to every game by mini-van. A shilling sweep was organised for the first goal scorer. Sir Roger was not playing so chances would be even. I drew the goalkeeper!

Banter was starting up and the solitary jovial policeman walked up and down behind the Kop goal. Beatlemania was in full swing – 'We Love You, yeah, yeah, yeah!' The Celtic crowd, seemingly many more than their 5,000 allocation, waved green and white flags chanting 'Celtic, Celtic', the Kop replying with 'Rangers' and 'go back to Ireland'. An hour to go before kick off and the Kop was jammed, packed with 28,000 fans.

No chance of getting out.

There were no refreshment bars or betting kiosks anyway. At last the heroes appeared on the field to a tumultuous welcome.

Names were chanted – Lawrence, Lawler, Byrne, Milne, Yeats, Stevenson, Callaghan, Strong, St John, Smith, Thompson. It was soon clear that the game would be a bruising battle. Tommy Smith hit the post and Chris Lawler of all people, missed from close in.

Soon after the half-hour Geoff Strong badly injured his knee and could only hobble about. Lennox missed a good chance for Celtic. Half-time passed with no goals scored. With time passing the crowd roared the team on: 'Attack, Attack, Attack'. Smith had been fouled heavily a couple of times and on the second occasion, just after the hour, he rose up to hit the free kick into the corner of the net to rapturous applause. A few minutes later a dribble by Thompson, a through ball to Cally and an immaculate centre for Strong to leap up on his one leg to head the ball past Simpson.

A nerve-wracking 20 minutes to go. Celtic got the ball into the net but the offside flag was up much to the relief of the home side and the ire of the away fans, raining bottles down at the Anfield Road end. A nail-biting last couple of minutes and we were through to our very first European final. Shankly was to remark later to his friend Jock Stein "would he take his share of the gate money or would he prefer to take the cash from the empty bottles?"

Memory and friendship
– Chris McLoughlin, The Kop Magazine, April 2005

> *Memoria e amicizia – in memory and friendship.*
> *15-4-89 – Sheffield – God Exists!*

You could say that the welcome Juventus fans got at Anfield was somewhat different to the 'welcome' Liverpool fans received in Turin – summed up by these contrasting messages.

While the supporters of Liverpool Football Club treated the Champions League tie between the two sides in a dignified, respectful and mature manner, Juve's Ultras used it as an opportunity to try and get some sort of revenge for what happened at Heysel.

A lot of Juventus fans, including some of the victims' families, have been moved by Liverpool's attempts to try and say sorry for what went on in Belgium and build bridges between the two clubs. They were the ones who warmly applauded the 'Amicizia' mosaic on the Kop and who have accepted that Liverpool's sorrow for the disaster is both genuine and heartfelt.

Those Ultras who turned their backs, whistled and gave a one-fingered salute to the 'Memoria e amicizia' banner that Liverpool fans took from the Kop down to the Juve end at Anfield were in a minority. The members of the Italian press inside the ground were deeply embarrassed by their reaction.

Kopite Pete Carney's 'Memoria e amicizia' banner, which contains the Christian names of the 39 victims and the symbolic Liver Bird and Juve Zebra, was particularly poignant and an important gesture on behalf of Kopites.

That banner was originally made in 1995, to commemorate the 10th anniversary of Heysel, and disproves any suggestions that Liverpool's fans only wanted to make peace because the two teams were playing each other. In addition to that was the excellent mosaic and a commemorative plaque, prepared by local sculptor Garry White, which Ian Rush and Michel Platini jointly carried alongside Phil Neal on to the pitch at Anfield.

Every Liverpool fan who attended either or both games deserves credit for their behaviour and conduct.

They paid their respects, acted sensibly and sensitively, and despite some intense provocation in Turin didn't react other than briefly returning some of the missiles, which any set of fans under such a bombardment would do.

They also helped to sway the tie in Liverpool's favour by creating an atmosphere at Anfield that, for all their experience, the Juventus players found too hot to handle

Fabio Capello must hate coming to Anfield. He saw his Roma team win on Merseyside in 2001 but go out 2-1 on aggregate before seeing them blown away in the Champions League a year later amidst a sensational atmosphere as Gerard Houllier made his emotional comeback. Now he's seen his Juventus melt in the Anfield cauldron in 2005 and sincerely believes Liverpool's fans play a huge part in their team's success.

Funny how visiting continental managers never say that about Old Trafford, Stamford Bridge or The Emirates, eh?

It confirms that we DO have an advantage over other clubs because of the noise we can generate.

Even before Juve came to Anfield Capello talked about how his players must "prepare for the atmosphere". But despite being warned about the wall of noise they would face, some of Europe's most experienced and talented footballers were still made to look like gibbering wrecks by a group of fans who constantly get reminded that that the atmosphere they create 'ain't a patch on how it used to be'. There goes another myth.

We've said this time and time again but when Liverpool supporters are up for it there is absolutely no other set of fans in Europe who can produce such a passionate, partisan atmosphere. Seats or no seats.

Like their players have done this season, the Kop saves its best for European nights.

Juve '05 is up there with the best of them. The noise levels were phenomenal. You could hear the Fields of Anfield Road being sung as far away as Athenry. There was a worry that with the build-up inevitably dominated by Heysel there could be a somewhat sombre atmosphere inside Anfield for the first leg. But after Liverpool's supporters had respectfully paid their tributes they proved those fears wrong by producing a cacophony of noise.

The old standing Spion Kop produced some unforgettable nights but for many Kopites the likes of Inter Milan and St Etienne came before their time.

For the current era of younger Liverpool fans Barcelona '01, Roma '02, Olympiakos '04 and Juventus '05 mean as much as the halcyon days of 1965 and 1977 do to older Kopites.

Leaving a ground knowing YOU made a difference is one hell of a feeling.

Leaving a ground and hearing your opponents' manager, who happens to be Fabio Capello, admit that is awesome. It's as close to getting out there on the pitch and scoring the winner as we'll ever get.

He thought I was a bird!
– John Aldridge, former Liverpool player

I started off on the Kop in the boys' pen and I can remember one funny incident that happened to me.

I was about 13 and at the time I had very long hair. I was down right at the front of the Kop and behind me was this big bloke, a docker or a bouncer or something.

Every time the Kop surged forward I could feel him pressed right up against me. I was worried he was going to roll up an Echo and piss down my leg but when the surge stopped he moved back a bit and said to me 'sorry, love'. He thought I was a bird! I'll tell you something, I got rid of that haircut straight away after that! There was no danger of me going on the Kop again with long hair.

I can well remember the first time I played in front of the Kop. It was brilliant. I was playing for Oxford United at the time and before the game I went on Football Focus and did a piece with them where I said what a big Liverpool fan I was.

We got tonked that afternoon. Liverpool were magnificent. It was 6-0 and I think Rushie got two. I got a great reception from the Kop though and I think we were about 4-0 down and all I could hear was them singing 'Aldo is a Kopite'. That was really nice. I really appreciated it.

I think I summed up what the Kop and those who stood on it meant to me in my final game for Liverpool. It was the night we beat Crystal Palace 9-0 and I scored a penalty after Kenny brought me on. I hadn't planned it, it was totally off the cuff, but I threw my shirt and my boots into the Kop. I didn't want to leave Liverpool and I know that they didn't want me to go either. It was a very emotional night for me.

When the Kop chanted Everton!
– Frank Walker, Kopite

I remember the time the Kop actually chanted Everton! It sounds like it can't be true but it was. It was a night match against Coventry City in 1977 in the old League Cup. There were Coventry fans in the Kemlyn Road stand right by the Kop. Somehow Coventry managed to score which was unusual in those days. Everton had just beaten Coventry 6-0 and when they started chanting '1-0' we all started chanting 'Everton'. It was loud and I'm still washing my mouth out with soap to this day!

It made me feel very proud
– Erik Meijer, former Liverpool player

I obviously knew about the Kop before I had signed for Liverpool. It has always been something special, especially when it was a standing area. To my knowledge, the only other place where you would get 26,000 people standing behind a goal like that was at Borussia Dortmund.

Liverpool, as a club, is something special to me. That's probably because I signed for them as a fan. And my first real experience of the Kop as a player was fantastic.

When I started the game against Leeds and I heard everyone singing 'You'll Never Walk Alone', I felt as though I was two metres 10 tall instead of one metre 90.

It made me feel very proud, because the people there were singing with their hearts. The Liverpool fans were always great to me. I got a good reaction from them, which is something every player looks for. That's what makes football special.

Parting of the Red Sea
— Bernie Swift, policeman who patrolled old Kop

I started off on the Kop standing in the Boys' Pen. They won the cup in 1965 and at the start of the following season they played Honved, a Hungarian army team.

What was the boys' pen like? Violent! I also remember as a kid standing on the Kop.

It was common for the bobbies, wearing those long rain-coats, to be spat upon, although thankfully I've never experienced this myself. You would see the odd policeman there and his coat would be showered in saliva. It was horrible, absolutely horrible, and thankfully I was never subjected to that.

I joined the police in the 1970s and in the late 1980s I was an inspector in the mounted section. At the Kop end they had cash gates.

This was all pre-Hillsborough and now it's very rare to have cash turnstiles but back then the Lake Street gates, and at flagpole corner, were cash gates.

I remember being in the mounted, not long having been in the department, and cutting my teeth on learning to control the queues. You'd get down to Kemlyn Road and Lake Street for 12.30pm on a Saturday afternoon and the queues were 100 yards long then and five deep. That was just the norm. If there's any sign of anything near that now we start to get a bit fidgety.

Some of the old mounted police officers were very sophisticated riders and would shout at people. The crowds would just accept this and do as they were told.

An awful lot of football supporters are not frightened of making their feelings known and can be quite stubborn when they want to but they can be very, very co-operative too.

We had one game, I think it was the Auxerre game, when some-one collapsed on the Kop.

A chap had suffered a heart attack and the paramedics wanted to get to him. I made a PA announcement to allow them to get through and it was like the parting of the Red Sea.

The crowd themselves made a corridor for the paramedics to get through to treat this chap. The Kop can be very co-operative when they want to.

A river down the steps
– Ray Edwards, policeman who patrolled old Kop

The big downside of the Kop was the toilet facilities. They were useless.

Of course, before the game everyone would go and have a couple of pints before coming into the ground but after 20 minutes they'd want to go to the toilet. That's where the old rolled up Echo would come in handy and people would think they were sweating because they were suddenly nice and warm!

It was even worse at half-time. They used to come out and go towards flagpole corner.

Because the toilet facilities were right down the bottom and couldn't cater for the thousands of people who wanted to use them, they'd line the walls of the actual steps going down and have a pee down the side.

When I was at the back of the Kop by the tea bar I'd try to make sure no-one was doing that in view of the girls who worked there.

I'd get complaints too. Some fella came over once and said "What are you going to do about this?" because it was like a river going down the steps.

He said he wanted them all arrested but it was impossible to arrest all these people because we didn't have sufficient bobbies on duty. The river would go down and it used to steam. It was totally inadequate the way the system was.

We didn't have the same equipment, in terms of clothing, as we do now. I remember that we only had thin Macs which didn't provide any warmth at all in those days.

At the time, some of the bobbies used to make scarves, which had your collar number in the scarf so no-one would pinch it, and on match day they'd wear them.

But one day the football inspector pointed at the scarves and said 'I don't want to see any of these in the ground today,' which meant he wanted to be able to see our shirts and ties which looked better.

But as time progressed we had sergeants coming from the Kop into the police control room carrying all these red and white scarves. They'd taken it as 'I don't want to see any scarves inside the ground at all' and had taken them off the fans as they came into the Kop. There were bundles, armfuls of these red and white scarves which they'd taken off people who had handed them over after they'd been told 'no scarves in here'. They must have took it as 'If you don't give us your scarf you're not coming in' but that's not what he'd meant.

You also used to be able to buy bottles of beer at Liverpool and take them on to the Kop. After drinking a bottle, some of them would be thinking what to do with it and see a copper on the pitch. 'He'll do' and they'd come flying down.

'Ejaculating' a male from the Kop!
– Tom King, a policeman who patrolled the old Kop

I remember well the queues at Lake Street and flagpole corner because it was a common occurrence that people would be locked out, particularly from the Kop.

It was cheap to get in and, apart from the Anfield Road end, the only area with cash turnstiles and also the area that was exceptionally popular. It was an art to see the way the mounted police turned the queues and snaked them to ease the pressure off the front.

No-one likes queuing but people would conform with what you wanted them to do because they wanted to get into the ground. If you asked them to do something they would do so without a problem. You'd get the odd moan – 'yer don't know what yer doin'– but you've just got to put up with that. You get that every week but in the main they were good natured.

If there was any trouble we used to have a system where by if somebody was ejected from the stadium the officer would notify the control room and give them a description of where they were ejected from or give their name and address.

When we first started this system we had a policewoman who passed a message to the control room that she had just 'ejaculated' a male from the Kop!

'Never look at the Kop'
– Stephen Shakeshaft, photographer

I first met the Kop when I was 17 years of age as a young photographer. It was 1966 and I'd never seen anything like it.

As a kid I'd been a Tranmere Rovers fan and spent my sixpence on a Saturday watching them. The first time I was introduced to the Kop I actually had to lie in front of it. It was an unbelievable thing to have had to do.

You'd dress for the Kop. It was one of the few football grounds that you'd actually dress for with protective clothing which was no use whatsoever because it was designed for the elements – not the Kop.

Putting a groundsheet down in front of the Kop then meant that you immediately obliterated any view of the people who had got in there hours before you and were right on the front wall. Their eye-level was grass and they'd be looking along the pitch.

You'd walk round to the Kop in trepidation, lay a groundsheet down and lie flat on your stomach before trying to make yourself disappear into the turf.

Fat photographers didn't stand a chance. They'd only be sat there for a few minutes before they'd be verbally destroyed by the Kop.

So you had to literally try and bury yourself in the ground and that's the most difficult position to try and take photographs because you're lying prostrate.

In those days you'd start off about two feet away from the goal-post. Conversations were regular with the goalkeeper. There were certainly goalkeepers who would talk to us.

John Osborne at West Brom would and Blackpool's Jimmy Armfield, a full-back, would come over and start chatting. It was uncanny being so close to the action.

Unless you got to the Kop pretty quickly you were the end photographer in the line and your elbow would end up on the white line. In really big games at Anfield, all the photographers would want to get down there. We'd all lie down but the angle meant you could only get a maximum of eight photographers.

If you got there too late you were on the touchline and that was the danger zone. Imagine being, and I'm not exaggerating, an inch away from the touchline.

One referee was concerned and stopped a game to move us. But the most difficult thing of all was when people like Steve Heighway and Peter Thompson played. They were wingers who would take the ball to the touchline before crossing.

The momentum of their body and the way they'd wait until the very last second before crossing meant that they couldn't stop. We were a natural cushion for them. When that happened there was a moment of fear. It was like being a sandwich between the action and the crowd. You'd close your eyes and wait for the crunch on your back. It was a regular occurrence. Steve Heighway used to give me nightmares.

European players visiting Anfield were worse. They'd never played in such a tight arena before and they couldn't work out how long it would take them to stop

They'd go over us and land in the Kop where hands would go up to catch them, except for a Bruges player who ended up landing on my back and knocking me unconscious! I was out cold and had to be brought round by the St John Ambulance people, much to the amusement of the Kop.

They thought it was great fun. 'Yer in for nothing, Mister, we've had to stand here for two hours'. So they'd like you to get soaking wet or whatever.

The Anfield Road end was luxury. On a hot day you could sit in the sun and the crowd were higher up. At half-time you'd walk round to the Kop and on a cold day it was like walking towards a convector heater.

You could feel the heat coming off the thousands of people who were stood together. It was extraordinary.

How comfortable we were depended a lot on the result of the game and what was happening. If there was a bad referee, a goalkeeper they didn't like or a full-back who'd fouled a Liverpool player, the obvious things happened.

You knew what was going to come. There was a shower of stuff. Everything you could imagine but coins mainly. We had old currency in my early days in front of the Kop.

If a fan was really angry he'd throw half a crown, which was a heavy coin and you wouldn't want one of them hitting you on the ear.

The golden rule was never to look at the Kop. If you did you'd take the chance of a coin hitting you in the face. I've also seen meat pies and other things I wouldn't care to mention come flying down. I remember one game when there had been a lot of aggro and I got all the coins together and photographed them. There was enough money there to go and buy a round of drinks which we did after the game.

For those who smoked on the Kop, there was nowhere to put their cigarette butts so they'd throw them as well. Many cigarettes landed on my back and burnt through my coat. You'd hear 'eh Mister, you're on fire'. If you were lucky a policeman would put the fire out with his shoe by standing on your back.

I also saw some awful things like darts being thrown, and I was once fired at with a pellet gun during a European game. Something was twanging off our heads and it turned out to be coming from a hand pistol. I handed a pellet to the police.

I've seen lads being taken out with darts in their faces so there was a side of the Kop that you had to take on board as one of those things you had to put up with.

The good side was the camaraderie. They were so funny. I've laughed so much at some of the natural wit from the Kop. It used to fascinate me how a song would evolve. Something would happen and a player would be singled out. Suddenly, the whole Kop were singing as one, a song that they couldn't possibly have rehearsed.

They all knew the words and some great songs evolved. I remember when they took the pop song 'The Mighty Quinn' and it suddenly became 'The Mighty Emlyn'. They seemed to be able to turn whatever the big pop song was at the time into a song about one of their players.

They'd have special songs for opposition players who they liked, such as Gordon Banks. Players like him would turn round and applaud the Kop although plenty of players would run off quickly because they weren't as popular.

I remember Tommy Smith once wearing white boots for the first time. As soon as he came on the pitch there was a song about it. He was in hysterics because they'd picked up straight away on it.

I don't care what anyone says, I know Rodgers and Hammerstein wrote 'You'll Never Walk Alone' for Carousel but that song has never been more poignant than when it's sung by the Kop on a European night.

Hearing the Kop and Gerry Marsden sing it together make the hairs on the back of your neck stand up. Every time I lay in front of them it was like being in front of a giant stereo.

There were some great characters on there too. I remember the woman with the bell. She'd always be in the same place behind the goal and she'd come in with a fire bell. It'd drive you mad.

Other strange things have happened. I remember losing my shoes once. They didn't have laces on and flicked off as I lay down. I had to persuade this lad to give them me back before I could leave the ground.

Those were the days when the Kop was very full and you'd see people, who had fainted or needed to be taken out, passed down over all the heads. They'd land on top of us too! Once I found a kid had jumped onto the groundsheet next to me and said 'don't tell anyone, Mister, pretend I'm a photographer'.

I told him that I wasn't going to shop him to a policeman but if he was going to lie next to me he'd have to be very quiet. Sure enough, as soon as Liverpool scored, he jumped up in front of me with his arms up. He was pulled out straight away.

Bill Shankly thought the Kop was everything. I was there one day when he was scattering a fan's ashes on the Kop with a family and he came over and asked me what I was doing there. He said I was being intrusive and it was a private moment. I said: "I know,

Bill, but the family have asked me to come along and take a picture". I took a picture and that was the only photograph of Bill Shankly scattering ashes on the Kop. No-one had ever seen a picture like that before.

He was very moved because it was one of his lads, one of his supporters who had stood on the Kop.

I remember the day when he stood on the Kop and watched a game. He didn't tell anyone he was going to do it. He was spotted by us. Could you imagine any other manager doing that? The Kop was Shanks' family. That's how he saw them. They were all his sons on that Kop and he was their dad. Everything he did was right. I never once heard one word against Shankly. He was their father. I don't think that could ever happen again.

The most difficult pictures I've taken in front of the Kop were on the morning after Hillsborough.

I got to Anfield at 7am, after being on Lime Street Station when the fans returned from Sheffield the night before, and they opened the ground up because so many people had arrived to lay flowers.

We walked in single file and I watched lads, sisters, mothers and fathers go to the spot that their brother or sister; son or daughter had stood on the Kop. They'd sit there and tie a little bundle of flowers around the crush barrier. I felt really intrusive being there with a camera but they were pictures I had to take because they recorded an event that you couldn't believe was happening.

It was so spontaneous. It would only happen at Liverpool. They had to go to the Kop. It was almost as if they were going to church and had to be there to identify with their son or daughter. It was the most moving experience. As I was taking photos, the Salvation Army had walked in with a band and they played 'Abide With Me'. I found it most tearful. I've never seen Anfield so quiet. It was like being in a Cathedral. It wasn't stage-managed, it was all a spontaneous and sincere reaction and took everyone by surprise.

The flowers and scarves were knitted together and it eventually came out to the half-way line. Liverpool rang me and asked me to come up and take a photograph for them.

I took a picture from the TV gantry to show this carpet. It was filled exactly to the halfway line. It was a tapestry of colour laid by people from around the country.

It was incredible.

On cloud nine – with only one shoe
– Mel Freeman, Kopite

I remember that famous night we beat St Etienne in March 1977. At that time, I used to travel to Liverpool from my home in Birmingham on the train. I was 17, just started work, and used to spend most of my £19 weekly wages on following the Reds.

That day, I caught the midday train to Lime Street and arrived at the ground at around 3.30pm. Some lads I used to meet on the train from Bristol joined me in the Sandon for some pre-match beverages. We used to cram into the tiny little room on the side of the pub.

At around 5.30pm someone came in and said the queues were all around the ground, so we decided to join the fray, in case it was a lock-out. From then on, with the French in their bright green wigs and swaying crowd outside the ground, it became my most memorable occasion of following the mighty Reds. I stood around the middle of the Kop and when the teams came out it was incredible. I'm sure the crowd blew Keegan's cross into the net after a minute.

Gradually though, it dawned on us that this French team were no pushovers and when they equalised, it was pretty much deserved. The Kop once again showed why we have the greatest reputation for getting behind our team and willed Razor's (Ray Kennedy's) goal to drag ourselves back. Then the moment that anyone who was there will surely put in their top 10 moments of life itself. Supersub scored. I will never forget the second it happened. We held our breath before he struck the ball. We knew this was it – the end of our dream if he missed, the realisation of our dream if it went in. Sure, there were more rounds to play but St Etienne were the best team left in the cup.

All I remember about the madness when it went in was – I lost my shoe! My brown platform heeled shoe shot off my foot, never to be seen again. I waited until the crowd cleared and looked every- where for it before happily resigning myself to limping home to Birmingham with one shoe. I had to catch the last train to Crewe at around 11.45pm, wait for a train to Rugby at around 1am, sleep at Rugby for a couple of hours then catch a mail train to Birmingham arriving at 6am. I would then go straight to work because I started at 7am. When I limped into work with one shoe I was still on cloud nine and no amount of mickey-taking could alter my mood.

A little piece of history I've got
– Ashley Neal, former Liverpool reserve player

I've always supported Liverpool. I was about six or eight weeks old when we moved to the city because of my dad so I was a big time Liverpool fan from a young age. I've got pure red blood and I used to stand on the Kop myself.

I was on it for the Auxerre game, which for me is one of the most memorable of them all, and I used to go and stand on it regularly before the club signed me up as a YTS lad.

There's one goal I scored for Liverpool reserves that I will never forget. We played Nottingham Forest at Anfield shortly before the Kop's last stand and drew the game 2-2. I scored Liverpool's second goal at the Kop end and it came from a penalty.

Of course, my dad used to take them for Liverpool so there was a little bit of pressure on me.

I remember there was a lad in our team, a Scottish lad, and he was fighting me for the ball. Luckily enough I was captain of the reserves at the time so I said to him: "Sod off, I'm having it".

I stepped up and stuck it into the right corner of the net.

I didn't know it at the time and luckily enough that was the last goal scored in front of the Kop by a Liverpool player.

It didn't occur to me at the time that I could be the last Liverpool player to score at the Kop end. The Norwich game was after ours and I expected the Reds to beat them. In the end they didn't do and Norwich won 1-0 with Jeremy Goss scoring the last league goal in front of the Kop.

What does it mean to me? I look at it in relation to my dad's career. He can turn round and say he's got these medals and those medals and that he's Liverpool's most successful footballer ever but I wouldn't swap that for the little piece of history I've got.

That's how much it means to me.

Gatecrashers at the Kop's big wake
– Paul Dove, journalist

One game that stands out in my memory was the first league match after Shankly died.

Me and my mate were new on the Kop that 1981-1982 season having finally being given permission to go to the match on our own. We arrived outside the ground before midday and queued up for the cheap turnstile along with pensioners and probably a few unshaven 'kids' not wanting to pay the full whack.

We got in and legged it up the steps before nabbing a prime spec perched on one of the crush barriers somewhere in the middle of the Kop before preparing ourselves for the long wait.

But things didn't go according to plan. Before 2pm we were pushed off the barrier. We were aware from the previous few games we'd been to that this could happen but it was usually around five to three that our 'seats' were under threat when everyone piled in before kick-off. My mate tried to sit back on but he was pushed off by a fearsome looking old Scouser who didn't look in the best of moods. We didn't argue with him.

All the other decent specs were gone by this time and the Kop appeared to be almost full. We were stuck and would just have to get a glimpse of the game as best we could by standing.

As the time neared 3pm, we were starting to feel uncomfortable. We were 12-year-old kids stuck in the middle of thousands of emotional, swaying Kopites. 'Shankly, Shankly' was chanted over and over again. We soon started to realise that seeing the game against John Toshack's Swansea wasn't even an option. Safety was now the number one priority as we decided we had to somehow get to the front of the Kop.

We tried to push our way through, ducking under the barriers and wading our way through a dense forest of legs. At times we felt like we wouldn't make it. Older Kopites offered to pass us above their heads. It took us the whole of the first half to reach the front and breathe fresh air again. It was such a relief.

The second half was viewed from the corner of the Kop, under the old café. The score finished 2-2 but that day wasn't about football. It was about the Kop paying an emotional heartfelt thank you to the man that had given them their faith.

We were Paisley kids. We worshipped Kenny Dalglish and cut our teeth on the glory of Rome '77 (and the agony of Wembley '77). On that dark October day, we had stumbled upon the passing of an era – like young gatecrashers at the Kop's big wake.

Until then, we knew about Shankly but didn't really understand his significance. We were left in no doubt after that.

In the beginning: Liverpool fans queue to get in Anfield around 1906

Flagpole corner: A similar scene on a match day in 1958

King Billy: Liddell in the 1950s, the Kop windows glimpsed in the background

It's there: Delirium on the Kop as Brian Hall celebrates a goal

Changing face: Early images; a new roof and the fences come down in 1989

All together now: 'The old Kop went back miles and miles ...'

The Kop loves a keeper: Gordon Banks' lap of honour (top); Everton's Gordon West gets a handbag (right) and (below) Kopites watch Bruce Grobbelaar in '80s derby action

One of us: Kevin Keegan ends up in the Kop – and receives a warm welcome

Anfield at dawn: A groundsman surveys the Kop in February, 1978

Kop job: Photographers in action

Standing together: A chain of scarves on the terrace after Hillsborough

Messiah: Shanks with a fan in front of the Kop

Gizza hand up: Climbing in to the Kop (above). **Left:** Being passed over heads to safety and Dr Fun

Overcrowding: A packed Kop spills on to the Anfield pitch in 1957

Who scored?: The Kop asked the Anfield Road End to tell them about Tony Hateley's goal in the fog

Kop heroes: 'Sir' Roger Hunt celebrates another goal in the 1960s and (inset) Kenny Dalglish heads to the Kop after a title-clinching goal in 1982

The Kop threw me a raw chop and said: 'Here's your dinner!'
– Tommy Smith, former Liverpool captain

I suppose my first memories of the Kop are linked with waiting outside the ground at three-quarter time with what seemed like an army of people, men and boys, who used to slip in for a taste of the action when the gates opened for the early leavers. I could never understand why anyone would want to go home before the final whistle.

Here we were, Liverpudlians on the outside, all desperately wanting to be on the inside. Many boys who couldn't afford to pay full whack to get in from the start gained their first taste of big time football by going in at three-quarter time. It was common practice and nobody stopped you.

The logic was simple. Once you had experienced life on the Kop, you would be hooked for life.

Of course, you didn't just go to watch the first team. I can remember going to watch the reserves.

It wasn't quite as crowded in the Kop and you could find your feet without being lifted off them as was the case in first team games when the fans surged forward.

You'd always try and get in front of a crush barrier, not behind one, but most people had their own spec, even though it was obviously a massive standing terrace with no reserved places. Somehow people still managed to stand on exactly the same spot every week.

It was an education in there and you always came away with a smile on your face. I remember when we had some quite chunky individuals playing down the left.

I remember this old Scouser declaring: "What do you see when you look down our left hand side? Ronnie Moran, Phil Ferns, Johnny Morrissey. When they're close together, it's like watching one giant backside powering forward like a ten ton truck!" What an image to lock in your mind. The Kop was full of jokers.

When I signed for Liverpool, I saw it from the other side.

I used to regularly have a chat with people in the Kop when the ball went dead. You got to know many of the faces in the crowd.

I can remember playing in a rough house of a game against Leeds, par for the course against them.

After one challenge, Terry Yorath came down heavily on top of me over by the corner flag on the Kemlyn Road side.

I pushed him off and was just about to crack him when I felt something hit me on the shoulder. I looked down and there was a raw pork chop beside me on the pitch, thrown from the Kop. This voice shouted: "Here's your dinner Smithy, leave him alone!"

I couldn't help but laugh. Another time, we were playing Coventry City. They had a lanky Scottish winger called Tommy Hutchison. He was having a nightmare and during a break in the play I was sitting on the wall talking to the fans in the Kop and taking the piss out of him.

He was about to go to the World Cup with Scotland and I was taking every opportunity to wind him up. Hutchison was going mad and it didn't help when we got a penalty and Alec Lindsay rolled it into the corner. "Lucky bastard", shouted the Coventry winger. I said: "Shut up you moaning Scottish twat".

This was all going on in the heat of battle. He suddenly said: "I'll tell you what Smithy, let's see who's the best. I'll race you to the halfway line. Twenty quid I beat you hands down". I wasn't the fastest of defenders. I used other tactics to hold my own.

"Okay, lad," I said. "I'll take your bet if you double it up to take mine. After we've had the race, we'll have a fight. I know who'll be going home with the money!"

The Kop was always quick to pick up on any banter between the players. When that roar went up it made the hairs stand up on the back of your neck. I was so proud when I later became Liverpool captain and would lead the team out on to the pitch.

The Kop would be singing 'You'll Never Walk Alone'.

It was so inspirational. Having been a Kopite myself, it made it extra special when they roared your name.

That bank of terracing was sacred ground. Once you became a Kopite, you didn't go anywhere else. You were part of a club within the club.

In the Sixties, Liverpool was the centre of the universe. The Beatles were just starting out and Merseyside was booming at that time. The Kop invented all these songs and chants that had no equal in football.

For me, it's where it all began. The whole world copied the Kop, but there was only one genuine article.

Leeds goalkeeper Gary Sprake threw the ball straight into his own net as he tried to launch it clear. The Kop were immediately singing 'Careless Hands' from the Des O'Connor hit of the day.

You'd go to take a throw-in and there were always hundreds of people shouting advice and telling you what do.

It was like having 25,000 coaches at one end of the ground, all very knowledgeable in their own right.

Liverpudlians know their football, no doubt about that.

The humour was never very far away. I remember Joe Corrigan, who was later to become a coach at Anfield, going in goal at half time at the Kop end for one of those penalty competitions.

Joe, a good keeper during his days with Manchester City, put on a bit of beef when he stopped playing. One penalty was stuck in the bottom corner and he dived and missed it. Someone shouted: "You would have got that Joe, if it had been a pie". Typical Kop humour!

When you look at footage of the standing Kop at its peak, it's an awesome sight. Of course, Bill Shankly was the undisputed King of the Kop. He loved them and they loved him.

Shanks always wanted to be one of them. He actually went in the Kop at the end of his career on one occasion. The thing I remember was one of those famous days when we paraded another trophy around the pitch.

Kopites were throwing their red scarves on to the track for us to pick up. Shanks already had a couple around his neck. A policeman kicked one aside and the boss was furious. He let the copper know in no uncertain terms.

Shanks demanded that the fans were treated with the utmost respect. The Kop was pure gold as far as he was concerned and it was the same for me. I've been lucky enough to travel all over the world. You can be thousands of miles away and walking down the street and someone will suddenly recognise you.

The first thing they ask is: "What was it like to play for Liverpool FC?" The second thing they ask is: "What was it like to play in front of the Kop?" It's an easy answer for me. "Absolutely wonderful".

The Kop was as much a part of Liverpool's success as the team.

Just like my old boss Shanks, I hold them in the highest regard.

Their football God
— Joe Mercer OBE, ex-Everton and Arsenal player;
ex-Manchester City and Aston Villa manager

From the moment Shankly arrived there's been only one way – up. And this endless success was mirrored in that amazing relationship with the Kop.

When he was at Anfield he was the city of Liverpool's answer to vandalism and hooliganism because the kids came to see Liverpool. They came to see those red shirts and Shankly was their man, their hero, their football God.

He belongs to the Kop. He's one of them. If he hadn't managed

Liverpool I'm sure he'd have been on the Kop dressed in red, singing and chanting 'Liverpool, Liverpool'.

'Where d'ya get dat sewt?'
– Mike McCartney, The Scaffold

When our kid and I were children, Dad used to take us to Liverpool's and Everton's games. I'll never forget our first visit to Anfield, complete with scarves, overcoats, vacuum flasks – the lot.

Many years later when 'Thank U Very Much' was becoming a British hit, we were asked to make a promo film for the United States. Our director, Jim Goddard, wanted to use the Royal angle and include a film of the Kop singing the last two lines – 'thank you very much for our gracious TEAM' instead of Queen (geddit?) Roger McGough was elsewhere on the day so just John Gorman (in loud check suit) and I (with long hair) presented ourselves at the packed ground on match day with very mixed feelings. What if they didn't like it? What if they didn't know it?

Our worst feelings were almost realised in front of that massive Kop audience when the record didn't play on cue. But we soon knew they were on our side – they roared together as one voice: 'Oh where d'ya get dat sewt? Oh where d'ya get dat sewt? Oh where d'ya get dat sewt?' ...'Getcher hur cut ... getcher hur cut'.

Then the song came on and they sang it better than the record – with the bonus of a massive sea of red and white scarves swaying in time.

'Why don't yer gerroff!'
– Stuart Hall, commentator and journalist

I was making a recording of the crowd during a European match. The wit was pouring off the Kop in torrents and I was semiconducting them. It was very emotional and when they finished I applauded them.

I was putting my recording gear away, still with tears in my eyes, when this little urchin on the wall called "Eh, Mister, come 'ere".

Thinking perhaps he wanted my autograph I went over to him. "Yes, son?" I beamed.

He looked me straight in the eye and said: "Why don't yer gerroff, yer short-arsed git!"

'Show us your arse'
– Mike Summerbee, former Manchester City player

Manchester City were winning 2-1 with six minutes to go at Anfield and I took a corner at the Kop end. They gave me some stick so I lowered my shorts. Minutes later they had gone 3-2 ahead through Roger Hunt and Ian St John and the Kop chanted: "Show us your arse, Summerbee". They were great fans though and fair to all visiting players who earned their respect.

'They just clapped my goal'
– Jeremy Goss, former Norwich City player

The Kop's Last Stand was a special day to say the least. I've put that day down as the proudest moment of my footballing career, to be honest, because it was such a huge event and such a huge day.

The whole world knows about the Kop end at Anfield. Norwich were in tremendous form going into the game. We'd had a brilliant season but we knew going to Liverpool on that day was going to be hard for us.

We thought with all the razzmatazz and all the hype it's going to be a tough game because they're going to be up for it in a massive way. We were all chatting about it before the game and we all thought Rushie was going to be the last guy who'd score in front of the standing Kop. He deserved to be the guy who'd score that goal at that end and rightly so, because of his services to the club and being the world class goalscorer that he was.

Unbelievably, I popped up from nowhere and suddenly it was my name that was down on the list as the last guy to score at the Kop end. It was the proudest moment of my life in football for sure.

I was quite fortunate that the good goals I scored were on the box. The Liverpool game was highlighted heavily on TV, the Bayern Munich games were live on TV and I was lucky enough to score twice against them and a goal I scored at Leeds won me the Match of the Day goal of the month award.

The best goal I've ever scored was at Leeds. No doubt. But the goal at Anfield was my proudest. It was just one of those things where I tried my best to shoot and score. I just tried to hit the target. I'd had one or two goals that season that had flown in and I was in a good vein of form. I was at the top of my game. It was the fittest I'd ever been, the strongest I'd ever been and I was confident in gambling and hitting things. Normally I'd take a touch and pass it on but during that spell I was just hitting them.

A corner was headed out to me and I chested it down. It took a bounce and I just struck through the ball and hit the target. It could have flown into the Kop but luckily for me I think David James was just standing there as it flew in. I've got two pictures at home on my wall from that day.

One is of that particular strike. The picture is taken from behind me as I've hit the ball and you can see Neil Ruddock closing me down and David James watching it fly past him.

I've also got a picture of me celebrating, running away with my arms in the air.

Again, another compliment to the Liverpool fans really, there are hundreds of people in the Kop end, with their arms outstretched, clapping. They were just clapping me and I remember that.

They just clapped the goal because they thought 'well played, good goal'. That's the type of fans Liverpool have got.

The atmosphere was electric. It really, really was special.

'Final goodbyes to a trusted friend'
– Alan Edge, author of Faith of our Fathers', 1994

The Saturday night was drawing to its unyielding close. I sat at the foot of our stairs, head slightly bowed, hands clasped consolingly down between my knees.

I was alone save for our dog. Albie, who lay prostrate alongside the front door several feet away. His skewed, doleful eyes peered up towards me, meeting my own gaze with somewhat bemused resignation. He was aware something was amiss if not sure exactly what. Certainly, he could tell a late night walk wasn't on the immediate agenda. He was right, too.

Scarcely pausing for breath, I began delivering my entire repertoire of Liverpool songs to our empty house and a by now disconsolate Albie who wanted none of it, having just had confirmed his worst fears concerning his walk, prompting him to slink off dejectedly towards the back kitchen.

Of course, both Albie and the house had heard those same songs resonate around every nook and cranny countless times before. Like the other members of the household they had grown accustomed down the years to my lusty exaltations of the men in red.

It was different this time, though. This time, the gusto that usually accompanied each exaltation was simply not there.

Instead, were just fleeting jagged remnants of defiance, almost as if I were making token efforts to claw back some redress for the emotions I was feeling. A few lines into You'll Never Walk Alone and the grim realisation of the day's events gripped me even tighter. Occasional tears welled up and spilled. Not a flood. No histrionics. But enough, nevertheless, to make our peerless anthem even more challenging to complete solo than usual, cramping my delivery and demanding intermittent droplets be wiped away.

Sure, the preceding skinful at the Thirlmere may not have helped on the waterworks front. However, it was not alcohol that was fuelling my sadness that evening. Several hours earlier I had bade farewell to a major chunk of my life.

The curtain had been drawn over the Anfield Spion Kop and like many thousands of others my heart was aching. After forty-odd years, final goodbyes to a tried and trusted friend are no easy matter. Even an equally forlorn Albie could, I'm sure, sense that.

Sore heads and proud hearts
– Chris McLoughlin, The Kop Magazine, May 2005

In 1985 Chelsea owner Ken Bates asked for planning permission to put electric fences up at Stamford Bridge to stop the growing hooliganism problem. The proposal was refused by the FA and Greater London Council.

Fast forward to the modern era and Roman Abramovich should consider trying to revive the plans as it may be the only hope he's ever got of witnessing anything that remotely resembles an electric atmosphere inside Stamford Bridge.

It was Liverpool's players and the travelling Kop who had made their noisy mark on the first game. How would Chelsea respond?

Such a show of Red would surely demand a similar response from the travelling Cockneys when they came to Merseyside?

Would they keep the Blue flag flying high above St George's Hall? Would Concert Square become a sea of Blue banners and a cacophony of Cockney chants? Er, no.

Chelsea fans were of the lesser-spotted variety on the afternoon of the second leg.

While Liverpool city centre was already buzzing with a sense of anticipation and a lot of Reds were fine-tuning their voices over a liquid lunch, Chelsea's fans were sneaking into Lime Street Station.

The night before the game Jose Mourinho and his players trained at Anfield. With the title now in the bag they looked relaxed and were pictured laughing and joking inside the empty stadium.

When they returned 24 hours later they found it to be a throbbing heartbeat of colour and noise.

Mourinho's dismissal after the first leg that 99.9 per cent of Liverpool fans already thought we were through was a gross insult.

Confident? Yes. Assuming we were through? No way Jose. If it was supposed to be a piece of psychological warfare then it back-fired spectacularly. All he had done was wave a blue rag to an already angry and pumped up bull. He should stick to bullshitting rather than bullfighting.

Mateja Kezman then showed a complete ignorance, or stupidity, by suggesting the atmosphere would just be the same for a Champions League semi-final on a Tuesday evening as it was for the 12.45pm kick-off on New Year's Day.

"Sure, they talk a lot about atmosphere at Anfield, but last time we played there I didn't see so much. It's more about history and tradition and we are not afraid of that."

We know you're crap but exactly what was it that made your legs turn to jelly as you completely mis-controlled a pass in front of the paddock just before the end of the game, Mateja?

Chelsea were in trouble from the warm-up.

Forty-five minutes before kick-off and the Kop was half-full with songs already being belted out.

At one point a clearly worried fat Frank Lampard Junior even turned to the Chelsea fans and gesticulated at them to try and gee them up in the hope they could out shout the Kop. There was more chance of him fitting into a medium sized kit.

As kick-off approached the noise got louder and louder and LOUDER. The intensity increased before a ball had been kicked.

You'll Never Walk Alone was sung at its spine-tingling best. Even by Anfield's standards it was sensational.

As The Mirror's Oliver Holt put it: "One of the great sights in world football right there in front of you. People stared at each other in awe."

Then came a sight that took everyone inside the ground back to the days of the old standing Spion Kop. With Ra-Ra-Ra-Rafa Benitez raucously ringing out, thousands upon thousands of Kopites began twirling their scarves, flags, banners and anything else they could get their hands upon above their heads. Almost instantaneously the rest of the ground followed suit.

The Kop looked like a giant food-blender that had been turned up to cyclone level after having a vat of tomatoes thrown into the mix. If steam had risen from the cauldron you'd have sworn it was still the old Spion Kop in its pomp.

It was a jaw-dropping moment. A moment of raw passion and desire that even the Anfield of old cannot have ever bettered. If it was a journey down memory lane then it was a journey with the car windows open and the stereo cranked up to full volume. The Chelsea fans stood there open-mouthed like slack-jawed yokels. They were shell-shocked. Like rabbits caught in headlights.

This wasn't just the Kop making the noise as it used to do in the past. It was the whole ground. Anfield was bouncing. It was better than anything we have ever heard inside the old place. Only Inter Milan '65 stands as a potential rival for such noise before a game. The question for those who attended both now is whether that Inter Milan night can still live up to Chelsea '05?

At some places that would have been the storm before the calm.

Not Anfield. The noise was continuous throughout as the game ebbed and flowed.

John Terry won the toss and turned us round. Anfield booed until Petr Cech trotted down to the Kop end and received the traditional and generous ovation.

He ignored it, just like on New Year's Day. More boos.

We always like to see Liverpool attacking the Kop end in the second half but so highly charged was the atmosphere that Terry's decision to make us swap ends worked in our favour.

Liverpool's players had no choice but to attack from the kick-off. The Kop demands it when you're kicking towards them.

Maybe with the Kop at their backs they wouldn't have been so openly offensive from the start.

Now they didn't have a choice and four minutes in came a moment of sheer ecstasy.

Stevie G plays Baros in and as he chips the ball over Cech the big lumbering keeper clatters him to the ground. PENALTY. PENALTY! Hang on. There's Garcia....yeeeeeeesss.....off the line but it was in...... what's he given?

Yeeeeeeeeeeeeeeeeeeeeeeeeeeeeeeessssssssssss!

Anfield erupted. Pure bedlam. The Chelsea players tried to argue that William Gallas had cleared it before the ball crossed the line but the Slovakian linesman was convinced, and still is, which was all that mattered. 1-0.

If such a thing was possible the noise levels went up again. Song after song rolled off the Kop.

Then the referee started playing up. Mourinho had described Slovakia's Lubos Michel as a good referee before the game.

The way the decisions were going for Chelsea in the first half had us all wondering if he was a good mate of Abramovich's. Put it this way. If he'd been eligible to vote in the general election then blue would certainly have been his colour.

Liverpool's players received a rapturous half-time reception and in the second half it was a backs to the wall job.

The noise levels continued but nerves were now playing a part. As Chelsea piled on the pressure, Anfield began to get edgy.

But Liverpool were defending magnificently on the pitch. Carra looked about seven foot tall out there. He was Ron Yeats without the muzzie.

A couple of pitch invaders, who turned out to be from Barcelona, briefly disrupted the play while substitutes Djibril Cisse, Harry Kewell and Antonio Nunez did their all to keep possession up the other end of the field and relieve the pressure.

All eyes were now on the clock and then the injury time board went up.

Six minutes. SIX? Six fucking minutes! What the hell? Either he's looked at one of the Hillsborough Justice Campaign's 'ninety-six' wristbands instead of his watch or he's Abramovich's brother, never mind his mate.

Then came the moment of heart-stopping agony when Eidur Gudjohnsen had the chance of a lifetime, deep into stoppage time, to wreck our night. But as the Icelandic diving champion struck the ball goalwards he didn't reckon on the 16,000 Kopites behind the goal blowing the ball out in the same way that they'd sucked Garcia's effort over the line.

Gudjohnsen reckoned the ball had deflected wide off Carra's thigh. It hadn't, although it did seem to take a slight deviation as it whistled past the post. Maybe it was the spirit of Shanks that kept it out. Perhaps it was the ghost of Shanks himself, popping up on the line to keep it out. Or maybe, as he once said, the Kop just frightened the ball away. Whatever the reason it didn't go in and less than a minute later the referee finally blew his whistle, prompting scenes of celebration so wild that they had to be seen to be believed. There were cheers and tears.

Cheers for the heroes in red. Tears for what it meant to be back in the European Cup final and for those, 96 of us in particular, who are no longer here to see it.

Abramovich got so caught up in the celebrations that he was stood in the directors' box smiling and clapping away in tandem with the jubilant Liverpool supporters. The word was that he thought the atmosphere was so good that he told Peter Kenyon to spend the whole of June dining in Liverpool City Centre restaurants to see how many of you lot he can sign up.

As the players joyfully celebrated on the pitch, making a mockery of anyone who suggests this current Liverpool side lack team spirit, a hugely emotional and heart-felt chorus of You'll Never Walk Alone rose into the night sky.

Even the early leavers waited until it had finished before getting off to beat the traffic.

That was then followed by chorus after chorus after chorus of 'we shall not, we shall not be moved, we shall not, we shall not be moved, just like the team that's gonna win the European Cup AGAIN, we shall not be moved' and 'we'll be running 'round Turkey with the cup!'

It was sung with a growing belief, a genuine belief that Liverpool can be kings of Europe again. The celebrations continued long into the night. They would have continued all night inside Anfield if Merseyside Police hadn't eventually put a message out over the PA system telling us all to go home because the players wouldn't be making a re-appearance.

The city centre had its busiest Tuesday night in years. People were queuing to get IN to pubs and clubs at closing time.

It was the kind of night that 24-hour licenses were made for. At 7.30am the next morning three lads were spotted staggering down the Dock Road still with half-filled pint glasses in hand.

It was sore heads ands and proud hearts all round that morning.

'Without it we're sometimes down to eleven'
– Jimmy McGovern, writer

I'm going to pick a match from Souness' disastrous time in charge. It was an evening game against Man Utd and it was to be the last time we played them in front of a standing Kop.

I went with Chris Eccleston and his girlfriend. At the time Chris was famous for two things: he was starring in Cracker and he was a lifelong Man Utd fan.

Not a chance of him going in the Kop. We got three seats in the Centenary Stand. Within minutes Man Utd were three nil up and Chris and his girlfriend were grinning from ear to ear.

Then the Kop got to work. A crescendo of noise.

I was only twenty yards away and I was getting it full blast. It was awe inspiring and even that crap team that Graeme had sent out responded to it. Even Nigel Clough, for God's sake, decided to get stuck in.

By half time it was 2-3. At the final whistle it was 3-3. We had fielded a lousy team, given the Mancs a three goal start, and still ended up with an honourable draw.

Believe me, that draw had little to do with that Liverpool team. Even less to do with the manager.

That draw was earned by the Kop, by its deafening reminder to the players of just what Liverpool FC means to its fans.

After the match Alex Ferguson said of the Kop: "It's a shame that such wonderful support is going to disappear."

He was right. That's not to say that Kopites should stand. Far from it.

Better a hundred years in the football wilderness than another 96 dead. But I do miss the old Kop.

It was, as Shankly said, a twelfth man. Without it these days, we're sometimes down to eleven.

Anfield erupted. It was pure bedlam
– Chris McLoughlin, journalist

I could smell it in the air as I walked up Walton Breck Road. It was like a crackling of electricity was passing through the night air and charging Liverpool supporters on their way up to the ground.

I had a sense of excitement and anticipation but it was tempered with a sense of trepidation. Evening games against Manchester United at Anfield are always more volatile. More highly charged. But this was to be the last time they would come to Anfield and play in front of the old Spion Kop.

I just had a gut feeling that we were in for something special, a night to remember. It was still an hour before kick off but I could hear the noise from the Kop filtering down Walton Breck Road. That had never happened before. Not since I'd been going to Anfield.

My first game was in January 1987 but that is the one and only occasion I can remember hearing such a noise before I could even see The Albert. I wasn't on the Kop that night. By then I'd got my season ticket in the Paddock – Kop end of course – and had become an avid admirer rather than a participant.

I've always loved the moment when I walk through the little tunnel-like area that leads you from inside the concourse to the Paddock seats. It's the moment when, as you fight your way past the Bovril buyers, you catch a glimpse of the luscious green turf for the first time.

It's just a glimpse, mind, but a glimpse that leaves you wanting more. It's Anfield's equivalent of cleavage. It doesn't give you that same breath-taking, awe-inspiring moment when you reach the top of the old Kop steps for the first time and see the Kop but, none the less, it was always enough to get me buzzing.

Not that I needed anything to get me buzzing that night.

As I walked out of that Paddock tunnel the noise slapped me in the face like a wet mackerel. It was astonishing.

The Kop looked full. Rammed. I just stood there, frozen to the spot, like I'd never been inside Anfield before.

There they were, enjoying an almighty old school sing-song despite the fact that we were playing our hated rivals who were strolling to their second title in a row and could, quite conceivably, give us a thrashing.

I looked towards the Mancs in the Annie Road end and most of their seats were full. That's the way it is when you're a Manc at Anfield or a Scouser at Old Trafford.

You don't hang around for long outside the ground and, true to form, the Mancs hadn't. Instead they were stood or sat in silence as the sea of red and white opposite made more noise than they had ever heard at their place. And this was before a ball had even been kicked.

Moments before the teams came out, DJ George played 'You'll Never Walk Alone' over the PA system. He could have switched it off after the first word because no-one could hear Gerry Marsden.

As I held my scarf aloft my eyes were firmly focused on the Kop. All of a sudden, the sea of scarves and flags were joined by two blazing red flares, which sent plooms of red smoke pouring towards the sky. It was a beautiful sight. An image I, and I dare say the Sky viewers tuning into the game at home, will never forget.

Had the Kop ever been more colourful?

United won the toss and, not surprisingly, turned us round.

The boos and howls of derision hadn't died down by the time Peter Schmeichel, with a nose as red as Liverpool's shirts, made his way down to the Kop end. Twenty-three minutes later and the only colourful thing I was aware of was the language around me.

United were 3-0 up and had, temporarily, silenced the Kop.

Early goals from Steve Bruce and Ryan Giggs had been met by

an increase in volume but Denis Irwin's third – a free-kick that seemed to make an almighty 'clunk' on the way in – was met with silence.

It lasted 90 seconds.

With the United fans still celebrating, Nigel Clough smashed in an unbelievable 30-yard shot that had us all believing again.

The noise levels exploded into life and, if I'm not mistaken, another flare or two lit up the Kop.

Clough got a second before half-time and by now the ground was rocking.

United had turned from arguably the best visiting side we'd seen for years into quivering wrecks. They were all over the place. The noise ebbed and flowed with the game in the second half. Maybe it is just a psychological thing, maybe it's true, but Anfield never seems quite as loud when Liverpool aren't attacking the Kop in the second half. Liverpool cranked up the pressure and with 11 minutes to go Neil Ruddock headed home Stig Inge Bjornebye's cross. It was like he'd dropped a tonne of dynamite into a volcano.

Anfield erupted. The place went berserk. I can't even remember the last 10 minutes – it was pure bedlam. Shortly after the final whistle sounded, 'You'll Never Walk Alone' rang around the ground as good as I've ever heard it. Everyone was engulfed in the moment. The Mancs, normally made to stay behind by the police so they could be safely escorted to their coaches, were allowed to leave immediately and trudged away in silence.

As they did it was to an impromptu and hugely ironic rendition of 'Always Look on the Bright Side of Life' being directed towards the away end.

Some people in the Paddock who I'd never seen move, let alone sing, were dancing jigs of delight. Others were stood on their seats. One or two were even crying. For me, that was the Kop's real Last Stand. The night games were always the best.

Given that we'd seen so many glorious triumphs as Liverpool supporters, celebrating a 3-3 draw was seen by some as a barometer of how our standards had slipped. It wasn't about drawing a game with Man United though. This was about the Kop.

This was a night of pride. A night of passion. A night of defiance. A night when a red and white Kop proved that it could still create the most inspirational, ear-splitting, partisan racket anywhere in football. A night when a point was proven beyond doubt to our visitors.

You might be the biggest club in England.

You might be the darlings of the media.

You might be embarking on an era of success that will one day threaten our own.

You might beat us on the pitch sometimes you play us but you never have, and never will, come close to creating an atmosphere that beats us off it.

No-one will. Ever.

'Where's your handbag?'
– Gordon West, former Everton goalkeeper

I remember my first derby game and I didn't know about the rivalry between the two clubs.

So I went down and stood in front of the Kop and they were all sticking two fingers up at me, poking and swearing, all aimed at me. I just couldn't believe anybody could be like that.

Don't forget, I was only a kid. I was only 19 and it was an eye-opener.

The year after I learnt and thought I would sort the Liverpool fans out so I started blowing them kisses and showing them a bit of bottom. I thought it was really funny. The following year, that's when I got the handbag. It ruined my life!

You ask anybody in Liverpool about Gordon West and they will mention Sandy Brown's own goal and the handbag – and I've played for England. It is unbelievable.

All my life I have gone out and had a pint and I have had people asking: "Where's your handbag?"

They threw leeks at me
– Neville Southall, former Everton and Wales goalkeeper

Sometimes I'd hear things they were shouting at me but it was never stupid. It was always good-natured.

I didn't mind that and I always looked forward to playing at Anfield because I thought it was a decent ground. There was always a good atmosphere and if you're any sort of footballer you always wanted to play in front of the Kop.

To be honest I don't remember my first game there. I was young and I was stupid so I never even thought about what type of reception I'd get as Everton's goalkeeper at Anfield. I just enjoyed playing there and it became a ground I looked forward to going to, even though they were our main enemies.

One game that sticks out in my mind came in the derby after somebody had thrown bananas at John Barnes.

When we played at Anfield the next time someone on the Kop kept throwing leeks at me. They didn't reach the goal though. They were crap throwers! I thought it was quite funny to be fair and there was no harm in it.

They appreciated what you did
– John Osborne, former West Brom keeper

I remember in one match there was a break in play because someone was injured. I was waiting to take a goal kick so I walked back and sat on the wall in front of the Kop.

As I was sitting there someone grabbed hold of my jersey. When the referee blew the whistle to try and play on I tried to get up but the fan still had hold of me and I over-balanced and fell right back into the crowd.

It left the referee and 21 footballers looking for a goalkeeper! That summed up the general friendliness of it all. In the late 1960s there was a feeling that they wanted to make the opposition goalkeeper welcome. If you turned it on, they appreciated what you did.

We knew we were living the dreams of the people
– Kenny Dalglish, former Liverpool player and manager

There was a unique bond between the people who stood on the terraces of the Kop and the players that they came to watch. It was a relationship that I believe was built on mutual respect.

The fans respected the players because they were successful. We won things almost every season and as a fan all you want for your team is for them to make you proud and to win silverware. The players gave their everything, every week and their efforts did not go unappreciated.

The Kop would accept defeat if it was defeat by a better team, because they were a sporting crowd but thankfully it was never something they had to get particularly used to.

There was no better lift when you were a goal down and chasing the game than the Kop in full voice. They got us through some tricky times and that unswerving support was part of what endeared the support to the players. But we, as players, also knew that we were living the dreams of the people watching from the stands. They would have traded everything to be where we were so we wanted success for them as well as ourselves.

You would go that extra mile for them because they would go that extra mile for you in return. Playing in front of the Kop was an experience few people will ever forget.

It was like steam coming out of their ears
– Keith Hackett, former match referee

The first time I officiated at Anfield I was running the line. It was Liverpool versus Burnley, sometime in the mid '70s. I remember my first visit well.

Tom Reynolds was the referee and during the game Steve Heighway came down the left wing and played it off a player. The ball went out for a corner kick, which I quite happily gave. Tom though, a bearded Welshman, gave a goal kick. The Kop went absolutely crazy. It was like steam was coming out of their ears.

I remember distinctly Reynolds, having given very firmly a goal-kick, hear the crowd's reaction. He shrugged his shoulders, looked in my direction and gave a corner kick. He got a ripple of applause after that. I realised that night the weight of the Kop.

The unity that rose from the Kop
– Dion Fanning, Irish Independent journalist

I went to Anfield for the first time in 1982. My father and I caught the boat from the North Wall Quay (Dublin) on a Friday night and arrived seven hours later in Liverpool at about 6.30 in the morning. Later, I would spend many more dawns at Liverpool having arrived by boat after all-night sailings.

We had travelled to see Liverpool play Luton. The game finished 3-3, I know who scored because I've looked it up, but all I remember of the day was being transfixed by the Kop and the way the terrace moved at times I couldn't predict. I didn't take my eyes off it. Later that day, we met Bruce Grobbelaar in the St George's Hotel and then we caught the boat home and I struggled but failed to stay awake to watch the highlights, but all I thought of was the Kop.

It was a few years before I went back to Liverpool, but from then on we started to go every year, and every trip affected me in the same way. I could remember incidents in the game, but more than anything I was infected by the need to belong to the spirit, the unity that rose from the Kop.

The night we arrived on the world stage
– Alan Edge, author

On Tuesday, 4th May, 1965 Liverpool entertained World Club Champions Inter Milan in the semi-final first leg of the European Cup. It was uncharted territory for the club and everyone connected with it.

The afternoon of the game half a dozen of us had skipped off school early to ensure that we would get in. On the preceding Saturday, amidst pandemonium, the team had lifted the FA Cup for the first time in the club's history, so everyone knew the Milan game would be a lock-out.

Arriving at the ground at 4.30pm for the 7.30pm kick-off, by that time the queues were already enormous. As we hurried frantically past the hordes queuing for the Kop along the Lake Street entry we caught wind that our intended destination, the boys' pen, was already closed.

At that point, we decided to try instead for the Kop end of the Paddock enclosure since we didn't fancy the length of the Kop queues. Mercifully it proved to be a wise decision.

By 5.20pm we had squeezed inside. All the standing sections of the ground were already crammed tight so we must have been amongst the last in. Such was our relief and exhilaration it felt as if we'd been the last through the pearly gates. Certainly with St John on our side we can't have been that far from heaven.

Inside Anfield that night the terraces throbbed with an excitement I have never experienced before or since. The buzz and tension tore at the nerve ends and sent untold adrenalin systems pumping wildly out of control. Fifty five thousand were crammed inside. Possibly half that number was locked outside.

The whole place bulged at the seams, threatening at any moment to burst apart like the crotch of Linford Christie's leotard.

It was an atmosphere that defied belief.

Over to our right was a 28,000 strong tidal wave of foaming humanity. Scarcely two years earlier it had re-defined the parameters of football support.

Now, as it tumbled and cascaded back and forth for the entire night like the endless swelling ocean at Cape Horn, the Spion Kop was re-defining those parameters once again.

From the moment we squeezed in you simply could not take your eyes off the ceaseless swaying and movement.

Looking for all the world like some vast bank of windswept corn it drew your gaze and mesmerised you, making it virtually impossible to look away for more than a fleeting second in case you missed something.

The Kop was centre stage and determined to lap it up.

Prompted partly by the sheer inspiration of winning the FA Cup for the first time, partly by the ensuing celebrations and partly by a genuine apprehension and fear of the unknown – namely a European Cup semi-final and whether they would make it to the pub in time after the game – the Kopites rose to the occasion with a unique concoction of noise, fervour and humour, which not even they have since been able to match.

Joined by the rest of the stadium to wield a four-sided attack, they created an incessant four-hour barrage of chants, songs and sheer glorious bedlam. Such was the din that a friend of mine later swore he was able to hear it in the city centre three miles away.

Giving their finest ever performance, they inspired their heroes to reciprocate and give theirs. The chemistry of fans and team together proved potent and irresistible.

The final score, 3-1, was a travesty of justice; it should have been at least 10-1, so total was the Red domination.

Eventually, long after the match had finished – by then fully four days after our Wembley FA Cup exultations – reluctantly and unwillingly, we all made our way home.

Desperate to prolong our high, we were still singing, still revelling, still savouring every last moment of our adventure. Sadly, inexorably, it was over; never to be repeated.

Since that time, in the wake of every ensuing Liverpool triumph, I have reflected, invariably, on that night in May 1965.

Whilst comparisons of this sort are inevitably invidious, so exceptional was that night I think special distinction is justified. Truth is everything else – no matter how great or important in its own right – really does tend to pale.

That particular period in Liverpool Football Club's history truly was unique and it was the night of May 4th that heralded the club's arrival on the world stage.

It was something new
– 'Sir' Roger Hunt, former Liverpool player

Liverpool were back into the First Division. We got into Europe for the first time; it was something that was new. Everything was on the up and the spectators were absolutely unbelievable. Every game was a sell-out.

For me, the Inter Milan match was the greatest atmosphere I

ever played in at Anfield. Gerry Byrne and Gordon Milne paraded the FA Cup because that was the first time that we had won it.

To come back a few days later and play against Inter Milan and beat Inter Milan was something else.

The atmosphere before the game when we came out on the pitch was incredible.

History in the making
– David Moores, former Liverpool chairman

When the team ran out with the FA Cup just before the Inter Milan game at Anfield you just knew it was going to be an immortal night. That's the only way to describe it.

We were watching history in the making.

Three broken ribs – but it was worth it
– Tony Barrett, journalist

The first time I ever stood at Anfield was in the Anfield Road end – in the visitors' section.

It was Easter Monday 1986 and Liverpool were at home to Manchester City and my dad had promised to take me on the Kop for the first time after years of watching the Reds from the Main Stand.

We queued up for almost an hour but 10 minutes before kick-off the Kop gates were closed and we were turned away. Being a resourceful chap, and with a heart-broken 10-year-old in his company, my dad decided to go around to the City end to try and get in there.

Despite having accents more Fairfield than Fallowfield we got in and watched Liverpool go top of the league thanks to two Steve McMahon goals.

I say watched, but the truth is the only thing I watched was the Kop. It was one of those special days when the League Championship loomed on to the horizon and the Kop was at its best.

Watching Liverpool wasn't good enough for me – I wanted to stand on the Kop. Our next home game was about a week later against Coventry and I was determined not to miss out again.

We queued up even earlier this time and got on to the terrace just as the Sayers cafe at the back of the Kop opened up.

There were only a few people there – it was 1.30pm after all – but just being there was enough. As it started filling up and the Kopites began belting out their songs, I knew it was the only place for me.

Liverpool won 5-0 that day and I've been on the Kop ever since.

Some of the most memorable moments in my life took place on that vast, somewhat ugly construction of concrete and wood. My most vivid recollection is of breaking my ribs when I got squashed against a crush barrier during a derby game in 1987-88.

That was the season of Barnes, Beardsley and Aldridge – the greatest team I've ever seen.

You had to queue up for hours before kick-off just to have a chance of getting in that year. But it only cost £1.80 on the kids' gate to enjoy some of the most free-flowing football played in the history of the British game. You can't even get a pie at the match for that price anymore!

Having gone in through the kids' gate I got separated from my dad but I knew where we stood at the back of the Kop and thought I would make my way up there. But I chose the wrong route. I took the shortest path – through the middle of the Kop.

At first I was happy to be stuck in the throng because I was at the heart of all the action.

The noise was incredible and with the constant swaying my feet were literally not touching the ground.

The game kicked off and Liverpool went straight on the attack and the Kop surged forward. Being 11 and about six and a half stone I couldn't really hold off 8,000 people at my back and I got trapped against a barrier. The pain was unbearable but then Peter Beardsley cracked a half volley in off the underside of the crossbar and everything went mad. As everyone celebrated I was able to free myself and even forgot the pain for a minute as I joined in with the pandemonium.

But as the game wore on the pain grew worse and worse and I can't remember seeing the rest of the match.

I ended up in Alder Hey with three broken ribs but it had all been worth it. Liverpool had beaten Everton but, even more importantly, I had graduated to the middle of the Kop.

In Italy it would be the place for the Ultras, the most fanatical supporters of the clubs in Serie A.

And at Anfield it was no different.

The stands always seemed a bit stuffy, there was no singing and supporters would do little more than clap when Liverpool scored – a sort of retirement home for ex-Kopites.

The middle of the Kop had a mind of its own. It was where songs started and where fans in the rest of the ground looked to for inspiration.

Although its best days had gone by the late '80s (according to everyone who had been there in the '60s anyway) there was still a buzz about the place.

My favourite memories are of watching one of Liverpool's finest ever performances, as we brushed Nottingham Forest aside in a stunning 5-0 victory.

Also, being in a crowd of 22,000 – most of whom were on the Kop – as we overturned a first-leg two goal deficit to beat Auxerre 3-0 in the UEFA Cup. The spartan crowd that night was obviously made up of die-hards because despite being only half-full the atmosphere was incredible.

I think the other 20,000 who didn't turn up must be the ones who never sing because the noise level didn't suffer without them. The Kop mark-two is not the same.

It still has the ability to truly inspire the team like no other stand in the country as countless European visitors (and Chelsea) can testify. I still sit in the middle of the Kop but more often than not you hear people muttering instead of singing and at times it is as quiet as Sunday morning Mass.

It reminds me of an aging boxer who was once King of the World but hasn't got the legs to make things happen anymore. But it has never lost its punch and every now and again can deliver a real knockout blow.

Kopites are football people
– Alan Smith, media pundit and former Arsenal player

The night Arsenal won the league at Anfield (1989) was the most memorable game I've ever played in. The way it turned out, it was one of those games to never be repeated.

Before that game Anfield had always been a lucky ground for me when I was at Leicester. We were something of a bogey team for Liverpool. I scored twice at Anfield one season although I think we lost that day. Ian Rush might have scored three and Liverpool ended up winning 4-3.

It was always a ground I loved playing on because it was such a football arena.

I remember the first couple of times I played at Anfield. I'd heard so much about the famous Kop and I remember just standing in front of it when I was attacking or defending a corner and feeling the hot air coming off it.

The Kop was standing and packed back then and standing so close to it and feeling that hot air was fantastic.

The Kop were always great to us, especially on that night in 1989. The game wasn't long after Hillsborough and before it we presented the crowd with flowers to show our respects. I think it was George Graham's idea to do that.

We won the game 2-0 to win the title but, even though they were disappointed, the applause we got from not only the Kop but the whole stadium meant an awful lot to be honest.

It made it more special than it already was because I think everyone recognises that Liverpool fans are football people and people who know their football. Even if an opposing player produces a piece of skill you'd always hear a ripple of applause. Players notice that.

I think they recognised that we'd given it our best shot to win the game and the reception we got was fantastic.

I can remember the Kop trying to get the ref to blow his whistle early. They started whistling for the final whistle a good five or ten minutes before the end. There was no clock at Anfield in those days so we didn't know how long there was to go. It went on and on but then Michael Thomas got the goal right at the end.

I think we went up there more in hope than expectation of winning that night. None of the papers that morning had given us a chance of going up there and winning 2-0 so in many respects the pressure was off. My goal gave us a platform and we got the winner but I don't suppose anyone expected it to happen.

I scored the winner in the 1994 European Cup Winners Cup Final against Parma and that was a very special night for me. But from the team's point of view, that night in 1989 was the greatest.

Even the lads who went on to play under Arsene Wenger and did the double still go back to the night in 1989 and think it's never going to get any better than that. It was just really special.

The Kop told itself to sit down
– Rogan Taylor, founder of the Football Supporters Association

I'll never forget Tommy Smith's testimonial. It was in 1977, just a few days after the great pilgrimage to Rome, where Smithy had scored the second goal with a wonderful header. He couldn't have timed his well-deserved pay night better.

The place was heaving with some still under the influence of Roman vino. That night witnessed one of the strangest pieces of mass theatre the Kop has ever performed. It began with a light-hearted attempt to make the (then standing) fans in the Anfield Road end sit down. The Kop sang 'Annie Road, Annie Road, all sit down' – and to everyone's amazement they did.

Much encouraged, the Kop turned to the Kemlyn Road and instructed everyone there to stand up. They obeyed immediately. Now thoroughly warmed to the task, the Kopites sought the next prime target – the directors' box. We all wondered: would the camel coats stand up too? Sure enough, they did. With a final flourish, and with a gesture that now seems prophetic, the Kop told itself to sit down. And we did.

'I couldn't see a bloody thing!'
– Brian Hall, former Liverpool player

I remember the first time I came across the Kop. It was in 1962, the year they went up to the First Division, and they had an epic FA Cup tie with Preston North End.

Preston were a good side at the time and had Peter Thompson playing for them. They drew at Anfield, drew at Preston and went to Manchester for a third game which Preston won by a Thompson goal.

But we were invaded at Preston by Liverpool fans on the night of the second game. It's one of the most memorable football nights I ever had. It was incredible.

The banter, the noise, the songs, the chants, the humour – it was just absolutely fabulous.

By 1965 I'd signed on as an amateur and after training Reuben Bennett came to us and said: "I've got some passes if you want to watch the game tonight". It was a European game, I can't remember who against, and I got there for half-time.

We went on the Paddock and I spent most of the 45 minutes watching the Kop. I'd never seen anything like it in my life. It was absolutely phenomenal. The songs, the noise and the steam coming off it – it was just out of this world.

I only ever went on the Kop once. I was an amateur player while I was at university and we were playing Manchester United who had Bobby Charlton, George Best, Denis Law and all the rest in their team.

One of my pals at university was six feet six. He was an enormous guy and a Manchester United fan. He asked if there was any chance of getting some tickets but I told him I couldn't get tickets for the Kop. I didn't have a game that afternoon so we went and queued.

So we went on the Kop. We didn't get anywhere near the middle but even so I hardly saw a damn thing. I'm five feet five inches and a bit and I couldn't see a bloody thing. I spent the 90 minutes listening to my tall mate giving me a commentary!

It was a fantastic experience though and I remember more about that experience of being on the Kop than I do of the match itself.

I can't remember my first game at Anfield but one which stands out was when we played Everton in November 1970. It was my first derby match and there was about five or six of us who hadn't played in derbies before.

Everton had a terrific side and we were the up and coming new side so I suppose they were favourites really. The atmosphere in the stadium when I ran out was electric. There were red and blue scarves everywhere, all over the stadium, and the atmosphere was wonderful.

Within about 10 minutes of the second half we were two down. We were getting beaten 2-0 at Anfield to Everton but the Kop stayed with us. They kept singing and urging us on.

When our first one went in there was a hell of a din. When our second one went in there was an unbelievable din. And when our third one went in, I'll tell you what, you couldn't hear yourself think.

We'd run back to the centre-circle and I was in the middle of the pitch and tried to say something to Chris Lawler, who'd scored the winner, but I couldn't hear myself. It was phenomenal. There were fans on the Kop roof and all sorts. I think the official capacity was about 55,000 but there was 60-odd thousand in there that day.

The Kop were part and parcel of the 'This is fortress Anfield' thing. It wasn't just the 10 red and one green shirts that ran out to play, it was the Kop as well. We were all in it together. It was a very daunting experience for teams and individual players when they came to us. They knew they were going to meet this barrage of sound.

The European nights were special. I always felt that Anfield in particular had a fantastic sense of theatre on floodlit games. The arena was lit, the crowd were literally three yards from your shoulder on the touchline and there was all the noise and colour. There was a huge piece of theatre taking place and that was accentuated by the floodlighting.

In those days we didn't know what to expect from the opposition and neither did the crowd. There was like an air of expectancy but also a sense of going into the unknown. When we'd overcome that unknown, it made it extra special. There was an edge to it and those nights were great.

I kind of rationalise it though. The Kop wasn't worth a goal start. The lads on the park had to put the ball in the back of the net but the Kop was very much an integral part of the event.

My understanding is that when Bill Shankly first came to Liverpool he felt something for the place. I think he actually saw himself there. He was so passionate about his football and he saw passionate people standing on the terraces who expressed their passion very openly. I think that's a trait of Liverpool people. They are very open, they are very honest, they do tell you what they think and often wear their hearts on their sleeves.

Bill could see that within the support. He saw their passion and saw that he was one of them. He came from a small mining village and a lot of people who came to the stadium had a difficult or poor upbringing. There was a lot of common ground that he empathised with. He'd do little things like stand at the players entrance on a match day and give out a few complimentary tickets here, there and everywhere to the kids. Those little stories used to get about so I think people looked back to Shanks and saw themselves. He was one of us.

Sheer bonkers ecstasy
– Mike Chapple, writer

Like its musical equivalent of seeing the Clash play at Eric's it was the game that even those who weren't there would swear was their greatest ever 'live' experience.

But 'early darts' arrival at three in the afternoon was not enough to get in and with an hour to go the gates were locked and I was still outside.

The game? It was 1977, the night of Supersub, and watching Fairclough's winning goal against St Etienne on the TV later was not enough to blunt one of the most bitter sweet emotions of my life and the ache felt on not being there to make the difference.

That's what being a fan on the terraced Kop used to mean – a suspension of disbelief in Shankly's old adage that we could actually suck the ball into the opponents' net by the sheer volume of our support.

I knew it to be true – I'd actually been lucky enough to be there to see it happen the season before.

Crushed in the favourite spec just below the narrow plateau halfway up and 20 degrees off the left-hand goal post, we'd watched Bruges emphatically put us in our place in the first leg of the UEFA Cup Final.

Lambert and Cools had crashed two great goals past Clemence and come half-time we were down, outplayed and almost out.

Except for the K factor ...

The chanting – a kind of low rumble – had already begun as the last man left the pitch. Ten minutes later as Jensen, the Bruges keeper, nervously limbered up between the Kop sticks the noise had become not so much a wall of sound as a psychopathic yowl, a collective clenched fist of defiance.

There was an incredible feeling that despite the deficit nothing – but nothing – was going to stop us turning this around. That recollection even now sends a delicious shiver of power shooting down the back of the spine.

And so it came to pass. Ray Kennedy clubbed in a 20-yard net buster on the hour.

Two minutes later he nearly did it again when the shot hit the post and Jimmy Case, who'd been brought on for Toshack at the break, slotted home the rebound.

Two-all and the ears were threatening to explode, the voice had cracked and the breath gone thanks to hyperventilation and frequent collisions between the solar plexus and the crush barrier as we swayed back and forth.

Then Bastyns chopped down Heighway in the area and Keegan stepped up to take the penalty. Bedlam, and many couldn't bear to watch as Mighty Mouse coolly placed the ball and smashed it home. I went down in the crush of bodies.

Seconds later the wave receded and briefly I was left on my knees in a briefly empty space hugging my twin brother laughing and crying at the same time in the sheer bonkers ecstasy of it all.

These are moments that will forever be frozen in time. And when my dreams are being tossed and blown as they seem to be all too frequently these days, I think back to that night for a little solace – and quietly celebrate at being a small part of what once were giants.

I felt I belonged. I was buzzing
– Phil Thompson, former Liverpool captain

That feeling of being admired by the people on the Kop is magnificent. From the first time they shout your name you automatically hold them in high regard.

I remember playing in midfield against Leeds when we won the championship in 1972/73. I was only 19 and Bill Shankly picked me ahead of Brian Hall at the time. I was just an up and coming young lad and I'd played quite well the week before. I was in the side and I like to think I was in on merit. Shanks had picked me and I thought to myself 'marvellous'. It was a great occasion. We stayed in a hotel overnight and I remember coming to the game along Anfield Road and I had butterflies.

To settle myself down I started singing to myself on the coach. I was sat there by the window and I started singing 'You'll Never Walk Alone'.

It sounds daft and everything but the passion was burning so much inside me. I was nearly crying. I'm looking out and thinking 'they're all looking at me here' and I was singing it. It gave me a great buzz and great belief to go into the game.

We played magnificently on the day and I was bursting with desire and pride. We won the game 2-0 which was magnificent. I had a fabulous game and I was so pleased to be part of that team at that time.

During the game it was all going off and I can remember going right through a tackle on Allan Clarke. I really did. It was a block tackle and I went right through and carried on.

I can remember the Kop, mid-game, started to shout my name. They broke out in song and shouted my name. Hearing them do that so early in my career was tremendous. I was limited as a midfield player but they understood the passion I had. They didn't chant players' names often during a game. It's something that has to be earned, but that day I felt I'd arrived. You don't hear things often in a game when you're playing but believe me, I heard that.

It was the first time I felt I belonged. I was buzzing and I'll never forget it. I was 19 and at a very impressionable age. I always remembered where my brother, Owen, used to stand on the Kop. I used to stand there myself.

So when I'd come out on to the pitch everyone would have their names sung. I was thrilled they were shouting my name but I used to save a special wave for Owen. I knew where he stood and I'd look at him and give him a wave and then he'd give me a wave back. The lads used to say to me 'how the hell can you see your brother. He's in amongst 26,000 people'. I'd say back: 'I know where I stood and I can look at my brother and pick him out'.

I think any supporters throughout the country who stood on their own terrace would know where they stood and if their brother was there. There was also a sporting side to the Kop and that comes with the knowledge of football.

Rowdy does the twist!
– Ron Yeats, former Liverpool captain

We drew with Honved 0-0 in Hungary and Bill Shankly said we could all go out for a drink after such a good result.

We went to a club – probably the only one in Budapest in those days – and the lads pushed me on to the end of a dancing troupe.

When we flew back home I told my family we'd had a quiet time, then television showed the pictures and there I was on screen kicking up my legs. Was I in trouble!

The Kop lads had seen those pictures too and sang at our next home game 'Rowdy does the twist!' The whole ground followed suit in song and I went the colour of my shirt.

It was a great experience to play before the Kop and those fans warmed to everybody, friend or foe, who gave 100 per cent.

I had to match their passion
– The late Alan Ball, former Everton and Arsenal player

We were awarded a penalty when we played for Arsenal and I picked up the ball at the Kop end and held one finger up to signify that I was about to put my team one goal in front. It was 0-0 at the time.

I scored but thought about that gesture later on. Can you imagine the flak the Kop would have given me if I'd missed? I was a former Everton player but the Kop showed respect to players who put in their full lot and I believe I had their vote.

They were wonderful people to play in front of and their power always turned me on.

I believe that I had to match the passion which they showed under that roof.

Nothing less would have done for them.

All the colour of a matchday but no people
– Chris McLoughlin, journalist

It's the queuing I remember. Queuing in an eerie silence I had never heard before. I can't remember exactly where we joined the queue. Somewhere alongside the railings next to Stanley Park car park, I think.

I just remember thinking how I'd never seen so many people queue at the same time and make so little noise. I'd only ever been to Anfield before on match days. It was always noisy outside the ground.

The hubbub of the crowd. The anticipation of the game.

The souvenir sellers shouting 'get yer hats, caps, scarves or yer t-shirts'. But this was different. Very different. It brought home to me exactly what had happened at Hillsborough.

I was 11 at the time. I wasn't at Hillsborough on April 15, 1989. I wasn't allowed to go to away matches. Too young.

In any case, my dad was a Blue so there'd probably have been more chance of me being taken to Villa Park that afternoon if we'd gone to a cup semi-final. We didn't. Our family went to buy a new washing machine instead. So I spent the afternoon watching the tragedy unfold on 20 tellys in the St Helens branch of Currys.

The magnitude of what was happening didn't initially sink in.

At first I remember being disappointed that the game had been called off and there wouldn't be any highlights on TV that night.

Then, as talk of a death toll emerged, that disappointment gave way to the realisation that Liverpool fans had died.

The following morning I turned up to play for my Sunday League Under-12s side, Parr & Hardshaw. All the talk was about Hillsborough. The older brother of one of the lads in our team had gone to the game.

He was okay. I can't say for sure but I think he'd been sat in the upper-tier of the Leppings Lane end. I remember feeling glad he was alright and that now I actually knew someone who'd been there. We held a minute's silence before the game. The silence of people queuing outside Anfield to pay their respects lasted a lot longer.

It was hours before we got into the ground. As we'd queued I'd thought to myself that for the first time I'd actually get to walk on the Anfield pitch and stand in front of the Kop.

That was an exciting prospect. I'm sure I was not the only 11-year-old in that queue who was thinking along those lines. My excitement immediately disappeared when I entered the ground.

Seeing Anfield's pitch and the Kop covered in flowers on the telly was one thing, seeing it with my own two eyes was another. It took my breath away.

This wasn't Anfield. Not the Anfield I'd been to before.

This was a shrine. A shrine of the like I'd never seen before and have never seen since. My mum laid flowers on the pitch that was now covered with floral tributes beyond the Kop end penalty box. My brother and I had taken our treasured Liverpool scarves with us. We'd only got those scarves quite recently. They were our 'best scarves'. Much thicker, warmer and redder than our originals.

I don't know about our Andy but I remember being reluctant to part with mine at first. It was only when we'd walked back down the touchline towards the Annie Road end that I decided to leave it there. I gave that scarf to a steward who tied it to the side-netting on the goal down that end. By then I'd only ever sat in the Annie Road end to watch Liverpool. It seemed somehow appropriate that my scarf ended up down there.

As we left the ground via the away terracing in the corner of the Kemlyn Road stand, I can remember looking back towards the Kop. It had all the colour of a matchday but none of the people. Weird. It's an eerie image I'll never forget.

Red place of worship
– Roy Gilfoyle, journalist

The last home game of the 1992-93 season wouldn't seem to be one that would stand out in many Liverpudlians' minds.

Under Graeme Souness it was becoming clear the Reds weren't really going anywhere as we embarked on the '90s – a period when our dominance of the English game would seep away.

But for some reason the match against Spurs seemed special. It might be that every game in the old Kop was special, with prices far more reasonable and the atmosphere brilliant for virtually every match.

It might be that we were playing a Cockney team – and we always loved to get one over on the Fwanks and Arfurs.

Or it might just be that it was the last home game of the season and a chance to celebrate the fact that we were still the best fans in the country, even if it had been a very mediocre season by Liverpool's standards. Whatever the reason, it seemed vital to get to Anfield as soon as possible and join the queue on Walton Breck Road to ensure you got in in time to guarantee you didn't miss a minute of the festivities.

So there we were, me, my mate Catty and my brother Kevin, having got the train over from Wirral and in the queue at 10am. Remarkably we weren't the first there, but the three-and-a-half hour wait for the Kop gates to open seemed to fly by.

Whether it was us taking it in turns to nip off to the local shops to get supplies, or whether it was carefully watching the mouth of the mounted policemen's horses to make sure the hanging drool didn't end up being shaken your way, 10am soon became 1pm.

Soon after you could hear the turnstile operators setting up and in the hustle and bustle of trying to make sure no scallies could jump the queue and the policemen shouting to make sure order was kept, you were swept into the ground and up the steps to the back of the Kop.

For as long as I live I'll always remember the overwhelming feeling I got whenever I reached the top of those steps and looked out over the gloriously perfect Anfield pitch.

Perhaps every football fan feels the same when they turn up at the ground they love, but to me there was no experience like gaining that first glimpse of my Red place of worship.

Like every Kopite it was then a case of making my way to my usual spot which was just behind the right hand goalpost, about 15 rows up on the new Kop.

At first you could sit down to rest your feet after hours of standing up, but within half an hour you had to get up to protect your patch, which for us was just behind a bar, next to a pillar.

The first action on the pitch came when the Spurs players stepped out of the tunnel in their suits to soak up the atmosphere on the brilliantly sunny day.

There were real boos – not the token effort you get these days when the opposition team is read out – and the likes of Teddy Sheringham, Ian Walker and Vinny Sideways stood on the halfway line with their programmes, looking calm but intimidated by the wall of sound they were greeted by.

As they milled around, captain Gary Mabbutt obviously felt he would strike a blow for his side by wandering on his own towards the Kop goal, in a show of defiance.

How dare he strut his stuff on our turf! We shouted abuse and blasted out all the Cockney chants we knew, and hoped he would be made to pay for his insolence by the misfiring Reds when the game got underway

The only other thing I recall, apart from the incredible repertoire of chants and songs that you just don't get before games these days, and the Kop being full an hour before kick-off, was the balloon that floated around on the pitch.

It seemed to come from nowhere and descended to ground near the halfway line. It made its way towards the Kop goal and we all went 'oooooooohhhhhh', then a gust of wind would sweep it off course and there would be boos. Then it headed towards the Kop again before ending up in the net and the cheer was as loud as if Torben Piechnik had had his contract terminated.

By kick-off the Kop were well up for the game, even though there was little more at stake than pride. Fortunately for the atmosphere on the day, there is a lot of pride among Reds fans and the noise was as if the match was a title decider.

But as exciting and compelling as the atmosphere was, standing behind our bar was becoming a struggle as the Kop swayed and the weight of hundreds of fans seemed to be directed towards us. As much as I wanted the Reds to win, part of me wanted the game to end 0-0 as I knew a surge of delirious Kopites could make me pass out. The game ended 6-2!

Fortunately, during the celebration of the first goal, we were able to duck under the bar and find a space where we could enjoy the rest of the entertainment in more comfort.

It was important to soak up every morsel of action as a long summer without football lay ahead. Thrashing Cockneys is always fun but after a season of disappointment a goal feast gave hope – false hope as it turned out – for the future and the three hours or so of almost non-stop singing made the entertaining game merely a bonus on a superb day.

In those days being a Kopite on a match day was a day-long experience. You couldn't stroll up five minutes before kick-off with a premium view seat waiting for you.

The best things come to those who wait and anyone who was mad enough to queue up with us from 10am for a top Kop spec that day will vouch for that.

It's one of my best memories
– Jim Beglin, former Liverpool player

It's a special place. If people ask me what's my favourite ground there's only one answer I can give – Anfield. Not because I'm trying to butter up Liverpool fans. It's because it is awesome and I was lucky enough to play there. I managed to get my name on the scoresheet in a European Cup semi-final at the Kop End, and I'll treasure that for as long as I live. It's one of my best memories.

Heaven was a No 68 bus ride to the Kop
– Roy Evans, former Liverpool manager,
Programme notes from the Kop's Last Stand, 1994

The 68 bus from Bootle to Stanley Park was full to capacity and it was match day at Anfield. I was seven years old and in the charge of my elder brother Malcolm. He was about to introduce me to the Kop. Excited? I couldn't hide it. Like everybody else aboard, I was gripped by the passion, the atmosphere and the expectancy. I had never been to Anfield before. I was decked out in red, of course, and I carried a heavy wooden rattle which would be classed as a dangerous object in 1994.

Once inside the boys' pen, I remember staring in bewilderment at the thousands who congregated under that famous roof.

Their feelings for Liverpool were ultimate and their humour was unbeatable. The best. I joined the Red Army that day.

That was my beginning and I'm sure that every Kopite will have his own similar story to tell.

There was the place where we stood too. A little piece of concrete, we felt, was our own personal property. I still look at the spot which was mine. Then came Bill Shankly and the greatest of all manager-supporter relationships began. It will never be equalled. The common bond and honest expression was unique.

Fans and manager were inseparable. After today, of course, the old Kop will disappear and the new all-seater stand will be erected. The bricks and mortar will be different, but the people will remain the same. They have been the heartbeat of this club and vital to its marvellous achievements. The volume of the Kop will be turned up to maximum whenever 100 per cent is given on the pitch. It has always been that way.

Meanwhile, we welcome Norwich City on this extra special day and the players are eager to sign off the season in style.

Football cannot be stage-managed but we will be aiming for an open thrilling game. Fortunately, our visitors also have a reputation for interesting and attacking football. I hope to see a performance which is fitting on this memorable occasion.

Finally, it is my duty on behalf of the club to thank everybody for their wonderful support this season.

I scored two and the Kop sang 'sign him on!'
– Ian Rush, former Liverpool player

The one game in front of the Kop that really stands out for me was my last Merseyside derby before I went to Juventus.

I needed two goals against Everton to equal Dixie Dean's record of scoring 19 goals in Merseyside derbies.

At the time everyone knew it was my last season at Liverpool and my last derby game.

I scored a goal in the first half and in the second half we were attacking the Kop end. At the time I didn't know I'd be coming back to Liverpool and the Kop were willing me on to score the second goal. We were 2-1 up and there was less than 10 minutes left when I scored a second past Neville Southall. It was great to equal a record like that and I'd say that the Kop made me do it. I still feel now that the crowd played a major part in me equalling that record. It was incredible after I'd scored. They were just shouting my name over and over again for the next 10 minutes.

I've got a great picture of me scoring that goal and on it you can see one of the stewards, who is meant to keep calm, jumping in the air with the Kop in the background.

I was very lucky to have a good relationship with the Kop supporters. They're clever people because even if you play badly, as long as they see you put the effort in they realise it and support you. The first goal I ever scored for Liverpool as a kid was at the Kop end. They gave me a great reception and I looked at that and thought 'I want to score down this end all the time'.

Bob Paisley used to say to us, and I'm sure this came from Bill Shankly originally, that they are worth a goal start. If we were drawing or losing, and in the second half we were facing the Kop end, it had a major influence on the team. They would get behind us and give us a little bit extra.

Another thing Bob used to say, and it was quite amazing really, was that sometimes when it was windy at Anfield you'd stand in the penalty area at the Kop end and it wasn't windy. The wind had somehow suddenly stopped.

I think that was to do with the design of the Kop and the people on it. Mind you, Bob would also say that if the ball was on the goal-line the Kop would suck it into the back of the net!

I remember the night when I played in Alan Hansen's testimonial in 1988. I was still playing in Italy at the time and I came back to play for Liverpool in a game against an England XI. I think I scored two goals and the Kop were all shouting my name and 'sign him on, sign him on'. It was incredible.

I was still a Juventus player but that was when I realised that I wanted to come back to Liverpool. I'd been in Italy for a year but coming back and pulling on a Liverpool shirt was very special to me. But really it was the Kop, and the way they made me feel welcome, which made me want to come back.

My own testimonial night took place in front of the new Kop which wasn't fully finished at the time. It was a superb night for me. Loads turned up for it and it showed how well I got on with them. It was a special night. We won 6-0 against Celtic and I scored one. When we were four or five nil up I hadn't scored and the Kop just wanted me to score. They weren't bothered about the result, they just wanted me to score.

When I did they were just so happy. It was a great occasion.

Like landing on a different planet
– Bernard O'Byrne, Liverpool fan,
former chief executive of the FA of Ireland

My first visit was for a match against Spurs back in the mid-'80s. The atmosphere really shocked me. Straight away I was in awe of the place. Having been born a few hundred yards away from St Pats in Inchicore, I'd naturally gone there as a kid. But transporting yourself over to Anfield and looking at the Kop really was like landing on a different planet.

A shadow of its former self
– Chris McLoughlin, journalist

Perhaps the strangest night I spent on the old Spion Kop was the last time I actually stood on it. It was the night when Robbie Fowler scored five against Fulham in the Coca-Cola Cup in 1993.

We'd won the first leg 3-1 at Craven Cottage and not many could be bothered with the second leg. Only 12,541 turned up for the game, which was played during the deepest, darkest days under Souness.

Jack Anderson (62)

Colin Mark Ashcroft (19)

James Gary Aspinall (18)

Kester Roger Marcus Ball (16)

Gerard Baron Snr (67)

Simon Bell (17)

Barry Bennett (26)

David John Benson (22)

David William Birtle (22)

Tony Bland (22)

Paul David Brady (21)

Andrew Mark Brookes (26)

Carl Brown (18)

Steven Brown (25)

Henry Thomas Burke (47)

Peter Andrew Burkett (24)

Paul William Carlile (19)

Raymond Thomas Chapman (50)

Gary Christopher Church (19)

Joseph Clark 'oey (29)

Paul Clark (18)

Gary Collins (22)

Stephen Paul Copoc (20)

Tracey Elizabeth Cox (23)

James Philip Delaney (19)

Christopher Barry Devonside (18)

Chris Edwards (29)

Vincent Michael Fitzsimmons (34)

Steve Fox (21)

Jon-Paul Gilhooley (10)

Barry Glover (27)

Ian Thomas Glover (20)

Derrick George Godwin (24)
Roy Hamilton (34)
Philip Hammond (14)
Eric Hankin (33)
Gary Harrison (27)
Stephen Francis Harrison (31)
Peter Andrew Harrison (15)
Dave Hawley (39)
James Robert 'Jimmy' Hennessy (29)
Paul Anthony Hewitson (26)
Carl Hewitt (17)
Nick Hewitt (16)
Sarah Louise Hicks (19)
Victoria Jane Hicks (15)
Gordon Horn 'Goffer' (20)
Arthur Horrocks (41)
Thomas Howard (39)
Tommy Anthony Howard (14)
Eric George Hughes (42)
Alan Johnston (29)
Christine Anne Jones (27)
Gary Philip Jones (18)
Richard Jones Bsc (25)
Nicholas Peter Joynes (27)
Anthony P Kelly (29)
Michael Kelly (38)
Carl David Lewis (18)
David William Mather (19)
Brian Christopher Matthews (38)
Francis Joseph McAllister (27)
John McBrien (18)
Marian Hazel McCabe (21)

Joe McCarthy (21)

Peter McDonnell (21)

Alan McGlone 'Gloney' (28)

Keith McGrath (17)

Paul Brian Murray (14)

Lee Nicol (14)

Stephen Francis O'Neill (17)

Jonathon Owens (18)

William Roy Pemberton (23)

Carl Rimmer (21)

Dave Rimmer (38)

Graham John Roberts HND (24)

Steven Robinson (17)

Henry Charles Rogers (17)

Andrew Sefton (23)

Inger Shah (38)

Paula Ann Smith (26)

Adam Edward Spearritt (14)

Philip John Steele (15)

David Leonard Thomas (23)

Pat Thompson (35)

Peter Reuben Thompson (30)

Stuart Thompson (17)

Peter F Tootle (21)

Christopher James Traynor (26)

Martin Kevin Traynor (16)

Kevin Tyrrell (15)

Colin Wafer (19)

Ian 'Ronnie' Whelan (19)

Mr. Martin Kenneth Wild (29)

Kevin Daniel Williams (15)

Graham John Wright (17)

I remember thinking that I'd never had so much space to move in on the Kop.

Fulham brought with them about 200 fans, who were sat in the middle of the Lower Centenary, and the atmosphere at kick-off was dire – 'You'll Never Walk Alone' was murmured so quietly that I began to wonder why I'd bothered going. The last time I'd heard the Kop so quiet in a cup game was when I watched Marine play Rochdale there in 1989 and the terracing wasn't even open.

I'm glad I was there though. It was a significant night in Fowler's life and I'm still proud to say I've seen every minute of first team football he's ever played at Anfield. The Toxteth Terror, playing in only his second game at Anfield, scored five goals – most with consummate ease – and made us all realise what a classy kid we had on our hands.

It also made me realise that the Kop was a shadow of its former self. There were still a couple of great nights, the last hurrahs, to come before the bulldozers arrived but that night it felt like I had a terminally ill friend who knew his time was up.

'Spion Kop End. Home Supporters Only'
– Ken Rogers, former Liverpool Echo Sports Editor

Those precious 16,480 terrace tickets, admitting fans to a very special Anfield farewell party, unwittingly said it all: Home Supporters Only. SPION KOP END.

The end it was. But only of an era. The demolition men can break concrete and metal but they can't destroy the spirit of the Kop.

I took my place for the 'Last Stand' on that famous mound as a salute to former Echo sports editor Ernest Edwards – the man who earlier in the century gave the Spion Kop its name. The Liverpool Echo has had a special affinity with the fans at the grassroots ever since.

The turnstiles for that game against Norwich in 1994 opened at 1pm and within minutes the central area of the Kop was a sea of red. One banner bade a nostalgic farewell in a dozen languages (those Scousers are well travelled people). Another carried the simple words: 'Kop's Last Stand – 1906-1994'.

The Kopites continued to pour in, greeting each other with the warmth of old pals meeting at a celebration party. They immediately made their way to their own personal two square feet of terracing, joining in with the singing and chanting en route.

This was no wake. It was an up-beat and defiant affair. The pitch was bathed in light, but there was suddenly a total eclipse of the sun as a legendary banner swept past. 'Joey Ate The Frogs Legs, Made The Swiss Roll – Now He's Munching Gladbach!'

Yes, a day for stirring great memories and the carnival was now in full swing. At 2.40pm a host of former Kop heroes were introduced to the crowd, including Albert Stubbins, Ian Callaghan, Tommy Smith, Steve Heighway and Phil Thompson.

Two names in particular inspired roars so ear-splitting, they threatened to shatter the glass in the executive boxes. Billy Liddell and Kenny Dalglish basked in this very special salute.

And then there was Nessie and Jessie.

When Joe Fagan – a great coach and manager in his own right – led out the wives of the legendary Bill Shankly and Bob Paisley, Anfield simply exploded.

'Shankly, Shankly, Shankly' bellowed the Kop as it paid homage to the man who built a Red Empire. The pace of the proceedings meant that Bob didn't get the same treatment, even though fans will never forget his unsurpassed trophy haul during his time in the hotseat.

They've got the Shankly Gates and the Paisley Lounge. Maybe the 'Shankly and Paisley New Kop' is not a bad thought either.

By now the fans were in full flight. They attempted and failed to match their Sixties counterparts with a rendition of 'She Loves You,' but it got better as the afternoon wore on. The famous Beatles song might now be re-introduced into the Kop's repertoire.

But these memories of great days and super heroes only seemed to emphasise the failings of the present side. The Kop won the day – the players didn't.

Emotion did not prevent straight talking on the terraces. "Three of the back four shouldn't be wearing that famous red jersey. The midfield are all sideways and backwards. There is no quality service whatsoever to the front two (We'd Walk A Million Miles For One Of Your Goals, Oh Kenny!)". Behind me, a young lad was rounded on by a girl companion who battered him verbally – and technically – on the question of wingers.

"We haven't got any," said the lad. "You can't expect full-backs to take defenders on. They haven't got the pace or the skill."

"They're supposed to be footballers, aren't they?" rapped the girl. "Just because you're a full-back doesn't mean you can't move wide to give someone an angle".

This vaguely technical retort from a female totally flummoxed the previously dominant male. "Yeah, well they're all useless," he said, returning to basics. "Seven or eight can go next season, no danger".

An older man behind, listening to this exchange, had the last word. "Let's just hope half of them swap shirts with the Norwich players at the end and then get back on the bus to East Anglia by mistake!"

Kopites are steeped in tradition, but they haven't got their heads in the clouds. At half-time, the humour returned. As one exhausted fan went to sit down on the terrace another told him, tongue in cheek: "Hey, NO seats!"

Behind us we could suddenly hear the sound of lump hammer hitting chisel, striking concrete. Someone was determined to take home his little bit of history.

On the final whistle the revelry subsided as the reality hit home that the Kop's Last Stand was finally over.

Hundreds dallied, reluctant to leave, and there was one final moment of theatre. The players had failed to score, despite chants of: 'Play your hearts out for the Kop'.

Fittingly, the last goal to be scored at that end was slotted home – by a Kopite!

Dressed in long khaki shorts and wearing a false moustache and a red fez, he pushed behind the ring of yellow-jacketed police and placed the ball on the edge of the box.

Roared on, he made an exaggerated dribble towards the goal and then punched the air as his shot found the target.

He was led away and the remaining Kopites drifted away, but the ghost of glories past remained.

As one banner said: 'The Spirit Lives On'.

Truth Day
– Chris McLoughlin, Kop Magazine, January 2007

If the six minutes in Istanbul encapsulated everything about Liverpool Football Club on the pitch, the six minutes for the 96 at Anfield during the FA Cup tie against Arsenal in January, 2007 told the world everything they need to know about us off it.

The 'Truth Day' protest was quite simply magnificent.

Organised to hit back against former S*n editor Kelvin MacKenzie after he once again tried to perpetuate the myths his paper printed in the aftermath of the Hillsborough disaster, the protest was carried out with military precision, steely determination and heartfelt passion.

The spectacle of the first six minutes of a massive FA Cup tie being played to the backdrop of a Kop mosaic displaying THE

TRUTH with incessant chant of 'justice for the 96' ringing around the ground was one of the most amazing, if not surreal, sights ever witnessed inside an English football ground.

When the six minutes (the amount of time played in the 1989 FA Cup semi-final before it was abandoned at 3.06pm) – were up, the cacophony of noise that followed practically deafened Thierry Henry and could be heard a mile away.

It got everyone talking, except Mark Lawrenson, which is what the protest had been designed to achieve in the first place.

There are a lot of people who can't get their heads around why Liverpool supporters don't let the whole Hillsborough issue go now. It's almost 18 years since those 96 innocent supporters lost their lives so why not move on? What they don't understand is that as long as scumbags like MacKenzie are around to try and drag our name through the mud we can't move on.

Truth Day wasn't about trying to find someone to blame for the events of April 15, 1989.

It was about defending ourselves, and those 96 innocents who can't defend themselves, against a pack of scandalous, scurrilous, sick lies that the perpetrator refuses to accept were wrong not far off two decades since he first told them.

And for those, like that horrible Manc Terry Christian, who claim Scousers wallow in grief and the protest was more evidence that we live in a self-pity city, then they need to remember one thing.

Truth Day would never have happened in the first place if MacKenzie hadn't brought the issue up again himself shortly before the game when he told a crowd of businessmen in Newcastle that "I was not sorry then and I'm not sorry now," while insisting that The S*n had told The Truth.

News that the BBC had commissioned MacKenzie to present a two-hour radio programme on Christmas Day inflamed the situation further so it was decided, with the official backing of the club, to make the Arsenal FA Cup tie 'Truth Day'.

MacKenzie claimed on the BBC's Question Time in the week after the protest that Liverpool fans are angry with him because: "They want to find somebody who caused the disaster."

You could read that as another sly dig (i.e. we're looking for a scapegoat to try and deflect the blame from ourselves) to further back up his lies while he then went on to claim that a senior police source, Tory MP and Liverpool press agency were the ones who had told The S*n that fans had robbed from and urinated on the dead. Trying to shift the blame on to other people, who he won't name after all this time won't wash here while his complete failure to realise what the point of Truth Day actually was only goes to prove how one-eyed the man is.

The Truth Day protest was about HIM. It was about defending the good name of Liverpool FC supporters against his lies and making the world aware that we will not sit back and let some scumbag denigrate the people of our city.

Thanks to the outstanding organisation by the 'Reclaim The Kop' group and the participation of every Liverpool supporter, and many Arsenal fans, inside Anfield, that aim was well and truly achieved in front of a worldwide BBC audience.

John Motson awkwardly gave it a mention but the BBC tried to largely ignore the six-minute protest, probably due to the fact that they'd received a petition with 11,000 signatures on calling for them to drop MacKenzie from their Christmas Day show on Radio Five Live.

However, great credit must go to Five Live's Alan Green who not only gave Kopites air-time on his six-o-six phone-in after the game but also publicly backed the protest.

Alan Hansen, another BBC employee, didn't comment live on air – much to a lot of people's disappointment – but did make a point of giving his views to LFC Magazine.

"I was proud to be sat inside Anfield and be a Liverpool supporter on Saturday night," he said.

"We never mentioned it on the television but what the Liverpool fans did in the first six minutes was absolutely unbelievable.

"I was in the ground early and the way the supporters had set up the Kop before the game looked absolutely fantastic. It brought a tear to your eye.

"Then, for six minutes, the noise was unbelievable.

"Six minutes is a long time to do something like that. It seemed like the chanting was going on for an eternity but when I looked at the clock there had only been three minutes and 28 seconds of the game played.

"It was a fantastic show of support and everyone involved, and everyone connected with Liverpool Football Club, can be proud of that support.

"I'll tell you something else as well. Liverpool supporters didn't just send out a message about Hillsborough and their campaign for justice but they sent out a message to everybody across the world about how good they truly are." Spot on and Liverpool supporters further enhanced their reputation 96 hours later when Arsenal returned to Anfield in the Carling Cup.

On a very different night, Kopites displayed two of the qualities that have set them apart from other sets of fans over the last 45 years – support and sportsmanship.

The last time Liverpool let six goals in at home was 1930 so almost certainly there wasn't a single fan inside Anfield that night who had seen the Reds ship six goals in a home game.

At most grounds it would have turned into a night of witch-hunts and recrimination but instead of slaughtering the players and manager, Liverpool's fans responded by getting behind them.

Jerzy Dudek did get some stick after making mistakes for the second and third goals while there were boos at half-time.

But a lot of those cat-calls were for the assistant referee who had failed to flag for Arsenal's blatantly offside fourth goal and when the players returned after the break they were cheered as if they were 4-1 up.

Liverpool showed a bit of fight in the second half and when Sami Hyypia made it 3-5 with 10 minutes to go there was a 'here we go again' feel about the place.

It wasn't to be and when Julio Baptista finished us off close to full-time the response was remarkable.

Up went the scarves and 'You'll Never Walk Alone' tumbled down from the Kop and into the night sky. Where else would that happen?

To be able to take the joint third worse ever home defeat on the chin and show support for a team that was responsible for the most humiliating and embarrassing defeat at Anfield in living memory is testament to the magnificent support that Liverpool receive.

Some Reds did leave early but they do that when Liverpool are comfortably winning and when the final whistle blew there were still 35,000-plus inside the ground.

Many even stayed behind to applaud Arsenal's young side off which, given the circumstances, was an outstanding piece of sportsmanship.

Contrast that to the scenes at Old Trafford after Man Utd's final home game of the 2005/06 season when, after seeing their team beaten 3-1 by Chelsea, just a few thousand Mancs stayed behind to applaud their own team as they did a lap of honour around the pitch.

Liverpool's fantastic support on the day was attacked by Paul Doyle, chief sportswriter of The Guardian Unlimited, the following day who claimed Kopites "are dumb" for "wallowing in failure" and that "rather than pledge their allegiance to the unacceptable,

Liverpool fans should have walked out en masse shortly after half-time."

It was a typical piece of anti-Liverpool journalism – wait until we're down before rushing in to kick us – from a man who evidently thinks those who attend football matches should act as customers rather than supporters and boycott products that aren't up to scratch. A bit like readers of The Guardian, Paul?

They say it's in times of trouble that you find out who your true friends really are and the same goes for supporting a football team.

It's easy following a team when everything is going well. It's when things are going catastrophically wrong that true supporters stand up to be counted. Liverpool fans did that twice in the space of 96 hours.

In the FA Cup they showed solidarity and passion to protest against Kelvin MacKenzie and remind the world what The Truth really is.

In the Carling Cup they showed support and sportsmanship despite paying £30 a go to witness a shambolic performance against a team of kids.

Quite simply there isn't a better set of supporters in the business and that, Kelvin MacKenzie, really is The Truth.

How the Kop became a stage of its own
– Alan Edge, author

Only very rarely is the Anfield Spion Kop ever accorded anything approaching a true representation of its real stature.

Sure, there will likely always remain a broad perception of its prominence, yet any attempt at conveying fully the essence of the Kop and its impact on modern football culture is inclined to fall someway short of its target.

Fact is with something so ethereal as the Spion Kop, mere words are never enough.

Back in 1964 the reporter for the BBC Panorama documentary covering what in those days was termed the 'Kop phenomenon' probably came as near as anybody to defining that essence.

Standing awestruck in front of the baying, swaying massed terrace prior to the 1964 title clincher against Arsenal he remarked briefly yet accurately how 'the Kop didn't behave like any other football crowd'.

Within his simple yet insightful statement perhaps lies the key to understanding just what the Anfield Spion Kop was about and how it came to revolutionise football culture.

Today, of course, we take for granted the modern global spectacle the game has become.

The singing, the chanting, the flags and the colour have become so integral a part of football that it is nigh impossible for most to envisage a time when such partisanship wasn't part of the scene.

Curiously, in Britain at least, that time was actually not so long before those Panorama cameras visited Anfield.

If the phenomenon the BBC news team came to witness that afternoon did not exactly happen overnight then it certainly only became prominent once that particular championship-winning season approached its climax.

Until that little period of football history in the making, the Spion Kop was, in truth, little different from any other crowded terrace. Possibly its patrons may have been slightly more exuberant and boisterous than most. Perhaps, too, more prone to sporadic outbursts and isolated chants from the odd cluster of fans. For the most part, however, everything was – collectively speaking – restrained and orderly.

Essentially, a gathering of like-minded enthusiastic individuals rather than the single homogenous excitable mass into which it was so rapidly to evolve. So what happened to transform things?

Well, this was early Sixties Liverpool we must remember. A post-war Liverpool that history confirms was a fertile cradle of exceptional creativity and initiative. And fast fulfilling it, too.

The Beatles had just emerged as the worldwide acclaimed vanguard of a veritable reservoir of talent – gumption too – that was to go on to permeate a broad spectrum of prime British cultural and business strata for several decades to come.

Released from the grievous restraints of war that had dogged preceding generations and fuelled by the increasing Sixties affluence that offered a diversion away from the drudgery of the workplace, the natural wit and exuberance of the Scouser suddenly found itself all manner of platforms on which to express that latent talent.

As it so happened – with the exception of the Fab Four's unique worldwide arena – the Anfield Spion Kop became the biggest stage of them all. Certainly it was the loudest. As the Mersey Sound resonated around the world, the full throttle of 28,000 of its own kind promptly amplified it.

Cocooned and isolated in a way you could never get today, the patrons of the Kop simply did what came naturally to them and – amongst other more base tendencies – swayed and sang along heartily with the pre-match tannoy. Here the Liverpool Irish pub sing-song culture was clearly to play a significant role.

Not many of the Kopites at the time were exactly strangers to belting out a communal tune from the comfort of their own ale-house on a Saturday night. The Kop simply became a giant extension of that concept. Soon more traditional melodies were hijacked and revamped with Liverpudlian lyrics reflecting the local vernacular and humour.

In no time at all, without any contrivance, all the ingredients were in place. Almost if not quite overnight it seemed the Kop had become a completely distinct and separate entity to all its peer terraces. Those orthodox and orderly flat cap characteristics of football crowds that had prevailed since the game's inception were now rendered old hat. The Spion Kop had found a culture all its own and was ready to unleash it on an unsuspecting audience.

In some ways what happened on the Kop can be viewed as a leap of creativity not dissimilar and certainly not unconnected to the spark that was igniting popular music around the same time.

Sure there was an element of evolution present yet what stands out above all is that impression of originality and spontaneity. What had taken place had been instinctive. Most certainly it was something to be cherished.

At this point, I'd like if I may to draw another musical analogy with what took place back then on the Spion Kop. I dare say some might consider it a somewhat tenuous one. Personally, however, I think it helps illustrate quite aptly the central point I'm trying to make about what transpired.

There's a song featured at the end of the film 'The Big Lebowski' as the credits are rolling. The song is 'Viva Las Vegas' by the new country blues artist Shawn Colvin.

It's taken from the 1995 tribute album to the acclaimed songsmith Doc Pomus who some thirty years earlier had been co-writer of the song with his writing partner, Mort Shuman. The original version you may recall was the title track for the 1964 film starring Elvis Presley.

That original Elvis interpretation had been quirky and upbeat, sprinkled with Hollywood-style pep and glitz. More than thirty other artists went on to record the song after Elvis. Each adheres fairly faithfully to the Elvis interpretation.

Mercifully, Shawn Colvin's version is the one refreshing and compelling exception. In Colvin's take the protagonist becomes as reckless and mysterious as the original was cheery and predictable.

Beguiling us to accompany her into those darker ruinous corners of addiction and obsessiveness that seam through Las Vegas, Colvin manages somehow to re-invent the song, bringing out hitherto concealed beauty and starkness of melody and lyric alike.

Her vocal innovation redefines the parameters of what Pomus and Shuman had written, giving us something completely distinctive; three or four smouldering minutes to savour.

The Kop's early Sixties spark of Scouse invention and innovation managed to pull off a similar trick to Colvin with regard to our spectatorial habits and, ultimately, our footballing culture.

In a way Shawn Colvin was to do with her song interpretation years later – though with the accent firmly on Scouse chirpiness as distinct from Colvin's Nevada darkness – it saw the Spion Kop redefine the parameters of football support.

Where once had been a banked dreary terrace no different to so many others, there was now a world-renowned and oft-imitated shrine where a congregation gathered to pay homage and sing its team's praises.

Individual voices may have paled next to Shawn Colvin's. Yet together in communion, those voices were even more exquisite.

Like with Colvin's song, the Kop's hitherto obscured beauty was able to blossom. Every other Saturday it afforded us not three or four but ninety or more life-affirming minutes to savour.

Demolishing Kop gave me mixed emotions
– Gary Morgan, Works Manager building new Kop stand in 1994

I started work on the demolition of the Spion Kop after the Norwich game. I was the works manager for McAlpine Fusiliers on there and worked right through the demolition of the old Kop and the building of the new one right up to its completion.

I was actually the assistant works manager on the Centenary Stand when that was built a few years earlier and also worked on the Stretford End at Manchester United before working on the Kop.

I'm a lifelong Liverpool fan and I stood on the Kop watching the great teams right through. I started going there as a kid in about 1965.

I went with my father and my granddad. My uncle, Phil Morgan, was a player at the club so we used to get tickets and go to the games nearly every other week. The reserves played at Anfield then so we'd go and watch them and then the first team.

When I was older I'd go with my mates. A big gang of us would thumb it from the lights at Bromborough right through to Anfield.

I've been all over the country and all over Europe watching Liverpool so to go from supporting Liverpool to working on the new Kop was really a dream come true.

Demolishing the Kop gave me mixed emotions. Knocking it down was quite sad but in terms of enjoying my work, in the sense of where I was working, it was excellent. We had a great team of lads working on it, all who were local.

We did all sorts as well as simply building it. We concreted in the time capsule which is under the Kop and we also, at the front apron of the Kop before you go on to the pitch, concreted in some urns of ashes in there.

The groundsman, Reg Summers, allowed people to come on to the pitch and walk around to scatter ashes but because we were concreting in at the time the people asked us if, instead of scattering the ashes, could we bury the casket in the concrete. We buried quite a few in there.

We built the new Kop in four main stages and we were under quite a lot of pressure.

When Man United rebuilt the Stretford End they closed it down completely while the work was going on. At Liverpool the fans were allowed on to the new stand as each section was built.

There was a time when stadium manager Ged Poynton and chief executive Peter Robinson said: "Listen lads, are we going to have it open for the Newcastle game?"

We had two weeks at that point to get the job done and there was quite a lot of work left to do. We did it though, which was a great achievement.

The Kop's time capsule
– Ken Rogers, former Liverpool Echo sports editor

Almost two months after the Kop stood for the last time, I would play one final part in the history of this legendary bank of terracing when I presented a 'Time Capsule' to the club on behalf of the Liverpudlian readers of the Echo.

In it was a 'Kop Roll Of Honour' containing the names of thousands of Kopites who had proudly sent their names to the Echo. A number of items were enclosed in an indestructible box and handed to the man who was Liverpool's Chief Executive at that time, the famous Peter Robinson. The contents included:

* *My own Kop ticket, used to gain entry for the Last Stand against Norwich City from where I reported the game.*
* *The matchday programme from that day.*
* *A song sheet used during the special Sunday Kop Concert attended by a host of players and stars.*
* *A Football Echo and Echo Kop Special edition – between them capturing the history of the Kop.*
* *A Kop video.*
* *All the players' autographs from the final day.*

Bill Pemberton, vice-chairman of the Hillsborough Family Support Group, was kind enough to donate his membership card –

number one – and a scarf which was carried by a fan all over Europe as well as on the Kop.

Liverpool FC placed the time capsule in the concrete under what became the new Kop Concourse running below the redeveloped stand.

The spot was subsequently marked with a brass plaque, carrying the inscription: 'Liverpool Echo Kop, saluting the fans who made Liverpool great'.

Champions – Yea! Yea!
– Liverpool Echo report, April 1964

Thousands were locked out of the ground at Anfield today when the gates were closed at 1.45pm with a capacity crowd inside to watch the league championship decision between Liverpool and Arsenal. A police official said: "It's worse than we expected," and by 12.30pm traffic was building up to a complete block.

Hundreds of motorists were parking their cars miles from the ground and making their way to the turnstiles on foot. Scenes bordering on chaos were reported at 1.30pm when thousands of vehicles were pouring into the vicinity of the ground.

Mounted police were busy controlling the crowds and other police were being reinforced by members of the special constabulary, said a police spokesman.

At 1pm a police spokesman from E Division at Westminister Road said: "We have every available man at Anfield and we are fully extended".

From 1.45pm onwards the ground was tightly packed with an exultant singing crowd waiting for kick-off.

"They're just singing their heads off – they love it," said an official. "But," he added, "with this big crowd it looks like being about 5pm before the ground is cleared".

The turnstiles at Anfield were opened at 12.50pm for the big game against Arsenal. By the time the gates opened the approaching streets were jammed with football fans. Lake Street, for instance, was packed 15 to 20 deep with queuing fans. Thousands of fans surrounded the ground as late as 12.30pm, pouring out of taxis and off buses knowing full well they hadn't a chance of getting in. "We know we haven't got a chance but we couldn't take the risk. We may get in," was the comment of one optimistic Wavertree fan. The queue started to form as early as 10 o'clock last night but by 9 o'clock this morning there were still only 50 fans outside.

People coming out of nearby public houses after closing time last night were staggered to see the fans armed with transistor radio sets, camp beds and flasks of hot coffee arriving at the Spion Kop end of the ground for the long vigil. The fans kept lively by singing 'Oh When the Saints Go Marching In' and shouting other football slogans.

First in the queue were 17-year-old Collegiate schoolboy George Hunter of Russell Road, Mossley Hill, and his friend, Alan Wilcock, also 17, of Holbeck Street, Anfield. By midnight the queue had grown to about 20 strong. Ticket holders found great difficulty in reaching their sections of the ground as the crowds surged from gate to gate in an endeavour to join the shortest queue. When one gate was closed there was a concentrated rush to other sections of the ground. Many people who arrived to find milling mobs of people besieging all the entrances decided to call it a day. They then trekked across Stanley Park to watch Everton's reserve game against Barnsley at Goodison Park.

Never heard noise like it
– Geoff Strong, former Liverpool and Arsenal player

I've never heard a noise like the Kop made that afternoon when we won the title against Arsenal. It made you want to stop and listen to them calling for their team to win.

So full of joy
– 'Sir' Roger Hunt, former Liverpool player

We were on top of the world as we did a lap of honour at the end. I was so full of joy that I could have played another 90 minutes.

'If you're all voting Tory ...'
– Dan Kay, journalist

My Spion Kop debut, having served my time for a good while in the stands, was Kenny's last game at Anfield, the initial Cup derby before the 4-4.

Running late and unaware that shortarses like myself would be better served by using the ground-level wing entrances, I raced to the top of the stairwells just in time to be greeted by the crescendo of Gerry Marsden's famous anthem and the teams taking to the field in glorious Spring sunshine.

Once the game settled down I realised that I had a great view of the backs of people's heads and jackets but precious little else, not really what I'd been queuing up for at 7am the previous Wednesday morning!

A bit of rugby-style jostling enabled me to manoeuvre my way to a spot where I was able to at least see some of the pitch, although for anything that took place beyond the penalty-box line at our end, it was a case of guessing from the oohs and aahs what had actually gone on. As it was, I had a decent view of the key moment in the game – Gary Ablett's lunge on Pat Nevin. I have always wondered how different things might have turned out if Neil Midgeley had pointed to the spot.

I was made to wait for my first Kop win as the next time I was in there was for a woeful 1-3 loss to QPR as the title started to slip away from us. "Ah well, next year", I thought, "We never go two years without a title" (gulp).

Dean Saunders finally broke my duck and his own goalless one when the Reds returned the following August and when that was followed up with a resounding win against the Beardo-(un)inspired Blues ("what a waste of talent"), there was no doubt in my mind that my proper first season as a Kopite would see us finish as Champions. Ho hum.

Those occasions when I was unable to make the game started to bite even deeper than before, now that I was missing out on the weird and wonderful experiences that took place behind that goal (anyone remember the fella who would wait for a lull and then start imitating a 1940's air-raid siren?!). The strongest pangs were felt the night against Auxerre when the Kop made up about half the crowd. The roar from Wally Walters' winner still left its mark though, even over the radio.

The Cup runs kept us going, with only Genoa's inspired goalie preventing them going the way of the French and of course we went all the way in the FA Cup in 1992. But the sweetest moment was when Rushie finally nailed the Mancs and their title pretensions, leaving us singing 'You'll never win the league' with, what was at the time, total conviction.

The stand-out memory that year though happened at a half-arsed end-of-season home defeat to Wimbledon in the League, the night before the General Election, when during a quiet moment in play, a lone voice sang out: "If you'll all voting Tory, all voting Tory, all voting Tory you're a twat!"

Must've been those Kemlyn Roaders who got Major re-elected.

Within months they'd become Centenary Standers and gazing up at them, in their new home, started to hold more appeal than watching the likes of Paul Stewart & co.

Maybe it was knowing the clock was now ticking on a terraced Kop, maybe it was that shower from down the East Lancs getting their act together or perhaps it was just the scale and speed of our own team's decline, but a new mood seemed to descend, with withering discontent towards the manager, not all of it of course due to on-field matters, being countered by enthusiastic support for the exciting crop of young players that were, at times, the only shining light.

At least the final terraced derby was also graced by drama worthy of the occasion as Everton's old nemesis, Ian Rush, boomed an equaliser past the Binman within seconds of Dave Watson's opener.

That was followed by Sir Robbie of Fowler marking his return from a broken leg with his first goal against the team he had supported as a nipper.

The three thousand or so non-season ticket specs for the Kop's 'Last Stand' against Norwich were naturally like gold-dust but thanks to the persistence of my auld fella (an Evertonian, no less!), I eventually managed to obtain one of those precious orange briefs.

The day itself was a bit of a blur but what remains clear in the mind is that the excuse for a match being played in front of us barely detracted from the genuinely unforgettable sense of occasion and history

The Kop was as jam-packed as even some old-timers could remember. The full repertoire of old songs, flags, scarves and other paraphernalia were on proud display but it was particularly the pre-match ceremony on the pitch that heightened the feeling that we were part of something truly unique, that would live on however we were housed.

Many famous names from years past were welcomed rapturously onto the pitch but the ear-splitting roar for King Kenny coupled with the singing as Joe Fagan walked out with Nessie Shankly and Jessie Paisley will live with me, and I'm sure many others, for ever.

The Kop Grandstand took a bit of getting used to but nowadays is still a match for anyone on a good day.

It has witnessed some brilliant moments of its own from the erratic flair of Roy Evans' side in the mid-'90s and those two 4-3s against Newcastle to electric European nights under Gerard Houllier against the likes of Barcelona and Roma and more recent games against Chelsea and others.

It remains the heartbeat of Liverpool Football Club and while a little holiday in a different part of the ground is nice every now and then, when the title finally comes back home there's only one place I'll want to be.

'We all agree Clemo is better than Tina'
– Keith Cunliffe, Kopite

The first game I actually stood on the Kop for was Chris Lawler's testimonial.

I don't remember anything at all about it though, apart from that I had to sit on the barrier to actually see.

Talking of barriers, the amount of times you got pushed off and then back on was unbelievable. Sometimes your legs would go numb and you were desperate not to get pushed off as you wouldn't be able to stand.

I then moved on to a milk crate in front of the barriers. This was pretty safe but was a chore walking to the ground having to carry it. I always enjoyed night matches at Anfield, especially the European games.

I took a day off school and went with my dad to queue down Kemlyn Road for tickets for the return leg against Forest in 1978/79.

We lost the first game 2-0 and although we had most of the game that night, we just couldn't score at Anfield. Forest were a good side then though.

The Kop used to have a great rapport with Peter Shilton. 'Tina, Tina, Tina' we'd shout at him and 'We all agree Clemo is better than Tina'.

He always took it in good humour though.

Around the early '80s, Ipswich were one of our main rivals and we had a couple of seasons when we played them in the League Cup.

I think one of those was when Mark Lawrenson made a tackle from behind on the penalty spot when an Ipswich forward, could have been Mariner or Gates, was through on goal. It was the best executed tackle I've ever seen.

I think it was in one of these games in the cup against Arsenal that went to extra-time and me and my mate nipped out to the chippy behind the Kop for a split and gravy, then back into the Kop to watch extra time with our chips!

Around this time there was talk of Eric Gates coming to Anfield in place of Craig Johnston and I remember the song: 'We all agree Skippy is better than Wurzel'.

One enjoyable afternoon was the time we beat Man United 4-0 in 1990.

Their favourite song at the time was 'Always look on the bright side of life' but when the fourth goal went in the whole of Anfield sang it back to them. It was immense, even the Kemlyn Road were singing it. I've still got it on tape.

And what about that huge tin of Crown Paint they used to put on the centre spot when Liverpool were sponsored by them?

About a dozen men used to get hernias carting it off before the game started.

That always used to give us a laugh on the Kop.

'Ten grand a week?'
– Andrew House, Kopite

Going to Anfield was a fantastic experience for me. I first stood on the Kop when I was seven and coming from Canvey Island in Essex I did not realise that my accent was not Scouse.

All my family on my mum's side lived on the Wirral and going to Anfield was a real family occasion. We would get the ferry across to the Pier Head and the bus up to Anfield.

Once in Anfield I would be dropped off in the Boys' Pen while my uncles took their place in the Kop half way up behind the goal. It was at half-time when the police were not looking that I would climb over the fence and find my uncles.

For me, the noise and fans were incredible.

The sheer volume was consuming and it was something that I looked forward to.

The humour of the Kop was something that I picked up on very quickly and the thing that stood out for me was in 1976 when we played Barcelona in the second leg of the UEFA Cup semi-final.

We had beaten Barca at the Nou Camp 1-0 with a John Toshack goal. On the return all I heard about was Johan Cruyff this and Johan Cruyff that so when I went to Anfield I was expecting to see some kind of god.

Half way through the game the ball was played to Cruyff who was on the side of the pitch by the Kemlyn Road (now Centenary) Stand when he went to control the ball and it went straight under his foot for a Liverpool throw.

Straight away one Kopite shouted out '10 grand a week?'

'More like 10 lots of shite a week' and everyone around us cracked up laughing.

For me though, the Kop was all about passion and support for Liverpool and when we sang it was all as one.

Shankly on the Kop
– Anthony Radcliffe, Kopite

When we were kids we went in the Boys' Pen. Going in there when you were aged nine or 10 was sort of taking a step into the Kop. It had barbed wire on the top with remains of clothes where boys had escaped out to actually get on the Kop. One of the bars was bent on the Boys' Pen but they used to put a copper on duty there because you could squeeze through when you were little.

It was a mad place to be though. There were girders on the top, part of the framework, and lads used to get up there from the Boys' Pen and walk along them. You'd see people above you walking along the girders. There have been stories which have changed over the years about Bill Shankly going on the Kop after he had retired.

Someone said that he went on in disguise. He never. Imagine Shankly doing that. He wasn't that type of fella. He'd also go to Everton and Man United games after he'd retired where he was treated as a VIP but at Liverpool they didn't allow him near the players so, even though he was Liverpool's greatest manager, he went on the Kop as a fan. That showed what an exceptional person he was.

I was there the day when Shankly actually went on the Kop. It was in November 1975, after he had retired, and I was 15 at the time. We played Coventry at home and drew 1-1. I used to get in the Kop early and I remember there was a bit of excitement in there. There was a bit of a buzz and they were all singing Shankly's name. When a player's name got sung you'd see all the arms go up and point towards the pitch where the player was. This time the arms were all pointing from both directions on the Kop to the centre. Apparently Shankly was on there and was getting shoved all over the place, from pillar to post.

When things had settled down I remember that he actually stayed on there for well over half an hour. I remember there was a fella who stood by him right through the game who had a red jumper on. The reason I remember it so well is that I actually shook hands with him. I shook hands with Bill Shankly on the Kop.

That was unbelievable because I was only 15 and I'll always remember it.

'Who's the Scouser in the black?'
– Jamar King, Kopite

I believe we were playing Man United during the great season of '89. Manchester fans were booing the ref for making some calls in Liverpool's favour.

They started to loudly chant 'Who's the Scouser in the black?' Without missing a beat, the Kop responded with a thunderous roar – 'Johnny Barnes, Johnny Barnes, Johnny Barnes', to which the away supporters were silenced. John Barnes clapped his hands to the Kop to show his support. You see it wasn't just the cheering and singing that made the Kop the Kop, it was the sense of humour. It didn't matter how the team was doing, someone in the crowd always said something to make the fans smile.

'1-2-3 puff!'
– Alan Powell, Kopite

I live now in a city in Canada that has the same name that I used to chant as a young lad on the Kop – Saint John. One of my greatest memories of the Spion Kop is from 1966, when Liverpool hosted Ajax of Amsterdam in a European Cup second leg tie.

Liverpool started the game 5-1 down from the first leg. I was 14 at the time and after surviving the crush at the turnstiles (thanks to a large gentleman who put his legs against the wall and his back against the crowd while shouting "there's a lad here, back off will yiz,") I took my place on the Kop to the left of the goal on the same side as the boys' pen. The attendance was 50,000 plus and the pitch was barely visible due to a thick fog. The Kop amused themselves by blowing in unison, probably after chanting something like '1-2-3 (puff)' to blow the fog away!

It wasn't long before the crush became too much for many in my area. I was near the front and many were being helped out onto the cinder track. One of the first aiders was at the front helping to pull people out and tried to help me out but I was wedged in firmly. I managed to crawl out under my own steam and the next thing I know is we are all being herded along the track. Good, I thought, we are being moved to another spot. Then the door opened and we were out in the parking lot. Anyway I got the bus home, and watched the game on TV if I remember correctly. Happy days.

The tunnel under the Kop
– Chris McLoughlin, journalist

There was a feeling that the atmosphere on the Kop was going down the pan somewhat in the 1980s.

Complacency from success, smaller attendances, largely because of unemployment, and the effects of the Heysel disaster all contributed to making the famous terrace quieter than it was in the halcyon days of the '60s and '70s.

What nobody realised though was that in 1987 part of the Kop was to go down the pan. Quite literally.

The builders were in during pre-season to strengthen the crush barriers on the Kop. They ended up on overtime when a giant hole, 20ft by 15ft, appeared on the terracing.

The work on the crush barriers caused a Victorian sewer, built in the 1860s, under the terracing to collapse, which in turn caused a shaft leading up to a manhole cover on the Kop to come crashing down with it.

Such was the scale of the repair job that Liverpool were forced to play their first three games of the season away from Anfield while the work was completed rather than play in front of a reduced capacity of what would have been around 22,000.

It was worth the wait. Kenny Dalglish's new-look Liverpool side, featuring new summer signings John Barnes and Peter Beardsley, finally played in front of the Kop on September 12 and won 2-0.

They didn't lose a single home league game all season, winning 15 of their 20 matches and scoring 49 goals in the process on the way to the title.

This was proof positive, if it were needed, that while the Kop may have gone down the pan in 1987, then the Liverpool team certainly hadn't.

Every underdog has its day
– Independent newspaper report, August 1999

It remains a rare pleasure to attend a match at Liverpool FC. The Kop makes it so. Long gone are the days when – assured of a prize per season (and a home win per fortnight) – that bank of Scouse passion might have been subject to accusations of only 'singing when they're winning'.

Only the relatively lean times test the strength of a support base. At Anfield, that base is strong and admirable. On Saturday (August 14, 1999) the colour, the noise and – most of all – the appreciation of footballing endeavour were magnificently vivid. Liverpool, meanwhile, lost 1-0 to the hot relegation favourites.

It is awkward when discussing the Kop – as it is with the Church – to know whether one is referring to a building or those who congregate in it.

In fact, neither would be anything without the other – a few thousand bucket-seats on a sloped expanse of concrete and a few thousand football followers with nowhere to gather – but it is the people who give life to the building. What a necessary service those people did for the game last weekend.

By 2.30pm the Kop was filling up. Scarves head-high and horizontally-taut, the Kop's first rendition of 'You'll Never Walk Alone' echoed with audibly genuine 'hope in their hearts'.

It drew applause from the Watford fans and created a momentum of support that lasted for much of the game.

Nobody booed when the Watford team-sheet was read out; everybody clapped when the Watford goalkeeper ran towards them for the start of the second half. Then at the end – and here was the highlight for anyone who clings anachronistically on to ideals of mutual respect, sportsmanship or simple decency – they stayed behind to applaud their victorious visitors.

Of course they are not perfect – what several-thousand-strong mass of humanity is?

Acknowledgement is duly made of very noticeable recent impatience among some Kopites which flies in the face of their fabled unconditional support.

Furthermore, there are, no doubt, some who would seek to recount less happy experiences of Anfield, and many more who believe their own club's support to be comparably good.

However, what happened at the weekend deserves to be held up as an example. It was sufficiently good and sufficiently rare to draw an affectionate word from the visiting manager.

Graham Taylor was right when he said: "In these days of all the tension, hype and pressure of the modern game, it was good to hear fans do that. I know my players were impressed and will remember it. It is to those fans' credit that they can do that.

"They weren't saying we were better than their players, but they appreciated how we had played".

I spoke on the subject to Ian St John who, having run out at Anfield more often and longer ago than he would probably prefer to recall, still rarely misses a match.

He described such conduct as 'standard'. His was one of the early names to be singled out for chanting by the Kop. Like 'Dal-glish' in later years, he was fortunate that his two syllables offered just the right emphasis to follow a rhythmic handclap.

That level of support added playing inches to a small man and the ethos of the Anfield crowd remains something of which he is proud.

"If an underdog comes up and plays the right way, with endeavour and organisation and without kicking lumps out of Liverpool, the crowd will appreciate that and they'll be applauded.

"I recall a famous Cup tie against Swansea in the early '60s when we absolutely murdered them. But it was one of those games in which their goalkeeper made about 25 brilliant saves.

"I got concussed and was blacking out but, in those days, they made you play on and, by the end, I think I was probably kicking the wrong way.

"It was terrible – but the Kop were great to them. At Liverpool, that's standard. It's tradition".

That tradition might have gone into decline after the installation of seats – (not, of course, that anyone at Liverpool objected to that) – and St John, like all devotees of the club, recalls the terraced Kop's "unique swaying and singing. After all, at rock concerts they stand. You do it better standing up".

But, through the dark days of the trauma which necessitated those seats, the tradition has survived and the perspective has sharpened. On the Kop, they love Liverpool but they understand that, without an opponent, there isn't a game.

Without Watford and Swansea, and even Everton and Manchester United, Liverpool is a pretty pointless entity. Pointless is precisely what Saturday became for Liverpool. Happily, the Kop offered that pointlessness some meaning.

'The best in the country'
– Bristol City fans' letters, 1994

* A very big thank you to Liverpool fans. I know I speak for all 7,000 Bristol City supporters in saying how moved and gratified we were at the fabulous reception we received at the finish of the FA Cup third round replay game on January 25, 1994. We were amazed and totally thrilled. Thank you again.

* I am a Bristol City supporter and was at Anfield. The best moment that night wasn't when we scored or even when the final whistle went. For me, the lasting memory will be of the reception the visiting players received after the game from the Kop. I've often heard that Liverpool fans were the best in the country – now I know it's true.

* I was fortunate to be one of the visiting fans from Bristol at Anfield. My lasting memory of the occasion was the magnificent ovation the Kop gave at the end. It was truly an emotional moment and the gesture will always live in my memory. There is no need to look beyond the Kop as the Sports Personalities of the Year. Thanks for the memory.

Walking off to a standing ovation
– Teddy Sheringham, former Tottenham striker

One of my best memories was the 2-1 FA Cup quarter-final win at

Anfield in 1995. It wasn't just playing and scoring but walking off the pitch to a standing ovation from the Kop.

Sportsmen of the century
– Telegram from Don Revie, former Leeds manager, 1969

Thanks for your very warm-hearted gesture. We nominate you as the sportsmen of the century. You and your team and wonder manager deserve one another. *(Written after Leeds clinched the title at Anfield on April 28, 1969 and received a generous ovation from the Kop).*

St Etienne of a new generation
– Chris McLoughlin, journalist, 2002

Roma 2002. Gerard Houllier's return. Rightly regarded as one of the greatest nights the all-seater Kop has seen.

Before the game Phil Thompson had said it could be St Etienne part two. Afterwards it felt like it was. It was certainly the St Etienne of a new generation and one hell of a night.

For me though, it was somewhat bittersweet because I wasn't on the Kop. I was in the Anfield press box, working for the Liverpool Echo, and didn't quite feel as part of the night as I could have.

I was on the Kop for the Paris St Germain game in 1997, right up in the back corner. The noise that night was sensational. Liverpool didn't quite do enough to go through but the PSG players, many of them internationals, were visibly frightened by the atmosphere.

My throat was on fire by full-time. It was a night of glorious failure and one that I'd felt very much part of. It's not the same when you're working.

The hardest part of watching the club you love and support from a press box is suppressing your emotions. Singing, chanting and celebrating goals isn't the done thing in the press box. You're there to cover the game, not lead the singing.

So whenever I've been sat in the press box and Liverpool have scored it's been a case of sitting there and simply watching the celebrations unfold around me. It's bloody hard.

Remember the 2001 FA Cup final when Michael Owen scored his superb late winner? While you were going bananas and hugging the nearest person in sight, I was sat in the Millennium Stadium's press box describing the goal down the phone for the Football Echo.

My immediate thought was how I was going to describe the goal for my report, which had to be finished and ready to print at full-time, rather than enjoying what in reality is one of the greatest moments I've ever experienced inside a football ground.

Don't get me wrong, I wouldn't swap working as a football writer for the world and I am very privileged to be doing it, but being professional under those circumstances isn't easy.

The Roma night was similar. We'd heard strong whispers that Gerard would make his long awaited return that night and on arrival at Anfield I was told that he was definitely there.

The noise when he walked out of the tunnel again was superb but with the scrum of cameramen around him, and Fabio Capello, only the people in the Paddock and Main Stand could really see him.

Early in the first half he came to the touchline to pass instructions on and everyone on the Kop saw him.

The noise was phenomenal. 'Allez, Allez, Gerard Houllier' rang around Anfield like never before. It was one of those goosepimple moments that I'll never forget.

With a noise like that against them, Roma, who were the Italian champions at the time and one of the favourites to win the

Champions League outright, didn't stand a chance.

Liverpool secured the 2-0 win they needed to go through to the quarter-finals thanks to a penalty from Jari Litmanen and a header from Emile Heskey.

In one sense it was good to sit there and experience the atmosphere, watching well-known members of the national press constantly gaze towards the Kop because they couldn't help it.

But on the other hand it would have been great to have been right in the centre of it all.

It was our Kop
– Tommy Fairclough, Kopite

When we were young and couldn't afford to get in, we used to climb into the Kop over the wall. We'd end up with cut hands and all the rest of it but that didn't matter. We just wanted to get in.

I'd go with my mates – Billy and Teddy Molyneux, Billy, Paul and Jimmy Collins and Charlie Daly.

Once we were in, there were these shrubs inside the ground and we'd go and hide in them.

About an hour before kick-off this 'arl fella would come along and start swinging a big stick into the bushes. We'd be getting smacked in the head, arms and everywhere else but none of us would shout out because if he found us we'd end up getting chucked out.

Once he'd gone we'd go into the Kop and watch the game. The Kop was great. People really would just take a piss wherever they were stood.

There was talk about you being able to see the steam coming off the Kop from the heat but it wasn't that, it was the steam from the piss hitting the concrete.

I remember when I started in the Boys' Pen. There'd be all kinds of scraps in there. We'd try and get out into the Kop as well. There was a bit where you could squeeze through and get from the pen into the Kop but I was a bit chubby so I'd go over the top.

We weren't hooligans or anything like that but we'd always be getting up to things. There was a lad who'd stand at the front of the Kop selling sweets at games. He was a bit like Everton's Toffee girl I suppose.

Anyway, I remember him getting dragged into the Kop once and we all grabbed as many sweets as we could and then legged off before anything could be done about it.

There were two lads who'd go around tipping (robbing) people. I remember one game when one of these lads suddenly let out a scream. We looked around and on his hand there was a mouse trap!

He'd tried to pickpocket a fella who had clearly been done before and this fella had put a mousetrap into his pocket! That was a classic moment.

There was this other fella who used to go on the Kop called Johnny Walker. He was the lad who used to run on and give Gordon West a handbag.

Anyway, he couldn't always afford to pay to get in so he used to go in The Albert before a game and chew glass for money! He'd hold a collection while he was doing it and then pay to get in.

I remember the time when Man United played Arsenal in a cup game at Anfield. We couldn't let either of them have our Kop so we paid to get in and went and stood right in the centre. There was about 350 of us with all these bizzies around us.

The United fans and the Arsenal fans both tried to get in the centre of the Kop but we wouldn't let them.

It was our Kop and there was no way we were giving it up for them. We'd go to away games when we were kids even though we couldn't afford to go.

We'd get up to Haydock where all the trucks were and we'd ask the drivers where they were going.

Say we'd be trying to get to Highbury we'd get a driver saying "I can take you as far as Leicester". We'd be like: "Well that's closer to Highbury than where we are now" and jump on the back.

We'd be under tarpaulin sheets and stuff in the freezing rain or snow going down the motorway on the back of a truck. We were only kids and I suppose we could've been murdered or anything but we didn't think about that.

We just wanted to go and see Liverpool play and would do anything to get there.

'Who scored?'
– John Pritchard, Kopite

Another great memory is from when Liverpool played Walsall in an FA Cup game at Anfield. The ground was covered in fog and there was a goal scored at the Anfield Road end. The Kop started chanting 'who scored' and back from the Anfield Road end came 'Tony Hateley'. Straight away back from the Kop came a chant of 'thank you very much for the information'. Great memories.

A symbol of the Kop
– Stephen Done, Liverpool FC Museum Curator

Behind the Kop stands a giant flagpole. It's a real piece of history, being one of the masts from the famous Great Eastern ship built by world famous engineer Brunel.

The ship, a piece of real maritime history, ended up in the docks at Rock Ferry and when the Kop was being redeveloped as a formal standing area in 1906, someone had the tremendous idea to bring the mast to Anfield and erect it as an enormous flagpole.

The mast had to be floated across the Mersey before being

hauled up to Anfield on a wagon pulled by three horses.

They went via Everton Brow and that must have been a real effort up that steep hill. For me, that flagpole is a symbol of the Kop, still standing proudly. The Kop is actually about people and it remains a very special place for those who sit in it and visit it.

The Boys' Pen
– Simon Hughes, LFC Magazine

A squealing colony of pimply-faced urchins stood expelled in the westerly corner of the Kop. Every other Saturday, little monsters – 'extras from Oliver Twist' as one fan described them – no older than 12, would shriek and curse their way through matches, knowing it soon would be time to graduate through the crèche of fandom and into the real world.

The Boys' Pen was meant to be a satellite community of Shankly's vision: Daycare for the offspring of seasoned Kopites – a place where sons deemed too diminutive for the genuine thing – would spend their Saturday afternoons cheering on the Reds and learning what it meant to be a Liverpool supporter. In theory. The reality was quite different. The Kop was an all-welcoming society. The Pen – a caged jungle – was a holding ground for frustrated juveniles and sometimes a lonely place for newcomers. Those that remained outside the clique, didn't hang around.

In one game some time in the '70s, as Liverpool cruised towards yet another comfortable home victory, the Kop was on its round of 'Annie Road, give us a song', 'Main Stand, give us a song,' before arriving at the Boys' Pen. 'Kopites are gobshites' yelped the hyena pups. Kids that stood in the pen were tough – the head to toilet flusher types from school. Regulars in the Main Stand, just across from the Pen, would witness and be the recipients of their ire.

"The Main Stand got a lot of abuse," said Mick Potter, formerly of The End fanzine. "There was a feeling that they looked down on the Boys' Pen. We were the underclass of Liverpool and they were the gentry."

Peter Hooton from The Farm, whose father acquired tickets through the son of former trainer Albert Shelley, started watching Liverpool from the obstructed view seats in the Main Stand.

"I was always fascinated by the Kop and this communion between fans and players," he said. "The Boys' Pen was different.

"You had to go in there with a mob to stand any chance."

There were some lighter moments.

In 1962, two goals from Kevin Lewis gave the Reds a 2-0 win over Southampton to hand Liverpool the Second Division championship.

"Just after the final whistle, everyone was going berserk and amid the celebrations I got thrown into the Boys' Pen," Ron Yeats recalled fondly. "We had a great sing-a-long. They seemed like a nice set of lads."

Great Escape from the Boys' Pen
– Mick Potter, Kopite

The 26 bus stopped right outside the ground so it was a convenient way of getting to the match. I went with a gang from Scotland Road but there were groups from Breck Road, Walton, Everton and Vauxhall. Many of them were hard kids.

There was only one objective in the Boys' Pen. And that was to get out. Every kid wanted to bunk into the Kop – it was like an obsession. I was nine when I first went. It was a night game against Man City and I think we won 3-2. My recollections are vague because I spent most of the game looking at people scale the barbed wire in an attempt to free themselves.

The system worked with one kid climbing over and deliberately getting caught by a steward manning the fence. The steward would throw the sacrificial lamb out of the ground and while that was happening, 20 lads would jump over and escape.

I probably missed some great moments on the pitch because I was so busy trying to get out. There were many routes – some of them more precarious than others. I think we sometimes annoyed the older fellas on the Kop but they must have been impressed by our determination.

It was the Great Escape. There were times when older fellas would pay the cheaper price to get into the Pen, then try and get into the Kop.

God knows how they got in. But two fellas brought iron bars and hid them under their coats. They managed to bend the steel on the fence of the Pen and lead a breakout. A screaming mob of kids broke free after them. For some reason, the club didn't fix the railings afterwards. They were bent for months and months and were manned by an extra steward or a copper.

The most adventurous attempt to flee came via the Kop toilets. They were directly below the Pen so you'd get some terrible smells wafting through. Hot air rises so there would be a bit of a pong. The sanitary conditions in the Kop were horrendous.

I eventually graduated to the Kop but times were hard so sometimes I'd bite the bullet, pay the cheaper price and try and go through the Pen and climb over, even though I was too old.

It was a great way to learn about football matches. It was where I started supporting Liverpool. You get a lot of people slightly younger than me saying they started watching Liverpool in the Kop. I think that generation has missed out. Human rights would have a problem with the original Pen. Its one saving grace was that it wasn't as bad as Everton's. The Boys' Pen in the Gwladys Street was like a monkey cage. The bluenoses had no chance of getting out unless they brought some cutting gear to the match.

After being in the Pen, the Kop was a reward
– Steve 'Mono' Monaghan, Kopite

Sometimes, a crowd of around 50-odd kids would sit there and listen every Monday morning. Everyone knew that I went to the match every week and my classmates respected that.

I would tell them about all the ways people managed to escape from the Pen and into the Kop. They couldn't get enough of it. One of my first games in the Pen was Liverpool's 10-0 win over Dundalk. My dad was mates with Bobby Graham so we got tickets. He'd sit in the stand and leave me with my mates to go our own way.

It was a difficult place to be at first for a kid trying to fit in, because unlike the Kop, it was suspicious of newcomers and outsiders. If you ever dared go in with a programme, it would soon be liberated from you by a bigger lad.

But after a while, when your face became recognised, you got to know all the other lads in there and it was a great place to educate yourself. A lot of the lads I met there, 30 years ago, I'm still friends with now. Skinny lads had an advantage when it came to escaping because they'd be able to squeeze through the fence. Others would be more direct and go over the 'Berlin' – or straight over the wall. I didn't fancy heights so I'd do my best to squeeze out.

The typical way out would be to crawl across one of the girders. It literally was like the Great Escape. If one of our own managed their way into the Kop undetected, a huge cheer would go up. If a copper got hold of him, we'd still cheer him on the way to the cooler. I was still a kid – 13 or 14 – but I felt liberated when I got my first Kop season ticket (in 1973/74). You were with the big boys then and the Kop looked after you. I used to sit on the bar and people would protect you from the crushing. After spending time in the Pen – it was a reward.

Missing out on an apprenticeship
– Brian Reade, journalist

I'd rather have waited until three-quarter time and go in the Kop than go in the Boys' Pen. It seemed like alien territory to me.

When you're a kid, territory is everything, it's not a nice feeling when you're an outsider. There was no ranking if you went in at three-quarter time because you charged in and found whatever space you could get.

Traditionally, geography played a big part in the side of the ground you stood or sat. I always arrived somewhere near the Arkles, so naturally, I'd find myself in the Anfield Road or the Kemlyn Road. We'd get a bus to West Derby Road then walk through.

I always liked the view from the Anfield Road because kids could get at the front and it seemed like a better spec than right at the back of the Kop in the Boys' Pen. Even if you were a kid at the front of the Kop, it was difficult to see the whole pitch because of the slope that subsides at that end of the ground. In the Annie Road, you could see everything.

I've never stood or sat regularly on the west side of the ground. For one year, I had a season ticket in the Main Stand and it just didn't feel right because I had to walk right round Anfield before the game to get to my seat.

Even when I did work in the press box, I didn't like it because it didn't feel natural to me. Psychologically, I think a fan gets used to a vantage point and anything different makes you think it might be unlucky.

In the mid to late '60s, the Annie Road was more dangerous than the Kop or even the Boys' Pen because all the away fans were there and there was no segregation.

With all the boot boys and the skinheads, there would be a lot of trouble. At 11 or 12, I used to take a stool to the game and on one occasion I went flying and hit my head on the barrier in front of me because of the movement of the crowd. I nearly ended up in hospital.

There was definitely more problems in the Anfield Road than at any other part of the ground. The atmosphere was cutting edge and I believe that we ended up singing a lot more because the away fans were so close and we wanted to prove to them that we were louder.

There's sometimes a stigma left with Liverpool fans who stood in other parts of the ground other than the Kop. But I always say that there seems to be more songs these days about the Annie Road than anywhere else in the ground, so it must have had something going for it.

I did feel later on that I missed out on an apprenticeship. I was lucky enough to have witnessed some great nights at Anfield and some wonderful trips abroad.

As a Liverpool supporter, I think I've experienced most emotions that go with the territory. Then someone will say, 'ah, but you didn't go in the Boys' Pen did you?' It didn't help because I was a bit of a shithouse.

I despair in the number of kids you see going to the game today. For me, it was the greatest time of my life.

When I started going between '66 and '73, we didn't win anything, but the atmosphere at Anfield and the thrill you would get going into the ground would be brilliant.

There would be hoards and hoards of kids. Now, when I walk up to the match, you see the odd kid with his dad that looks privileged.

Instead, they've been replaced by fat, 45-year-old men who are trying to squeeze into replica shirts. That's just plain weird and wrong.

A heartfelt plea for harmony
– Chris McLoughlin, The Kop Magazine, 2007

'You are the custodians but the club is ours. Rafa stays'.

The whole essence of the support march from The Sandon to Anfield before the Porto match in 2007 was summed up in that one banner. If George Gillett and Tom Hicks wanted to know for certain how the supporters of the club they bought perceive them, the nine words on that banner said it all.

The final two words also made it blatantly obvious whose side Kopites were taking in the escalating row between owners and manager. And if those two words weren't enough the 2,000 fans who went on the march added a bit of extra weight to them. At the front was the Rafatollah – the gold-framed picture of Rafa that was first seen in Cardiff '05 and had become a symbolic image of Liverpudlians' fanatical support for their manager.

The last time we saw the Rafatollah around the streets of Anfield was before the Barcelona game (March, 2007) when they 'canonised' Benitez. This time they were singing to save him. Outside the Paisley Gates I heard a Kopite calling: 'Rafa's going nowhere, Rafa's going nowhere' and 'allez allez, Rafael must stay'. It was a truly bizarre sight.

You're more likely to see fans gathering outside a football ground calling for their managers or chairman's head, but then we've always been different at Anfield.

This was a march in support of a manager, not a protest against anyone. There were no calls for Hicks or Gillett to go, no anti-American abuse and no trouble.

Instead it was a dignified, heart-felt, passionate plea for some harmony inside Anfield. It was a protest that made the news and it must have made interesting watching on a couple of surround-sound, widescreen TVs across the Atlantic.

Concrete evidence!
– Carl Williams, Kopite

I remember the day when we played Norwich on what was the Kop's Last Stand in 1994. I am a season ticket holder and I took my usual standing position on the Kop with my mates and watched the match as usual.

However, after the game, as the crowds were beginning to leave, a fan standing next to us produced a hammer from his coat and proceeded to chip away at the famous steps. He then collected some of the rubble and put it in his pockets.

At this point some stewards and police officers started to move in our direction to help disperse the crowds. Seeing this, one of the culprit's mates' chirped up "Hurry up, before the police collar ya".

He then added, "Just tell 'em you can't arrest me officer because you need some concrete evidence!" This put a smile on all our faces at the end of an historic match that had ended in defeat.

You'd always end up at the front
– Carol Boddington, Kopite

The thing I remember most about the old Kop was the way that we'd all stand in a neat line, fan by fan, waiting for the kick-off.

That would all change when the Reds scored. As soon as the ball hit the net those immaculate lines would seem to crumble and fall down like soldiers. Everybody would go forward towards the front as we cheered, screamed and jumped up and down.

Then we had to march back up to our line again and stand neatly, side by side, waiting for the next goal so we could all fall down to the front again. It didn't matter how close to someone or where you were standing, you'd always end up at the front. It's something I'll always remember.

The 'reaction test'
– Paul Hughes, Kopite

Whilst a schoolboy, throughout the glorious '80s, I travelled to each home game on the train from North Wales.

Not believing me that the atmosphere on the Kop was like 'being on another planet' for 90 minutes, a number of mates would accompany me to the odd match.

I would make a point that every newcomer had to undergo my self-devised 'reaction test'. I would wait until about quarter to three then proudly lead them in through the turnstiles. I would then lead them up the steps and approach the Kop from the side, past the old food/drinks bar. At this point, I would make them wait 30 seconds so I could run on ahead and stand just inside the Kop, facing their approach.

When the 'newcomer' appeared around the corner for their first glimpse at a full Kop, I would look directly at the expression on their faces. I instantly knew from that first look whether or not they were permitted to return with me to my other 'planet' across the border. A group of blokes who stood regularly at this spot must have caught on over the years. Every time I ran ahead of one of my newcomers they would shout: "More fresh blood on the way then, Taff?"

Ooh aah . . .
– Peter Sharples, Kopite

One of the best bits of song improvisation I heard on the Kop was against Aston Villa in the early '90s.

The Villa fans had been droning on with their 'ooh-ah Paul McGrath, ooh-ah Paul McGrath' song which goes on and on and on and sounds like that hymn.

Anyway, Jamie Redknapp completely skins him and scores a beauty. After the celebrations die down the Kop finally shut the Villa fans up with their own rendition of the song. It just started off as: 'Where was Paul McGrath? Where was Paul McGrath?'

That was funny in itself but then a new verse was added: 'He was in the bar, he was in the bar,' being a reference to his reputation as a drinker. But then the piece de resistance at the end was the closing line of: 'Jamie Redknapp superstar!'

It was instant creativity, unique to the Kop and the best bit was the collective laugh at the end as we all stood there thoroughly pleased with ourselves.

Like being in a Turkish Bath
– Kop Magazine, December, 1966.

(Written after it was suggested the Kop was too dangerous and should be partitioned following overcrowding issues at the Liverpool v Ajax game)

The suggestion is enough to make the regular patrons of this Very Important Place to get steamed up all over again. The trouble last Wednesday does not take a scientific probe to work out.

24,000 people huddled together, chummy but chilly, sheltering from the rain. Nothing is more natural than that steam should rise from the damp bodies. That, added to the smoke spiralling from thousands of cigarettes formed a man-made mist.

It was like being in a Turkish bath. Those at the rear who could not see moved forward causing crushing and alarm.

There wasn't too many people in the ground. There was no breaking of crush barriers.

There were no smokebombs thrown as has been reported – although one nit-wit threw a firework.

A host of emotions in five seconds
– David Grice, Kopite

I stood on the Kop for the first time in the mid-1920s. There was no other place to be if you supported Liverpool and I spent 60-odd years there.

One great memory I have is Billy Liddell's 'goal' in 1956 against Manchester City that was disallowed just as the ball entered the net.

The Kop experienced a whole host of emotions in the space of five seconds – from the heights of excitement to the depths of despair. We were gutted when the referee indicated he had already blown his whistle when the ball was flying in the net.

Henry Newton or Isaac Newton?
– Martin Walker, Liverpool

As a Liverpool supporter since the famous Cup win over First Division Burnley in 1960, I can recall quite a number of famous matches.

There was the fan who fainted in the middle of the Kop, was passed head first DOWN the crowd to the edge of the pitch. He was then revived and, at his request, was passed BACK UP the crowd to his regular spot!

My favourite story dates from 1969 when Everton already had on their books one Newton (Keith, an England full-back signed from Blackburn Rovers) and had just brought in another (Henry Newton, a slim, cultured wing-half from Nottingham Forest).

Liverpool were playing at home and Everton were at Arsenal. At the end of the game (which Liverpool won), we were heading out when the tannoy announcement came: 'The final score from Highbury – Arsenal four, Everton nil'.

After the cheers died away, I said to Paul: "It looks like Henry Newton had a good debut then!" As quick as a flash, a huge docker in a flat cap behind us, responded: "Yer know what it was, dey got the wrong fella – it was ISAAC Newton they wanted!"

I even applauded a Tommy Smith tackle!
– Steve Collier, Evertonian

Picture the scene. It's 1967 and the crowds throng the turnstiles outside Anfield for the annual derby clash. With only minutes to go before the kick-off, things look desperate for three 14-year-olds – diehard Evertonians who have somehow found themselves stuck with three Kop tickets. Can they swap them to be with their mates in the Anfield Road End? Can they heck!

No alternative. In we go, through a sea of red – slam, bang in the middle of the Kop. This didn't deter us. We chanted our songs and displayed our colours throughout the first half. Even the venom of a huge mountain of a man several yards in front of us didn't bother us. Between him and us was the crush barrier.

With the start of the second half, something dawned on us. Man Mountain had vacated his spec – but where? You've guessed it – right behind us. From then on, butter wouldn't melt in our mouths. I think I may even have applauded one of Tommy Smith's tackles!

Proving the point that in any other ground, we would undoubtedly have been pasted from pillar to post. Not on the Kop. Great atmosphere, great people.

The safest place
– Steve Tootill, Evertonian

I am an Everton supporter but I've been on the Kop countless times. Even though I am a Blue, it wasn't difficult to see why the

Kop was so famous. The crowd were loud and humorous and were quick to praise the opposition where appropriate.

I don't recall seeing any trouble on the Kop and, as an away fan, I can say the Kop was the safest place for opposing supporters.

Wark on
– Matthew Griffiths, Kopite

One funny memory I have is John Wark on his Liverpool debut staring into the Kop with admiration and being told in no uncertain terms by a Kopite to turn around because he was frightening his kids! The midfielder had no choice but to obey, amid the ensuing hilarity.

Eerie in the Kop
– Bill Arnold, Liverpool Echo

I was born on Venmore Street on the doorstep to the Kop in the days before it had a roof on. One of my pals at Venice Street school was a lad called Riley, whose dad was head groundsman for many years. One Sunday, young Riley had got hold of a pass key for the Walton Breck Road entrance to the Kop.

Here we were, four young kids with a tennis ball, kicking it into the net. The only snag was it went through the netting and it was a case of jumping into the Kop. I still recall how eerie the great stadium was with just four kids in.

Pulsating, raw passion
– Chris McLoughlin, journalist

Chelsea 2007. Better than Chelsea 2005? Probably not, but it's hard to say for definite. What you could say is that the atmosphere was different to when we beat them two years earlier.

Before both games the singing of You'll Never Walk Alone followed by an ear-drum bashing Ring of Fire with scarf-twirling aplenty made for one of the most spectacular sights and sounds you'll ever see in world football.

Football fans across Europe tune in for that spectacle. It's totally unique. Like nothing you can see anywhere else. It's the type of genuine, heart-on-sleeve, pulsating raw passion that they wish they had at their clubs. In Seville, which is recognised as having the most passionate stadiums in Spain, they urged their fans to try and 'recreate Anfield' for their UEFA Cup semi-final. That's one huge compliment to us.

As far as comparisons to 2005 go, though, the different natures of the games made for different atmospheres. Luis Garcia's early goal in 2005 sparked wild celebrations but then led to a 'backs-against-the-wall' atmosphere.

There was far more booing and whistling when Chelsea players were on the ball than this time and also more of a nervous tension in the air.

In 2007 we needed to score to stay in the competition and then get a second without conceding. That resulted in Kopites urging their players to go forward more and naturally leant itself to more songs getting an airing than whistles for Chelsea players at both 0-0 and after Daniel Agger had made it 1-0. By extra-time everyone knew it was next goal winner with nerves and throat fatigue (a condition found in Liverpool but not London) taking over and there being the odd lull in the atmosphere.

Everyone picked themselves up for penalties though and even though they were taken at the Anfield Road end, the cacophony of noise inside Anfield ensured it was the Chelsea players who had the wobbly legs this time rather than the Liverpool keeper.

The celebrations when Dirk Kuyt struck the winning penalty

were as good as 2005. They lasted long into the night in Liverpool city centre. Once again, Liverpool's 12th Man had played its part and the Reds had reached another European Cup final.

They kissed his feet
– Mark Grimes, Kopite

Bill Shankly's testimonial match in 1975 is one that stands out in my mind. I was totally bemused, numb, when Bill announced his retirement. It was like someone had died, someone important. I was 15 years of age and the lads from my dad's Sunday team had offered me a lift to the game.

It was a total sell-out. Thousands of people locked out and rightly so. We played a Don Revie XI (I think?) and back then Liverpool were always better than England. To be honest the game was incidental. Before the game the Kop was in full voice, new flags and banners paid homage to (Sir) Bill Shankly. Just before the teams came out and YNWA started, Bill started talking over the PA system. The ground fell silent immediately.

I'm sure there was no introduction. You know – 'Ladies and Gentleman, Bill Shankly'. That was typical Shanks. No fuss. He spoke and thanked us for all we'd done for him and Liverpool. The result didn't matter but we roared Liverpool on, like it was a derby.

The final whistle blew and it was over, quite literally, over. The players shook hands and applauded the crowd, Bill did a lap of honour. There were no tears from Bill but oceans of tears from every other part of the ground. Some managed to break free from the police and stewards and ran on to the pitch. They shook his hands and draped scarves around his neck.

He stopped and picked every scarf up. They kissed his feet. This was a messiah, and a man of the people, for the people. Shanks went down the tunnel, and everyone bar the Kop left the ground.

We stood there and sang and sang for Shankly (The Amazing Grace tune). Then I saw him.

He must have come back up into the directors' box, climbing over the press box and walked along the Main Stand. He stood there, his hands clasped like in prayer. We sang and sang his name, tears blinding us. Then, he held his hand in the air, turned and walked back. We were emotionally broken. Boys became men and men were reduced to tearful boys. I had to run like the wind back to the car.

I was using up their valuable drinking time. I told the lads Shanks had come back to see us. They were gutted they never stayed. It's my worst memory of being on the Kop but the most emotional and memorable.

'Koppers' take action
– Alan Marsh, Kopite

The Kop had its own way of dealing with invaders. Most of the time the only rival fans that found their way into the Kop were Bluenoses on derby day and that was never a problem. But I remember one day a Geordie managed to get himself in the wrong end.

However, rather than keep quiet and out of the way this particular Geordie – who looked like a skinny version of Oz from Auf Wiedersehen Pet – had overdone the Newcy Brown and was in no mood to keep quiet. The occasion was the third round of the FA Cup in January, 1984 and the high-profile visit of Keegan and Newcastle in front of the TV cameras.

'Oz' was obviously caught up in the excitement of it all so he comes down to the front of the Kop and turns to face the Kop. He raises his hands above his head and starts giving his best rendition of a Toon classic or two.

That was the cue for the unofficial Kop police to take action. Without a hint of fuss two 'Koppers' came down from the middle and took the offending Geordie to the side of the Kop by the cafe where he was 'dealt with'. That was the last we saw of him.

Goodbye to all that
– Article in 90 Minutes Magazine, April, 1994

The Spion Kop ceases to exist after Liverpool's match against Norwich this Saturday. The celebrated cinder banking that has pulsed with life for 90 years, supporting millions of dockers' boots, winkle-pickers and Reeboks, will be bulldozed into myth. Maybe it's just as well.

"The Kop was full 90 minutes before kick-off," read the match reports after a recent fixture against Newcastle, before describing how the home team were outplayed on their own turf by the visitors.

The terrace has become an anachronistic reminder of Anfield's illustrious past. On the Sunday immediately following the Norwich game, Liverpool fans will have the chance to pay their final respects at a specially organised 'Kop Party', in which Gerry Marsden and a host of local celebrities and pop stars will provide the entertainment.

Then the demolition men move in.

The new stand, by all accounts, will be a single-tier construction with a capacity of around 12,000. 'By all accounts' because the club are notoriously backward about coming forward.

Bill Shankly once said: "We created an institution – something more than a football club, something alive and vibrant, and warm and successful."

Times have changed. These days, Hercules would have trouble breaching Anfield's red tape. But enough about the club. Back to the Kop, which, as early as 1957, Manchester United boss Matt Busby described as, "Liverpool's most prized possession".

Built in 1906 to coincide with the Reds' second Championship triumph, the Spion Kop was named after a hilltop in South Africa where 300 British soldiers, the majority from Merseyside and Lancashire regiments, lost their lives during the Boer War.

It was extended and roofed in 1928 to accommodate close on 30,000 spectators, making it the largest covered terracing in the country.

It earned its reputation, though, in the '60s. Shankly was installed, the music scene was swinging and the Kop was swaying. Among the sea of faces standing on its yawning slopes were future stars like Phil Thompson, Joey Jones and Jimmy Case.

Shankly, too, when the mood took him. "One night we ran out on the pitch for a European game and we thought the Kop was on fire," recalls former Liverpool striker Ian St John.

"It looked like smoke was bellowing up out of it, but it was steam. It was raining, the fans had all gone in soaked and the heat from all the bodies was drying out their clothes".

The fervour and fanaticism may have been watered down over the years, and fathers may tell sons that it's not the same any more, but the Kop still has over 10,000 season ticket holders and gates at Anfield regularly exceed 40,000 to this day.

More to the point, the hallowed cave has remained a relatively safe place to watch football.

One of the most serious injuries to have occurred there happened when a woman broke her hip when she slipped on one of the greasy blackened steps during a Billy Graham sermon when the American evangelist toured Britain in 1984.

"When I was a player, I was privileged to be cheered on by some 26,000 on the Kop," says former favourite Kevin Keegan, who returned to Anfield in triumph as manager of Newcastle. "For the current players, it's 16,000 and now it's going to be down to 12,000 when the seats are in. For me, Liverpool Football Club nor the ground will ever be the same. It was the Kop which made Anfield a special place to play and watch football and I'm terribly sad to see it go".

Modern thinking and safety requirements have rendered the Kop obsolete. But the question now is: Can Liverpool become great again without it?

Every Kopite has a regret
– Chris McLoughlin, journalist

Better than the Brazilians according to Sir Tom Finney and I hadn't been there to see it. Gutted.

Every Kopite has a regret. A game they never made it to that turned out to be a classic. An early goal they missed after taking too long on that final pint in The Park.

This is mine.

I'd been to a lot of home games in the 1987/88 season – not all of them – but many of them.

We were originally scheduled to play Forest on the Saturday but our FA Cup semi-final game with them at Hillsborough fell on that day so it was moved to the Wednesday. It gave me a fixture clash. I was playing junior football back then and, with the nights becoming lighter, we had a game that same evening.

There wasn't really a choice to make. I was 10-years-old and far more interested in playing than watching so Carr Mill Juniors came before Liverpool FC. I can't remember who we played – or how heavily we lost – but on the way home I remember hearing on the car radio that Liverpool were winning.

I didn't think much of it. Liverpool were always winning. By full-time it was 5-0 and I remember looking forward to the highlights, which I was allowed to stay up and watch.

At what point I regretted not being there, I'm not sure, but I look back now and wish I'd actually been there, in the flesh, to watch King Kenny's men destroy Forest.

Forest were no mugs.

They were one of the best three sides in England and one of only two teams to beat Liverpool in the league all season.

They were ripped to shreds. Aldo got two. Ray Houghton, Peter Beardsley and Gary Gillespie one each.

That wasn't half the story though. The Echo described Forest keeper Steve Sutton's performance as like 'the kind of display Gordon Banks used to do for Leicester in the 1960s'.

All in all, it was the finest display of football I've seen from a Liverpool side in my lifetime. I just wish I'd been there to see it.

The lock-out
– Paul Dove, journalist

There was one experience from the old Kop that I do not miss: The dreaded lock-out.

In these days of all-ticket, all-seater games, you more or less know three or four weeks in advance whether you're going to the match. That wasn't the case in the era of the cash turnstile.

As a keen youngster first starting out on the Kop I would roll up before the gates opened, just before midday on a Saturday lunchtime.

A few years later I became less keen to stand on a cold terrace for the best part of three hours with only a cup of hot water masquerading as tea and a Wagon Wheel for comfort. My arrival times on the Kop became later as I developed a regular spec (a quarter of the way up to the right of the goal) and learned more about when the prime spots started to disappear.

One day I totally underestimated the demand among the fans was the first game of the 1986-87 season. Kenny's men were up in front of the Kop for the first time since claiming the Double during that unforgettable month of May, 1986.

As the 26 bus snaked its way around Anfield just after two o'clock, the first glimpse of the stadium roof over the terrace tops always sent a shiver of expectation through your body. However, the second emotion was more head-numbing than spine-tingling as I saw the size of the queues.

My heart sank as I joined the end of a seemingly endless line of heads in front of me. As time neared kick-off the queue developed in to more of a crush. A few more shuffles closer and I was nearly there – and then it happened. The doors shut.

That moment was hard to take.

Just over that little wall with the broken bits of bottle cemented in to the top was a joyous, singing, swaying Kop welcoming the mighty Reds on to a luscious green turf for the start of another epic campaign. And I wasn't invited to the party.

Different Kopites had different ways of coping with the closing of those little wooden red doors that were like football's equivalent of the pearly gates slamming shut.

Some banged on the doors distraught; some turned on their Samba heels ready to execute Plan B and others bombarded the mounted coppers with questions.

As I stood there coming to terms with the disappointment, I bumped into a lad I'd known at school who had suffered the same fate. This lad was normally mild-mannered and likeable with an easy-going temperament. He was Mr Nice Guy with a soft Runcorn accent who never harmed anyone.

But today was not just any day. He had been struck down by the lockout madness. His eyes were wild. "They can't lock me out," he mumbled. "No-one keeps me out." He wasn't going to take it.

That's when he came up with *the plan*. We were going to pool our entrance money together, he insisted, and he would buy a hacksaw from one of the nearby shops. He would then saw through the iron above the Walton Breck Road bogs and then we would be in the Kop. Easy.

He even showed me how he could scale the wall and where he would be sawing. No problem.

Despite my own frustration, I wasn't buying into the hacksaw plan. Probable arrest and detention in the local nick would have had something to do with this.

I started to head home, beginning to come to terms with the agony of a long football-free afternoon. My mate disappeared into the crowds disgusted at my failure to go along with his cunning scheme.

Jumping on a bus, I sat on a near deserted top deck feeling sorry for myself as it juddered and jolted down Everton Valley towards the city centre.

I arrived home just before full time and only then found out that the Reds didn't score – the game ending 0-0. I'm ashamed to say a small part of me was pleased – it almost served them right for locking me out. Whether it was any consolation to my would-be partner in crime, I never found out.

The Kop mosaics
– John Pearman, Editor of Red All Over The Land fanzine

The mosaics were first suggested by Rick Parry. He was very impressed with what he had seen in places like Milan and Barcelona and came up with the idea. They used to take Andy Knott, who designed and organised them, four to six hours to do.

They are normally done the day before the game and usually there is an appeal for helpers. Sometimes you get quite a few come down to help. A lot of school kids have come down and helped out.

There's a lot of legwork involved – running up and down the Kop and making sure they're in the right places. When you've got 70 steps it tires you out.

The club pay for the mosaics. It's not a whim of the crowd; they're sponsored by the club. We did the first one against Manchester United in 1998 but the next one against Sheffield Wednesday drew a lot of attention.

On previous seasons we had been to Sheffield and been treated like dirt. They wouldn't let Liverpool fans take floral tributes into the ground because they were ridiculously seen as 'a danger'. People were told they couldn't even take single roses in to put in the Leppings Lane end. Instead they put tables, the sort of thing you'd see at car boot sales, outside the ground to put the flowers on.

They also put a statement out saying they wouldn't put a plaque or memorial up as it would be seen as a sign of guilt. So when Sheffield Wednesday came to Anfield we organised a mosaic on the Kop, consisting of red cards, which was aimed at the Sheffield Wednesday directors. When they saw it, it stunned them. They could not believe the strength of feeling.

It was a tribute to the people who had died at Hillsborough and a statement that we wanted Sheffield Wednesday to erect a memorial in a suitable place. There's now a memorial there – we like to think that one worked.

Two others which stand out are the Shankly day and Paisley night. Bob's wife, Jessie, came out on to the pitch on the Paisley night. The following day she rang me up and wanted to thank me for organising it. I told her that was the wrong way round, it was me who wanted to thank her, but she sent me a tenner through the post for some fanzines! I couldn't believe it. I sent it back. That just shows the person she is.

The Shankly Day, against Coventry in 1999, probably meant the most to me. That was incredible. The mosaic was a picture of Shankly that day. After the game there were parties across the city. It was a fantastic celebration.

The most famous mosaics are probably the 'GH' one and the 'Allez, Allez' one from the 2001/02 season.

They were incredible. The 'GH' one was at the Manchester United game, just after he had been taken ill.

It wasn't deliberately aimed at the United game, it just fell that way, and Gerard later said he saw it on the television.

The 'Allez, Allez' one was for the Roma game, Gerard's home-coming, and it was a very emotional night.

No-one else in this country does tributes like that.

We've tried very hard to let the past live on and keep it going. We've tried to keep the Kop unique.

Things have moved on and during the time of Rafael Benitez and there have been more glorious European nights at Anfield. When we played Olympiakos in the now famous 3-1 game – that in truth set us on the way to Istanbul – the Kop mosaic paid tribute and remembrance to fans that had died at Hillsborough and also at a game in Athens when 29 Olympiakos fans lost their lives.

At the game in Athens Liverpool fans had shown their respect and laid flowers at the Olympiakos memorial and that had been well received by the fans and people of the Greek club. When they came to Anfield and saw the '96 and 29' mosaic everyone in the ground was moved. It created a bond of friendship between the two sets of supporters and in the current hostile world of football sup-port that means a lot.

During the run to Istanbul there was the game against Juventus, a game that brought back many sad and, for the Italians, bitter memories. Rick Parry suggested that we do a mosaic that in some way showed how we felt about things. We couldn't say sorry or

apologise in any way but we could show some respect and therefore we had the 'Friendship' mosaic.

Unfortunately it wasn't too well received by the visiting fans, but
not all of them some appreciated the effort and it drew a mixed
reaction from the media in this country.

Our media saw it as either an attempt to show our regret and
some thought it was typical of Liverpudlians going over the top in
search for sympathy. It was never meant to be like that; it was a
genuine effort to build a bridge or two.

There have been several other Kop mosaics and it is noticeable
how other clubs have tried to follow the idea.

However, the Kop ones are still fan based whereas others appear
to be stage managed and almost choreographed.

There have been many associated with Hillsborough and, of
course Michael Shields. There was the very heart-warming Ray
Kennedy mosaic that showed the Kopites never forget and at the
end of the 2008/09 season there was a tribute for Sami Hyypia,
who would be leaving the club.

Although I don't get involved now, seeing the Kop in colour, be
it in a Flag Day style or a mosaic creates a sense of pride. Back in
the early part of the last decade it was possible to select the ones
that stood out and for what reason. Looking back as far as the late
'70s, St Etienne was an amazing night.

There were all those French fans in the Anfield Road end and
people had never seen those vast numbers of away fans at a
European game before, apart from when Celtic came down in
1966. That was the night where the 'Allez, Allez' came from.

For me the best night at Anfield during that period was the Roma
night.

That's because of the whole emotion of the occasion and that
night we were playing against a team who were possibly the best
in the whole of Europe and we gained a famous victory.

Shankly Day in 1999 remains in my mind as something very, very special because of what it meant. Listening to the crowd almost whispering the name' 'Shankly' to the tune of 'Amazing Grace' brought tears to the eyes; it was almost ghostly, maybe even spiritual. You needed to be there.

Whether they've run their course now, I don't know but being involved from the start and working with wonderful people such as Andy Knott and John Mackin, plus Rick Parry – because without his help and support and enthusiasm they just would not have been possible – has been an honour. They've been a mixture of the history of the club, the sadness, the success and the humorous, which maybe summed up the meaning and legend of The Kop.

Tale of Scouse Columbo
– Dave Randles, journalist

As a Kop season ticket holder throughout the '90s I, like many Kopites, have many great memories of the famous old stand. I could go on about the Auxerre's, Genoa's and Roma's, plus the banter we've all experienced and taken part in at some point but this particular recollection actually occurred on our way to the ground.

The hilarity of what was witnessed was typical of many of the sights and, more importantly here, sounds encountered along the way and sent us into Anfield in tears of laughter as we assumed 'our' usual spot on what was still the old terrace at the time.

Remember Columbo? The famous old hardboiled detective played by Peter Falk, but more famously in my eyes his Scouse double who used to (and maybe still does) sell burgers and hotdogs from his stall outside Anfield.

'Scouse Columbo' was a local legend with me and my mates for over a decade, and as we trudged through Stanley Park onto

Anfield Road, the anticipation always grew as to whether he would be there in his 'pitch' between Skerries Road and the Shankly Gates.

Of course, he always was with his knee length Columbo coat on (only in hotdog vendors white instead of camel brown, plus the obligatory mustard stains, of course) and the famous cigar had been replaced by a cigarette – great with ketchup I believe!

This day, it must have been about 1991-92 – I can't remember the match but that's incidental. Out of The Park we emerged as one of the lads spots our hero: "There he is, there's Columbo, never lets us down..."

As we got closer to him the usual buzz of his presence flowed through us, but this time it was to be special as 'Scouse Columbo' implanted himself firmly in our memories forever – and how!

None-deterred by the waft of boiled onions, we shuffled alongside him to get as close as possible but as we drew near, our man looked to be composing himself for something big.

Bending his knees and crouching forward, 'Scouse Columbo' proceeded to let rip one of the loudest farts you could ever wish to hear.

Forget those nasty silent things you would have to endure on the Kop with no warning whatsoever after some docker had downed 20 pints of bitter the night before, this was the real deal.

With a pained grimace spread across his face, 'Scouse Columbo' then turned to his arse and with a waft of his hand uttered quite simply "Get out and walk yer bastard!"

This was absolute poetry in motion, and as we burst into fits of laughter, our hero rubberstamped his legend status with a quick wink (with his good eye) and a smirk in our direction before getting back to work: "Get yer burgers and hotdogs 'ere..."

Not today thanks Columbo, but you'll always be a Kop legend in our eyes mate.

Red stars and Red Rums
– David Moen, Kopite

Liverpool FC v Ipswich Town, 9 April 1994. That was the game I had earmarked to finally experience the Kop atmosphere for the first time. Although I had been at Anfield before, I had yet to stand on the famed terrace for a game.

Once we arrived in Liverpool (from Ireland) we headed to the usual haunts. The Lord Nelson Hotel, all the hotels on Mount Pleasant Street, even The Moat House was tried, as if I could afford it. Everywhere was full. All I could hear from my mate was something about it being a huge weekend in the city and horseracing.

After three Red Rums we headed to Lime Street where there was always an assortment of B&Bs. The fact that many of these establishments were available on this, the Grand National weekend, should have been a clue to our abode, not that I cared too much. We were relieved to get anywhere to put our heads down, and at £12 a night we shouldn't have expected too much, although a light bulb would have made the weekend extra special.

It was a tradition for Liverpool or Everton to play their home game on Grand National Saturday as an 11.30am kick-off so the locals could attend the great racing spectacle later in the afternoon. After waiting until dawn, so we could have some daylight in the room, we got ready for the game. We had to get there early, as the Kop was not all-ticket, and cash was being taken at the turnstiles; even so, a large crowd had gathered to get in early and grab their usual vantage points. Plenty of out-of-towners like us were in the vicinity, but I was in and that's all that mattered. At last I was on the Kop for a game, and there would only be two more games after this for the standing Kop as well. What a close shave.

The banter was as I had expected it to be. We weren't setting the world alight that season, but Ipswich were having an awful time and would finish bottom. 'You'll Never Walk Alone' took on that extra bit of significance for this supporter; I was used to holding my scarf up and singing towards the Kop, but now I was one of them, a Kopite, one small part of the most famous terrace in world football. Nothing can describe that feeling. I can remember it as if it was just last week. Liverpool won the toss, another good omen; we would be attacking the Kop in the second half, yippee! I was sure there would be goals galore in the second half and I would be there to suck the ball in along with the rest of the famous Kopites. Or so I thought at the time.

Well, what a dire affair my game turned out to be. Not only that, but it was a very cold April morning. We had snow, hail and rain, and I was just freezing, despite being surrounded by fellow supporters. I shudder to think what the Paddock and Annie Road end would have been like.

After a forgettable first half and equally forgettable second, it was looking bleak until Don Hutchison, who had replaced Robbie Fowler, was bundled over in the box in the 75th minute and the ref pointed to the spot. Happy days. "Knock it in yourself, Don lad!" I roared, only for Julian Dicks to amble forward and grab the ball, as a few gasps were heard from the Kop. "Just drive it down the middle, Dicks".

He delivered, bang, straight down the middle it went. Get in there! It was the last meaningful action in the game to be fair, but I was happy enough. I got my goal at my end, and the three points were in the bag.

Before we knew it we were in a taxi across to Aintree racecourse. Having as much knowledge of horseracing as Everton have of European Cup victories, I was in need of inspiration. Local comic Freddie Starr was on the monitor and I overheard a few punters saying he had a runner in the big one.

That'll do for me, so it was Freddie Starr's horse Miinnehoma at

£20 on the nose. He romped home in style and it was only when I went to collect the winnings that I even bothered to look at the odds: a cool 16/1. This betting lark was a doddle.

What a night in town we had after that. We drank most of it, of course, although I did treat myself to a little something: a spanking new 100-watt light bulb for the hotel room. Well, I thought I might as well splash out!

Nothing will hurt more than this
– Michael Harkin, Kopite

May 20, 1989. We'd just beaten Everton 3-2 in a dramatic and emotional FA Cup final, and we were ecstatic.

Amid the euphoria, my dad promised we'd go to see history being made next Friday night against Arsenal: the first-ever double Double. I was 11 years old.

We set off on Thursday morning: my dad and sister came along too. It was quite a trek from Northern Ireland to Liverpool as, about a year earlier, the Belfast to Liverpool ferry stopped operating, as did the Dublin to Liverpool ferry. It meant a five-hour bus journey from Derry to Dublin to catch the ferry to Holyhead in North Wales. The ferry docked around 1.30am on Friday morning after a short crossing.

Then we had to wait at the Holyhead train station, which is right on the docks, until 4.30am for the train to depart for Chester. About an hour-and-a-half later we arrived in Chester, and it was already beginning to look like a scorcher of a day. The sun was blasting through the glass roof as we waited for the train to take us to Hooton.

From there we got the underground to Lime Street, arriving at 7.30am, 20 hours after our journey first began. Once there, we had only one thing on our minds: three match tickets. We didn't have any and there were rumours on the boat that there would be a cash turnstile. At 9am, we went up to Anfield and checked the Kop. All we could find were 'ticket only' signs. We paid £60 in total, which left us with a fiver for the whole day. It didn't matter; we had tickets to see history being made.

Everyone knows we didn't make history that night thanks to a certain Michael Thomas.

But the two abiding memories that will live with me forever are coming out after the game in floods of tears and my dad saying to me: "Well son, no matter what you see in football during the rest of your life, nothing will hurt more than this." I looked up at him and thought: "What's he on about?" But over the years, as I understood more, those words rang true.

I cried when YNWA was played
– Liam Mulcahy, Kopite

My buddy and me travelled from Limerick to Dublin, got the boat over to Holyhead and then headed up to Anfield. I couldn't wait to get there. After we dropped off our bags at the hotel, we went straight to the ground – the atmosphere was crazy. I cried my eyes out when 'You'll Never Walk Alone' was played. I was in the Kop. My friend was actually a Villa fan and wouldn't sing or cheer for the Pool. Gary McAllister scored a penalty to win the game as we sang all night and partied until 6am.

A mark of respect to the people who had been good to me
– Bill Shankly, former Liverpool manager

Liverpool was made for me and I was made for Liverpool, and I knew that the people who mattered most were the ones who came through the turnstiles.

A manager has got to identify himself with the people. Football is their whole life, and for the last twelve seasons Liverpool have played two games most weeks, which is hard on the pocket.

The encouragement the supporters of Liverpool Football Club have given their team has been incredible.

When there is a corner-kick at the Kop end of the ground they frighten the ball! Occasionally I would have a walk 'round the ground before a match, and I went to the Kop one day before it had filled up.

A little chap there said, "Stand here, Bill, you'll get a good view of the game from here!" I couldn't take him up on that offer because I had to look after the team.

I have watched a match from the Kop since I retired as team manager, and that was just the start of going to see the supporters in all parts of the ground. I didn't go to the Kop for bravado or anything like that. I went as a mark of respect for the people who had been good to me.

They used to chant my name as much as they chanted the names of the players, which was unusual. I am a working man and I went among my own kind.

Liverpool played Coventry that day, and a crescendo greeted the Liverpool team just as I went into the ground.

It wasn't a great game and we only drew that day, so there wasn't a continuous din.

But when we scored our goal the noise was deafening.

'Ye Beeyutay! What a hit, son!'
– Mike Chapple, writer

The power and the glory of the Kop explodes on those nights of European competition when its wall of sound – built on the foundations of a collective will to win – can leave those wrapped up in its thrall tingling with a mix of euphoria, crazed adrenalin and nervous hyperventilation.

The cream of these great nights are when the stakes are highest and it becomes that vital 12th Man, that extra edge which fans of other European football giants can only aspire to.

These are the nights when the Kop made the difference between success and having those dreams tossed and blown away. The Champions League group game second leg against Olympiakos on December 8, 2004 was one of those such nights.

The demise of the standing Kop and the 10-year enforced exile from Europe, following the Heysel tragedy, made many Kopites wonder if it could all ever happen again.

Memorable full-voiced victories in the new century against the might of the likes of Barcelona and Roma, the dispatch of the latter inspiring the controversial if hilarious Kop rendition of Arriverderci Roma to the disgruntled Italians, eased that discomfort.

But with Liverpool 1-0 down to a Rivaldo goal at the end of the first half, Liverpool needed three goals to qualify for the final stages. Past experience of never say die performances both on and off the field, however, prompted an inspired comeback.

There was confidence that one early goal would turn the tide and this was provided on cue by Pongolle, sending the Kop into a screaming anticipation that rose to critical mass when Neil Mellor got a second with 10 minutes left.

With just four minutes remaining and the roar leading him on, Steven Gerrard unleashed an unstoppable shot into the corner, sparking jubilation of golden years proportions.

Afterwards, the icing on the cake for Kopites was watching endless repeats of Sky commentator and arch 'Bluenose' Andy Gray forgetting himself and screaming with delight "Oh ye Beeyutay!" as Gerrard's shot ripped into the onion bag.

The roof almost came off
– Andrew Bland, Kopite

My earliest memory was sitting on a cold barrier watching a young Robbie Fowler score five on his debut against Fulham.

Others include sitting in a half-built Kop watching Robbie score the fastest hat-trick against Arsenal; attending the Hillsborough Memorial service; Mark Wright bulleting a header in against Paris St Germain, and the second half of the Olympiakos game when Gerrard scored 'that goal'. But the game that will never be beaten for atmosphere and result was obviously the game called 'The Twelfth Man' against Chelsea (in 2005).

As the teams came out of the tunnel the atmosphere was electric. I've never heard singing like it. Then the goal went in at the Kop end and the roof almost came off. In the second half it got louder, until the ball landed at Eidur Gudjohnsen's feet in the last minute – and then he put it wide.

We were soaked in urine
– John J, Kopite

I am Malaysian Chinese and arrived in Liverpool in 1976 for a reunion with my family.

My first game was against St Etienne in 1977 with our kid. We did not know the layout of Anfield, but followed the masses of fans into the Kop end.

We squeezed into the middle, thinking we would have a good view. How wrong we were! All night, we were pushed down and up the steps. The banners, scarves and the flags were flying, the singing 100 times the decibels a human could endure. Worst of all, we were soaked in urine.

We were only able to watch five per cent of the game because of our height (five feet six inches). But it was truly a night you will never experience again anywhere on this earth.

Great days, great stand
– Steve Hopkins, Kopite

My first game on the Kop was when I was about 12. My mum had got us tickets for £8. What made it even more special was that it was a Merseyside derby and we won 1-0 with a last minute goal from Ronny Rosenthal! From then on I was a Kopite. Great days, great club.

When a child is born ...
– Debbie Foxcroft, Kopite

One of my treasured memories was at a game one Boxing Day in the Seventies when the Kop sang the whole of 'When A Child Is Born,' by Johnny Mathis. The whole ground applauded us when the song came to an end.

I still get a tingle
– Keith Sayle, Kopite

My grandad, Harry Fishwick, got me hooked on the then Second Division team.

I still get a tingle when I think of my first match and seeing the Kop draped in red and white. I had arrived at Lime Street with my mate, Gordy Raisbeck, great grandson of Liverpool's first Championship-winning captain, Alec Raisbeck, and we caught a bus up to Breck Road.

The game was Kevin Keegan's debut. Needless to say, he scored and Liverpool won 3-2.

Dad lost his false teeth!
– Graham Laverty, Kopite

Who can forget the moment when an injured Geoff Strong leapt to head the winning goal against Celtic in the 1966 Cup Winners' Cup semi-final? The Kop surged forward. Three of us were pushed toward a crush barrier behind the goal. Then, the crowd which had pulled back from the initial surge, came spilling down the steps again. My dad was again trapped against the crush barrier.

As the breath was forced out of his lungs he gasped loudly. This time something flew out of his mouth. His false teeth! They disappeared into the crowd in front of us. At the end, we waited for the crowd to leave, but never found them.

A cat called Emlyn
– Elaine Wade, Kopite

Me and my dad went in the Kop in 1970 when I was 14. My favourite player was Emlyn Hughes. I even called the cat Emlyn.

I saw all the league victories from our famous stand and did the Kop sing in those days!

'We are the champions,' and some great witty songs I will always remember. I still go now with my husband and sons and witnessed the special atmosphere of Olympiakos, Juventus and Chelsea. It was like being back in the 1970s and 80s!

Teams were physically frightened of it
– Mark Lawrenson, former Liverpool player

As a player, it didn't hit me but when I got an opportunity to speak to visiting players after a game, I began to realise just how daunting it was for them.

Teams were physically frightened of the Kop. Nothing can compare to it. The nearest is the Stretford End at Manchester United but they never had the humour.

It's amazing, when you meet Liverpool supporters all over the country, the one thing they all want to do is get to Anfield and stand on the Kop. It has an aura.

10p to see a European final
– Dave Hewitson, Kopite

On a night of torrential rain, the game was abandoned with the scores level at 0-0.

The match was being replayed the following day and I found out that it would only be 10p to get in.

The year was 1973 and Liverpool were playing Borussia Moenchengladbach in the UEFA Cup final.

I had to convince my dad to take me, but my sister was ill in hospital and we had to visit her in Alder Hey. I used a 10-year-old's powers of persuasion, repeating every 30 seconds 'dad, can we go the match? It's only 10p to get in?'

After visiting my sister, we made our way up to the ground. It was nearly half-time and my dad informed me we can get in at the 'half-time gate'. We handed over the 5p each and I ended up on my dad's shoulders. We won 3-0 and the crescendo of noise that reverberated around the roof almost split my eardrums.

Give Peter the ball back
– Gaz Stevens, Kopite

Sunday, September 16, 1990 and the days that followed will always live long in my memory for the 4-0 victory over our arch rivals Manchester United.

A Peter Beardsley hat-trick and a John Barnes goal were richly deserved rewards for a performance that led to a United player kicking the ball into the Kop in frustration at the final whistle. There was a plea in the Liverpool Echo to the person who claimed the ball to return it to Peter, which he promptly did, getting his photo in the Echo handing it back.

You're supposed to let us win!
– John Ormandy, Kopite

I remember the last game of the free standing terrace, watching Goss score from 25 yards. Singing 'You're supposed to let us win,' was fantastic. However, it was a tearful ending when 'You'll Never Walk Alone' rang out.

Mystical place
– John Quirk, Kopite

Growing up in Australia I always saw the Kop as this mystical, if not heavenly place, not really thinking that one day I would ever get the chance to stand on it.

I was lucky enough to have spent the last few months of the 1989/90 season on the Kop and was swaying and heaving with thousands of glorious Scousers when LFC won the game that gave them the championship.

I even got lucky that night at The Grafton Ballroom. Great days.

'Walrus, walrus, walrus!'
– Dick White, Kopite

In the late Sixties and early Seventies, I recall a larger-than-life police sergeant who was a very imposing size. He had grey hair and a large grey moustache.

One cold November night against Ferencvaros there was snow on the ground. As the Kop filled, someone decided to throw a snowball in the direction of the sergeant, who, walked straight into the Kop and up the steps. The bloke had scarpered, the policeman casually looked around the fans, then calmly walked back down the steps onto the track. The Kop acknowledged him with a loud chant of 'Walrus, walrus, walrus,' and he was acknowledged nearly every game after.

My first game – did we lose?
– Robbie Ashcroft, Kopite

On Christmas Day in 1965, my dream came true. My best Christmas present ever. The day after, I was finally going to Anfield to watch the Reds.

I discarded my 'Popeye break a plate' game and other Christmas presents and sorted my best clothes and my Liverpool scarf out in preparation for my very special day.

On Boxing Day, Liverpool took on Leeds United at Anfield and all our family were going. I was made to eat some dinner beforehand but I had no appetite. I was too excited. We waited for what seemed like an eternity before we set off to the ground. I can remember what seemed a horrendous cold and long walk for a seven-year-old boy from Clare Road to Anfield. Walking up I can remember being amazed at the numbers of people walking up to the match and they all seemed to know each other.

We arrived at this place called Anfield. It was dark and gloomy on the outside, and inside was something else. We made our way into the Paddock right by the Anfield Road end. I can remember sitting on the wall of the old floodlight stanchions and watching a mass of people at one end of the crowd.

This end contained the most people I had ever seen in my life. It was huge. It was incredible.

It was just a wall of noise and very colourful.

This turned out to be the Spion Kop, one day to be the love of my life.

As both teams ran out side by side, the noise was deafening. It was a wall of sound that hurt this young boy's ears. Suddenly, as if prearranged, the majority of the Spion Kop held up their red and white scarves and started to sing 'You'll Never Walk Alone'. I had never seen or heard anything like this in all my seven years on this planet. It was a sea of colour, a bastion of invincibility.

Throughout the game, the Spion Kop moved and sang as one. Early on, Liverpool nearly scored. I fell off the floodlight wall and suddenly the earth moved. I was put back up on the wall.

After a while Leeds scored and the couple of hundred Leeds fans in the Anfield Road end waved white hankies up in the air in acknowledgement. The Liverpool supporters around us clapped the Leeds United goal. At the end of the match, I can remember clapping in appreciation to the efforts of both teams, my hands hurt for ages afterwards.

It finished Liverpool 0, Leeds United 1 but the funny thing is, I was told it was 1-1. It wasn't until years later that I found out we had been beaten.

My brother and Dad had said Liverpool had scored while I had gone out to the loo. Maybe they thought I would be too upset if I thought I was a bad omen or something?

In time, my own mates and I decided we wanted to go into the Spion Kop.

The Spion Kop had a reputation of being full of drunken, high-spirited young Liverpool men and was not for the faint hearted or the weak. Our first game in the Spion Kop was to be Roger Hunt's testimonial.

For a week my mum, dad and brother kept saying: "I hope you know what you are letting yourself into".

On the way to the match none of us mentioned the Spion Kop but I think we were all nervous but wouldn't admit it.

When we got to the Spion Kop even the fella on the gate said "Are you sure you want to come in here?" We moved near to the middle and claimed a barrier to sit on. Easy. What is all the fuss about?

As the crowd began to build up we noticed how cramped our space had become. We must have climbed up and got knocked off the barrier two dozen times at least.

What a night!

Suddenly, all of us seemed to know all the words to all the Liverpool songs. We sang our hearts out. For the first time in our lives we were independent and had been fully introduced and accepted into the world famous Spion Kop.

The smell of sweaty dockers, urine and tobacco will never be forgotten. 'Sir' Roger Hunt was my first Liverpool hero and I will never ever forget him or his testimonial.

Jammed in like sardines
– Nev Smith, Kopite

Sir Roger Hunt's testimonial (Reds v England X1), an extra 3,000 to 4,000 jammed in like sardines. I started to sway during YNWA and everyone else had to go with it. Fabulous memories.

Never been on the Kop but I'm a Kopite
– Nessie Shankly, wife of Bill Shankly

It was Bill's life. Liverpool Football Club and the Kop, that is. Bill felt close to the Kop from the start.

It was the instant humour and the singing of the songs all together that appealed to him. I only went to a few matches at that time but I knew how close Bill was to the Kop. He would have been very, very sad to see it go but it is progress, out of the ashes will come a great new stadium.

I've never been on the Kop but I'm a Kopite.

I might have dropped the ring celebrating
– David Martin, Kopite

The first time I sat on the Kop was for a game against Sheffield Wednesday in December 1996. We lost 0-1 and Guy Whittingham scored the only goal. The only other incident I remember from the game was Jason McAteer hitting the crossbar.

The reason I was not concentrating on the game so much was that I had an engagement ring in my pocket and was petrified of losing it amongst thousands of people.

I had planned to propose to my fiancee over dinner in the hotel during our weekend trip, but when I collected our match tickets from the Secretary of the Dublin Supporters Club the night before the game I realised that we would be on the Kop and decided to do the deed after it had emptied after the game.

Within minutes of the final whistle the entire Kop had emptied and I produced the ring. My fiancee, Liz, was totally shocked and all she could do was nod 'yes'.

We made our way to The Park and Liz quickly made her way to the toilets, still without actually speaking. Eventually she came out, recovered from the shock and accepted my proposal. She told me later that there were bars on the windows of the toilet and she could not escape!

The Kop may mean special things to all Liverpool fans who were present at famous European nights but I was thankful

We won it five times: Famous Kop banner updated with Istanbul triumph

Oh, what a night: The Kop reaches fever pitch against Chelsea, 2005

Burning passion:
The Kop ignites for the visit of
Manchester United, 1994.
Below left: Nigel Clough celebrates
a goal in the 3-3 draw

Famous night:
Gerard Houllier's return
v Roma, 2002

Comeback:
Mark Walters scores on a classic
Kop night against Auxerre, 1991

Mourning: The Kop flag at half mast on the day Shankly dies, 1981

Cash turnstile: Queuing up to get in the Kop, 1994

Terrace's time is up:
Demolishing the old Kop
during the summer of '94

Dawn of a new era: Shafts of sunlight illuminate the new Kop stand

Mosaics:
YNWA (top); a
message of
support for
Michael Shields
(above, left) and a
tribute to Ray
Kennedy

King of the Kop:
Steven Gerrard

Shrine: Turning the pitch and the Kop into a sea of flowers after Hillsborough

Euro night to remember:
Jubilation at the final whistle against
Barcelona in 2007 (right) and (above)
the Torres banner in the corner of the
Kop and Ian Rush

Kop's Last Stand:
Norwich's Jeremy Goss
scores the last goal (above)
and (below) Kopites are
reluctant to leave. Left:
A Kop End ticket stub

Pride and passion: The famous giant banner unfurls on the Kop, 2007

Memorabilia: Flag Day flyers, a Kop season ticket and a programme cover from the last stand v Norwich

Liverpool never scored that day as I may have dropped the ring when celebrating.

The proposal of marriage being made on the Kop was very special to us both and it turned out to be a good luck charm for the future as on our wedding day Michael Owen scored a hat-trick at Anfield against Newcastle. A week later on our honeymoon in Orlando, we both watched the Reds win the FA Cup and the second week of our honeymoon was spent finding a pub in New York to watch the Alaves final. Some may put the second and third legs of the treble down to Michael's goals, Gary Mac's brilliance and Delfi Geli's own goal. Not us. Myself, my wife and our son Jamie all know that the Kop was the reason behind the success because of the part it played in our engagement, wedding and honeymoon – another very successful treble.

They're great when it's not going well
– Steven Gerrard, Liverpool captain

We've had great times at Anfield in recent seasons. You look back at some of the famous nights here and think of the games against Chelsea, Arsenal, Inter Milan, Juve and Olympiakos in the Champions League. But you really appreciate the Kop and our fans sometimes when things aren't going so well. I remember against Benfica in the Champions League in 2005/06. The noise levels when we came out for that game were up there with the very best and the fans stayed with us, urging us on all the way to the end of the game – even though we ended up going out.

I couldn't see a sodding thing
– Ian McCulloch, Echo and the Bunnymen

I must have been about seven for my first game at Anfield. My

Dad took me and our Pete who was three years older.

What game was it? I haven't got a sodding clue. I've got a crap memory. It was packed. I think it was the Kop, I'm not sure.

I went once or twice a season at that age. When I was at primary school me and my mates started watching from the Boys' Pen when I was about 10. I remember thinking 'Oh my God'. It just seemed like a load of criminals were in there. It felt like a prison and I couldn't see a sodding thing. I would go to every game and my Dad would say: "Who scored then?" I'd go: "I think it was Roger Hunt," and he would say "No it wasn't you dozy sod." I was already going blind then and I never wore specs until I was 16.

I don't know how I moved that far
– Ray Annal, Kopite

My first visit to Anfield was in 1968. I watched the game against Newcastle from the Boys' Pen for the first and last time!

Then we played Wrexham in the FA Cup so my friends and I (13 years old) decided to go on the Kop. We queued up at 1pm and the gates opened at 1.30pm. So in we went, straight to the front right hand side of the goal on the edge of the eighteen yard box. It was a great spec.

The game kicked off at 3pm with nearly 50,000 in the ground and I was still standing in the same spot. By 4.40pm Liverpool had won 3-1 and I was now standing near the corner flag! To this day I still don't know how I moved that far. I must have been standing in someone's place I reckon. I also remember the guys in red coats who sold chewing gum/sweets in a tray at the front of the Kop. People used to throw their money down and they threw the gum or sweets back up. They were great shots and always threw them at least half way up the Kop. I wonder if they ever reached the right person?

Blue mate sang You'll Never Walk Alone
– John Valente, Kopite

It was Liverpool's first season back in Europe and was the time when my mates and I had started going to the home games on a regular basis.

Our 'gang' consisted of four Reds – myself, Michael Smith, Graham Clarke and Phil Whewell – and two Blues – Stephen Dunn and Martin McQuid.

Anyway, in those days, the two Evertonians would come to the Liverpool home games whenever we went and the day consisted of taking the piss, watching the game and generally having a laugh.

On the night that we had to beat Auxerre by three goals to go through and seeing the odds were against us, the two Blues decided to come to hopefully laugh at our cup exit.

Dunny decided to act the idiot and ripped the bobble off a Liverpool hat and then made a home-made scarf out of that orange tape you see around traffic cones.

Looking like a right idiot he pretended to be a Red and acted well over the top at any cars going past his 'hat cone'.

We all know what a glorious night it was and the two Blues weren't happy at giving Liverpool their hard earned cash to see us go through.

But what was funny was watching the game back home and seeing Dunny stood on the Kop singing his heart out to 'You'll Never Walk Alone'.

At the game it was clear he was taking the piss but on TV he looked so committed to the cause. The Blues in school gave him some shit the next day.

In fact, I think the school bully (a Blue) ended up giving him a punch.

Kop still behind me despite own goal
– Nick Tanner, former Liverpool player

I would go for the UEFA Cup game against French club Auxerre at Anfield as my most memorable night in front of the Kop. We were two goals down from the first leg and not fancied to win. But we turned it around and won 3-0 to go through. The atmosphere was unbeatable that night. It's the game I cherish most from my Liverpool days.

I also remember the day I scored an own goal down at the Kop end. The fans were stunned in silence but they never gave me any stick. They were still behind me when the game resumed.

That showed me that they were good people and good to have there even when things were going the wrong way.

18,000 faces cheering and jumping
– Lee Johnson, Kopite

I was about 12 when I stood on the Kop for a game between Manchester City and the mighty Reds in the 1993/94 season.

City went 1-0 up after around four minutes at the Anfield Road end but we managed to equalise just before half-time, much to the Kop's delight.

My dad Paul was stood behind one of the stanchions and I was stood just beside him but not directly behind the stanchion.

Rushie scored in the 89th minute to give us a last gasp winner. I was pushed to the front of the Kop by the sheer crowd surge. I turned around to find my Dad and all I can remember seeing is the Kop going nuts. There were 18,000 faces cheering and jumping up and down.

At 12 years of age that should have been a terrifying scene but it was sheer heaven. I was completely in awe of the whole moment.

Magical to touch the great man himself
– Philip Ball, Kopite

I've always been a Kopite although my first match was standing on the Annie Road with my dad.

I was dumbstruck when I first set eyes on the mighty Kop and longed for the day I was allowed to stand on it. In 1973 I was 13 and allowed to go to the games on the coach with my mates. We lived near Wigan so this was a big adventure for me and my mates.

That season we never missed a home match and viewed every game from the Kop. It was awesome. Every game got better. After a full season on the Kop I then longed to view a game from the Main Stand just to see what it was like to sit and watch a match. I scrimped and saved, even worked during school holidays in my Dad's butchers shop to earn extra cash to give me a good start to the season.

That year King Bill Shankly retired. I was devastated like so many other Reds. The new season soon came round and I remember being excited and apprehensive as it was the start of a new era. My first match that season, I decided to watch the game from the Main Stand. I was the envy of all my mates. I was sat close to the Kop so I was able to still absorb the special Kop atmosphere and I remember, not long before kick-off, the Kop erupted. There he was. The great man himself. Shankly was walking amongst his disciples and I was sat in the Main Stand!

I had to be in there. I had to touch him. I made my way down to the Paddock where I skipped over the barrier and I was now on the pitch. Oh my God. I couldn't believe my luck. I was so nervous but my adrenalin kicked in and no one could have caught me even though two stewards tried and failed. I jumped into the Kop and eventually touched the great man himself.

As a young lad it cost me what seemed like an arm and a leg to get into the Main Stand but to end up in the Kop and to touch the great man himself was magical. The memory will live with me till my dying day.

Extra-time drama
– Mike Smith, Kopite

By the age of 15 I had become an avid Red and had been going to Anfield with my mates Phil and Vaz to watch Liverpool for a few years. I had secretly been standing on the Kop for a couple of years without the consent of my parents.

Not only did they object to me standing on the famous Spion Kop but any suggestion of me going to see the Reds on a school night was a complete no-go. For me Liverpool FC came first and anything after that was a distant second. So when, during a playground discussion, I heard Vaz and Phil were planning a trip to Anfield for a mid-week FA Cup tie against Ipswich I knew I didn't want to miss out. But how could I convince my parents?

After minutes of rattling my brain, I knew that the only solution was to explain to my parents that an important rehearsal for a 'drama' exam was required at Vaz's house. It worked a treat. Within hours I was sat on the bus with Phil and Vaz on the way to my beloved Anfield.

To me, standing on the Kop was the best place on earth. It was cheap and the atmosphere was great. The FA Cup fifth round replay against first division Ipswich was a fantastic game but the script didn't exactly go according to plan.

With minutes to go, Liverpool found themselves 1-2 down but a belting free-kick from Jan Molby took the game into extra-time. I now had a dilemma. Should I leave Anfield there and then or cheer on the Reds in extra-time and risk severe punishment from my parents?

A winner by Steve McManaman sent me and the lads home happy. Unfortunately, my season finished that night because after returning home at 11.45pm, a phone call by my parents to Vaz's old man was not enough to convince them that the drama rehearsal had also reached extra-time!

I sensed the night would be special
– Nigel Clough, former Liverpool player

The Kop were unbelievable to me right from my first pre-season game against Newcastle.

My abiding memory is of my official Liverpool debut against Sheffield Wednesday and running out in front of 44,000 people who generated so much noise – most of it from the Kop.

It was good to know they were on your side.

The Kop was packed week in, week out, and the people on it have helped Liverpool win so many games over the years. My dad used to be amazed by the consistency of those supporters.

Whenever you came to Anfield as an opponent you'd find them getting right behind Liverpool and making things very difficult for the away side.

The Kop was intimidating, not in a nasty way, but by its level of support for the home side. It made Anfield like a fortress and that meant getting a point was deemed as a great result.

The 3-3 draw between Liverpool and Manchester United was the best game I've ever played in. I'm not from Merseyside or Manchester but it was impossible not to feel the passion among the supporters. I'd not experienced anything like that atmosphere at club or international level.

As soon as I saw the flags and banners waving on the Kop, I sensed the night would be special. I couldn't have been more right and I can honestly say I was privileged.

I'll never regret coming to Liverpool
– Paul Jones, former on-loan Liverpool keeper

The fans in the Kop when I came out – I will never, ever forget that. The applause I got was incredible although, to be fair to them, they had always given me a good reception when I was the away keeper. It was very special and that summed the Kop up for me. I could have gone down the road (to Portsmouth) for two years but that's why I'll never regret coming to Liverpool for a month.

Just to get that feeling.

Coming back was emotional
– Ray Clemence, former Liverpool keeper

When I first joined Liverpool I sat in the stand and marvelled at 20-odd thousand people singing and swaying together on the Kop.

Their humour was incredible and topical. The singing of 'You'll Never Walk Alone' was another experience. I look back on the derby games I enjoyed but the win over St Etienne is the one which stands out. It wasn't just the Kop which gave ultimate support that night, the whole stadium was gripped in a tremendous atmosphere.

My other memory is coming back to Anfield as a Spurs player for the first time. The reception I was given can only be described as a very emotional experience for myself. But I have no individual memories because I closed my ears in order to concentrate on goalkeeping for 90 minutes. I heard deafening roars but that's all.

Mound of dirt started it all
– Stephen Done, Liverpool FC Museum Curator

The laying of the tramlines on Arkles Lane was a fairly big project and at the end of it all there were these huge mounds of dirt that needed removing. Someone from the club spoke to the corporation and asked them if they wouldn't mind dumping the earth outside the Anfield stadium at the Walton Breck Road end. This was duly done and it was this dumped earth that turned into the terrace.

If you mention the Kop to football fans from anywhere in the world the first place they will think of is Anfield. There are Kops at Blackpool, Sheffield Wednesday, Leeds United, Birmingham City and several more but none have the same tradition or reputation as the one at Anfield. It is a reputation that spans the globe as well. Paris Saint Germain were so impressed with the Kop at Anfield that they tried to create their own version and fans of Inter Milan hold the Kop in such esteem that they actually made a tribute record in honour of it.

All of the exhibits we have which are connected to the Kop in any way are always extremely popular with visitors. We also have a piece of rock from the original Spion Kop in South Africa, an authentic Kop turnstile, through which so many Liverpool fans will have passed over the years, and a programme and ticket from the last game of the standing Kop against Norwich City. We have been fortunate to have many, many great players at Liverpool but players come and go – the Kop will always be here in one form or another. It is a symbol of what the club is about.

Kop debut day ritual
– Kevin Keegan, former Liverpool player

I was surprised by one of the fans' rituals prior to my debut back in 1971. The self-appointed representative of the Kop came on the field to greet me. He gave me a kiss, and the smell of booze on his breath almost knocked me off my feet.

He needed a shave as well, as his beard was rough. The police accepted this ritual whenever there was a new player.

This Kopite was a nice old fellow with no harm in him. He kissed me, then kissed the grass in front of the Kop and went back to join his mates in the crowd.

Wipe yer arse Stevie!
– Gareth Roberts, liverpoolecho.co.uk

I'd actually 'sneaked' to the match as there was no-one in my family who was really into footy like me – and my mum and dad didn't like the idea of me going without an adult.

But I just had to go – and it didn't disappoint.

I can still remember getting to the top of the steps of the Kop and seeing the inside of Anfield for the first time 'or real'. It was great, I had butterflies in my stomach – I can still picture the Annie Road – without the second tier and a Wonderfuel Gas advert on the top of the stand.

From there on I was hooked, and I got to as many games as money would allow. Myself and a couple of friends from school in Huyton stood in the same spot on the Kop for years and we'd see the same felllas week in, week out. We were soon up to speed on the rules, too – how to avoid the crush barriers, how to be aware of the fellas just out of the alehouse who'd soon be dying for the toilet and wouldn't think twice of aiming their piss down a rolled up Echo and into your pocket!

We followed the same routine before every Saturday home game – visiting my mate's grandad near the ground beforehand and avoiding his dodgy scones (the same ones were put on a plate week after week).

Then there was my 'nan sweets' – a bag of éclairs my nan gave me before every game which I dished out to my mates at half time.

Back then everyone would pile in the ground hours before kick-off – I stood on the Kop as early as 12.30pm for some of the big

Saturday games (which were all 3pm kick-offs then).

But it was all part of it – booing the opposition players as they come out for a first look at the pitch, studying the warm-ups, baiting the away fans and so on.

We used to dare each other to shout things – if you got it wrong you could almost hear thousands of people scowling down at you at once.

I got it right once, someone threw a bog roll at Nottingham Forest keeper Steve Sutton (a bit of a thing at the time) and on my own I shouted: "Wipe yer arse Stevie".

He did, and I'm sure he gave us a little wink. I was buzzing – and everyone was grinning at me – for that moment I was the funniest lad on the Kop.

We still lead the way when we want to
– Dave Jones, Kopite

Part of our match-going ritual used to be getting the sweets in. There were always loads of great sweet shops around Anfield and one of our gang would take it in turns to get two ounces or a quarter of pear drops, chocolate limes or eclairs. If we won that day, we would have to stick with that sweet until we lost (which didn't happen very often in the 1970s and 1980s) or drew. We also had the same celebration every year when the title was in the bag (we didn't realise how lucky we were). We would get in a small huddle and jump up and down, big smiles on our faces. We knew who would stand by us each game and they all had their own little habits.

One fan would shout 'Liverpool, Liverpool hurrah, hurrah, hurrah' in a plummy piss-take voice like that bloke from the Panorama programme. Another lad used to whistle 'der-der-der der-der-derr' (not Ring of Fire) which used to be heard at every game when the crowd went quiet.

Everyone used to have their own nicknames for the players as well. Some of them can't be repeated, of course, but most were just funny. The full-backs in the '80s both had nicknames – 'Barney Rubble' (Alan Kennedy) and 'Zico' (Phil Neal). There used to be a buzz of expectation when Barney got the ball because you were expecting him to do something stupid, like fall over the ball. He was a great player but he did get himself in some funny situations.

Brucie Grobbelaar was another one who made us laugh. We would sing 'Brucie, Brucie what's the score' and if it was 3-0 and we were defending the Kop end, he would hold up three fingers behind his back and we would give a cheer. At Christmas, we would sing the song: 'On the first day of Christmas my true love sent to me a Brucie Grobbelaar in our goal' and then we would go through the whole team – two Phil Neals, three Barney Rubbles, four Stevie Nicols, five Ron-nie Whelans and so on.

The humour hasn't gone, some of the old Kopites have made sure it is still around. I went to a Portsmouth game recently and Herman Hreidarsson was playing. Every time he got near the crowd, one fan would shout in a low voice: 'Herrrmmmannn, your tea's ready!' (I think it's from the Addams Family). I also remember one time in the '90s when Steve Harkness was playing. He was going through a phase where he had designer stubble. This one day he was having a bad game and when he came near the Kop someone shouted: 'Fuckin' sort it out George Michael!' which was the cue to fits of laughter all round.

Some of the foreign fans pick up on the humour from the Scousers too. One Scandinavian lad who was stuck right in the top corner of the Kop in a terrible spec recently started joining in with the 'Oh Sami, Sami' song for Hyypia and then added at the end: 'Where the fuck is he – I can't see him!' because he had an obstructed view!

So although I miss the old Kop, I think the new Kop has some good moments too. The sight of all those scarves swirling for Ring Of Fire on a European night is totally breathtaking.

I notice that everyone else has copied the Ring Of Fire chant – as they do with other songs that we invent. So we still lead the way when we want to.

'Oh I do like to be beside the sea!'
– Mike Chapple, writer

'Oh I do like to be beside the seaside, Oh I do like to be beside the sea, Oh I do like to walk along the prom, prom, prom, where the brass bands play, fuck off West Brom!' The above was a personal favourite from the Kop that had no relevance even when conceived many moons ago. However, it is occasionally dusted down and bellowed at Anfield to celebrate its sheer stupidity – whether the Baggies are playing or not!

The Brazilian handclap
– Ron Yeats' Liverpool Echo column, 1962

I have some more information about the origin of the 1960s Kop war cry (the famous 'Liv-er-pool' chant followed by three staccato handclaps).

At a holiday camp in North Wales, contingents from Liverpool, Bolton, Blackburn and so on are always present and last year there was a lot of friendly rivalry during one particular fortnight between the Liverpool crowd and one from Blackburn. On any pretext whatever there would be a shout of 'Liv-er-pool' or 'Blackburn' from the appropriate quarter.

When the finals of the dance competition were being held, the Liverpool supporters emphasised their encouragement by adding three claps in time with the music, which then became the signature tune on all occasions and was eventually brought back to Anfield. Another correspondent, Billy Edwards of Norris Green, says that it originated from the World Cup in Brazil (the World Cup was actually in Chile in 1962). When Brazil were on TV their supporters would chant 'Brazil, clap, clap, clap.'

I treasured the Kop roar
– Billy Liddell, former Liverpool player

I cannot recall who said that a city is not just bricks and mortar and fine buildings. It is the people in it and this expresses what I think. I was always happy at Anfield where we had the staunchest bunch of supporters in the land. I do feel the Kop is very biased at times, but in this sport which is fast becoming commercialised, the fans have a part to play in the team's success. I treasure the relationship I had with those fans and recall with pleasure the feelings that I sensed when the Kop roar was in full flight.

I've just been in the Kop with the boys
– Peter Thompson, former Liverpool player

It was a quarter-to-three on match day at Anfield. We were in the dressing room and there was no sign of Shanks. Suddenly, he came in. His shirt's torn, tie undone, jacket hanging off, hair all over the place. One of the lads says: "What's happened boss?" and he replied: "I've just been in the Kop with the boys." He'd gone in with 28,000 of them and they'd been lifting him shoulder high, passing him round, and he loved that.

We had Shankly and the Kop at Liverpool and the partnership made you feel you could do anything. We were brainwashed into thinking that we could win everything. It was a great feeling.

Feeling a part of something
– Neil Macdonald, Kopite

I can still remember the thrill that ran down my spine when my dad said to me "come on then, we're off to the match." It mattered little that the opponents were some foreign team I'd never heard of – I was going to Anfield, the promised land, for the first time.

It was a night match – which I have always preferred attending ever since – and my first impressions were how dark it was on the Kop, and how far away the pitch seemed.

But when the players ran out, the noise was deafening and the red of the kit shone against the vivid green of the grass. I also remember that Oulu had a bald player, which made me laugh then and still does now.

Liverpool won the match 7-0 and the game was played the day after Bill Shankly died.

The Kop chanted his name throughout the second half, but back then it was just noise to me. As I had only started following Liverpool a few months before, I thought they were singing for one of the players.

But that feeling of community, of being a part of something greater than yourself, has stayed with me from that day to this.

The tie that binds
– Ian Donohue, letter to liverpoolecho.co.uk

This story comes from my dad, Tony, and dates back to 1969 when he and a few of his mates were working in South Africa. They were helping to build the Civic Centre in Johannesburg when they decided it would be a good idea to visit the original Spion Kop.

One of their mates, Mick Ferry, was in a wheelchair so they decided to club together and fly him out so he could make the trip with them. It was 600 miles away to the site of the Spion Kop but, as die-hard Liverpool fans, it was a trip worth making.

Once there, they pushed Mick to the top of the hill where they took photographs of them all with the commemorative banners and ties they'd made. They had made 11 ties with one in mind for a special recipient back in Liverpool. When they got back, a dinner was held to mark the trip, which the Liverpool Echo covered at the time. My dad and his mates invited Bill Shankly to the dinner but when he couldn't make it, he agreed to go and meet them all at the Supporters Club. It was there that they issued Shankly with the 11th tie. It was emblazoned with the words 'Spion Kop 1969' woven into it in gold letters.

Shankly kept the tie and even wore it on various occasions. He took time out that night to chat to my dad and his mate about their trip and all things football. They were amazed at just how much he knew about the origins of the Spion Kop. It was a fabulous moment for them to present Shankly with the tie.

Block 1892
– John Mackin, editor of 'The Rattle' website

The diaspora that resulted from the seating of the Kop meant that the old core – the 500 to 1,000 who regularly formed the nucleus, and who stood together shoulder to sweaty shoulder, between the stanchions on the world's greatest terrace – was no more. They were now scattered all over the Kop and all over Anfield.

Going all seater also meant that fans are not getting into the ground until the last 20 or 30 minutes before kick-off.

The long hours that we used to spend standing and waiting for kick-off used to be filled by having a laugh, inventing new songs, practising the old ones – there was a real sense of comradeship and belonging.

What we've tried to do with the 1892 (singing section on the Kop) is to get some of those people – and likeminded supporters from all over Anfield – back together again and encourage those younger ones who want to be a part of it to step up to the plate.

It's not for those who want to soak up the atmosphere, it's for those who want to generate the atmosphere and ratchet it up several notches. It's for supporters, not spectators.

Kop love triangle
– Gareth Roberts, liverpoolecho.co.uk

The Kop also influenced my love life. My comprehensive school crush asked me to take her to the match but her dad didn't want her standing on the Kop. So we watched from the Anfield Road.

As the Kop cheered every home player's name, I sulked. It wasn't right sitting there.

"What's up?" she said, "What's different about the Kop?" "Well they cheer the players' names for a start," I said. "We can do that here" she said before proceeding to cheer at the announcement of the much-maligned Barry Venison.

"Ar, ey love, you don't like him do yer? Where'd you get her from lad?" boomed a burly bloke in front. The shame – that was it, the next date was the Kop, no matter what her old fella said!

Outside our school at 12 I'd told her – it was Spurs, the last game of the season and bound to be a sell-out. One o'clock she turned up – we didn't get in and a tout wanted 70 quid for a ticket. That was it, back to Huyton, not a word to her, other than to snub her offer of watching a video at hers. And that was that – we never went out again – she'd got between me and the Kop!

I always remember a derby on the Kop when it was still standing. Just as the game kicked off I spotted a Bluenose I knew. "What you doing here?" I shouted, to which he responded by chanting

"EVER-TON" and raising his arms in triumph.

With that we took the lead, David Burrows, I think it was, banging one in after just a few seconds. 1-0! I'll never forget his face – the shock – it was priceless – how to silence a Bluenose in one easy step! Since those days, I've sat in every stand at Anfield but I still find myself studying the Kop when You'll Never Walk Alone kicks off – it's not the same anywhere else in the ground – I'm not sure half of them even know the words in the Main Stand.

I make sure I'm back on the Kop for the big European nights and, for me, Chelsea in 2005 was the best ever. That's the loudest crowd I'd ever been a part of in 17 years of going to Anfield.

It was unbelievable – everyone sung, everyone stood and everyone was everyone else's best mate – I was hugging strangers left, right and centre on the final whistle like I'd known these people all my life! No-one wanted to leave – we were in the European Cup final – the stadium announcer had to tell us all to get off in the end, almost half an hour after the final whistle.

Tributes to Dr Fun
– Liverpool Echo

For generations of Liverpool fans he was an unforgettable part of the match experience.

Dressed in a red top hat and twirling a rattle, Lenny Campbell became one of the Kop's best-loved characters.

Today (January 23, 2007) relatives of the super-fan famously known as 'Doctor Fun' spoke of their sadness after his death on Saturday, aged 63. Father-of-two Mr Campbell, of Rupert Road, Huyton, died from cancer at Whiston hospital only hours after his beloved Reds beat champions Chelsea at Anfield.

The former Butlin's Red Coat became well known on the Kop during the '80s and '90s for his flamboyant outfits, rattle and hand-puppet called Charlie.

His niece Sandra Baker, 36, said: "Uncle Lenny was the best character I've ever met. He was an ambassador for the club he loved and he embraced life and football with a passion.

"He sat on the Kop from the age of 13 and fell in love with it, then he went to be a children's entertainer in Butlin's and Pontin's.

"Because he had such a great way with kids at the holiday camps, he got the nickname Mr Fun and when he came back he just kept it going. Apart from his family his two loves were Liverpool FC and the Beatles. He even had Strawberry Fields on the gates of his house."

Volley of beach balls
– Robert Gillies, 'The Jury', Liverpool Echo

The match against United (in October, 2009) encapsulated the best of being a Liverpool fan.

The volley of beach balls raining down from the Kop showed our ability to laugh at ourselves, deal with adversity and completely steal the thunder of the visiting fans.

The support and passion for the team was palpable and will be difficult if not impossible to replicate if we ever move to Stanley Park.

I was proud to move here
– Pepe Reina, Liverpool goalkeeper

Something that will always stay with me is the special reception I got when I made my way to the Kop goal when I played for Barcelona (against Liverpool, UEFA Cup semi-final, 2001).

Everyone was clapping. I thought it must be for some of the Liverpool players, so I turned around but there was nobody there.

When I realised it was for me I started applauding the crowd. I returned their respect and the Kop cheered loudly. It was magnificent. I have never seen anything like that anywhere else. I was an opposition player – I didn't imagine I'd be on the other side in a couple of years.

When Rafa asked me if I wanted to come to Liverpool, that was something I immediately thought of. I was very proud to move here because we have some of the best fans in the world.

Banks tribute so emotional
– Michael Donnelly, Kopite

The memory of the reception that Gordon Banks received when he walked around the ground with Shanks for the visit of Stoke (I think it was the first game of the '72-73 season) after he lost his eye and was forced to retire from football was an unbelievable and proud moment that I will never forget.

I was only twelve at the time and I was my school goalkeeper (St James and Bootle Boys – just like Carra). Banks, Bonetti and Clemence were my boyhood heroes.

The emotion and passion that rang out as Shanks raised his arms and walked around the entire ground to salute Banks – not even a Liverpool player! It was totally inspirational and it brought home to me for the first time, the special warmth that the Kop has displayed many times since for special players over the years. If you are a great player or a good team – you are respected and we salute you.

Off the wall
– Neil Jones, Kopite

It was September 1978 when we beat Spurs 7-0. I was sitting on the wall at the top of the stairs under the Boys' Pen. It was the great goal scored by Terry McDermott to make it 7-0.

We scored and I jumped up, fell off the wall but landed on my dad and uncle who put me back up. It was the best and most scary moment of my life. I was only ten years old and the Kop was scary indeed.

'We're not going till he's here!'
– Mike Maxson, Kopite

My best memory was in 1986. The championship had just been won (at Chelsea) and we were a few days away from playing Everton in the cup final.

Norwich were the visitors in the final of a competition which was designed to replace the loss of European football. I think it was called the Screen Sport Cup or something.

At the end of the game (which we won) the Kop refused to leave until Kenny came out to be applauded.

'We're not going till he's here' was sung around the Kop by twenty-odd thousand people until Kenny was forced to appear to take the applause.

A great night to finish a great season and a fitting way for the Kop to show their appreciation to the greatest Liverpool player of them all.

There goes my contact lens
– Ken Cattrell, Kopite

Dalglish cuts the ball back to Souness 25 yards out, thump, GOOOAAAL! The Kop erupts around me.

A flailing arm catches me in the eye, ouch! There goes my contact lens – knocked clean out. Sod it!

Keep celebrating in unison, thousands jumping up and down. I look down. There's the lens on the floor!!

'MAKE A SPACE!'

Fifty people push back around me making a big hole in the centre of the Kop.

The Main Stand are looking over, the police are looking – where's the fight? No fight here officer, just picking up my clean intact contact lens.

Sore back in the morning
– Baz, posted on liverpoolfc.tv

It was the 1989/90 season. We used to travel on the bus from over the water. 30p return and £4.50 to get into the Kop end.

My memories of the Kop at that time – a standing tier system, no barriers, no fences, simply a sea of bodies, as one, chanting, the smell of pie and chips and the occasional spliff in the air.

It became interesting when there was a corner at the Kop end – we couldn't see to the corner of the pitch from our vantage point, evidently neither could a few thousand others.

Suddenly there would be an almighty surge towards the corner as people leaned towards it, trying to get a view of the ball being crossed in.

Being a lanky youngster of just 16 years, I often found myself being literally lifted from my feet and carried with the ripple of bodies.

Sometimes I would find myself 20 feet from where I had been standing with my mate and would have to wait for a corner at the other side of the pitch before being reunited with him again.

Some great moments, interesting characters, fantastic songs and the occasional sore back in the morning.

Class.

Stinking headache and a big smile
– Andy Stewart, posted on liverpoolfc.tv

We were 2-0 down to Auxerre and no one gave us a chance in the second leg. Only 23,000 in the half-full ground, but 17,000 on the Kop – what a noise!

I've never heard the Kop that loud before. It was frightening! Marsh, Molby and Walters deserve a mention but the Kop won that game for Liverpool and were the real heroes on that famous night! I left Anfield that night with a stinking headache and a smile as big as the Kop.

We were 'the four'
– Adam Hollowood, posted on liverpoolfc.tv

Myself and three friends only ever stood on the Kop once and that was for the opening game of the season in 1993 when Nigel Clough scored twice on his debut against Sheffield Wednesday. Nothing special about the match, but we were just pleased that we'd had the unique experience before the seats came in. The attendance that day was particularly poignant – 44,004, and as it was our first (and last) time standing at Anfield – we considered ourselves to be the '4'!

'Sitting down' ... 'Going down'!
– Jason Andrews, posted on liverpoolfc.tv

I was was fortunate enough to be on the Kop during two historic 'standing' occasions before it became all seated. The last Merseyside derby. Superb occasion with Everton fans singing 'sitting down, sitting down, sitting down'. The Liverpool faithful replied, 'GOING DOWN, GOING DOWN, GOING DOWN'.

I was on the pitch and I thought: 'Christ, what's this?'
– Alan Hansen, former Liverpool captain

The Kop were always fantastic to me. In all honesty, I think I was a sort of quiet hero to them whereas others were vocal heroes. When I came out on to the pitch, and they were chanting people's names, they never chanted my name.

There was a mutual respect there, though, and they were great to play in front of.

Funnily enough, one of the games that showed me what the Kop was all about came when we got beaten at home by Birmingham. It was January '78 and we were 3-0 down. Trevor Francis was a scorer.

Anyway, we were 3-0 down and all of a sudden the Kop went ballistic. We got two back in the last 18 minutes or so and I tell you what, if the game had gone on we'd have won by six in the end. I'm not kidding you, it was unbelievable.

I remember playing in my first derby match at Anfield in September '77. When I went on that pitch, I tell you what, I couldn't hear myself think. The noise levels frightened me. I was on the pitch and I thought to myself 'Christ, what's this?'.

When people talk about Liverpool supporters, and talk about their vocal support, then in the main they talk about the Kop. That's true but I think there was a general malaise in the Liverpool supporters in the 1980s. They just won too much. We'd be coming off after winning 2-0 or 3-0 and they were groaning.

I remember playing and we'd be 2-0 up and the bench are shouting 'give it back to the keeper'. We'd keep hold of it across the back four and the first time we did it they'd start counting the passes or whatever. The second time we'd do it you'd start to hear the grunts, the groans and the dismay.

They were always fantastic to me though and my testimonial at

Anfield was extra special. We'd just been beaten in the FA Cup final by Wimbledon but 33,000 turned up. It was frightening. There was a great atmosphere. Rushie had come back to play and Kenny played with him. The crowd loved it.

'What's it like to queue for bread?'
– Dave Lennett, posted on liverpoolfc.tv

My personal favourite Kop memory is the year before the original Kop was torn down. It was the one and only time I stood on the Kop. We had to pay £35 each for £7 tickets from a tout due to a ticket mix up. It was a UEFA cup game against Spartak Moscow. We lost the game but it didn't matter as the atmosphere on the Kop that day was the best I have experienced in my life, all swaying and singing. The funniest and best song I have ever heard, sang to our Russian brothers – 'What's it like to queue for bread'. You can't beat Scouse humour.

The unwritten code
– Graeme, Kopite

I recall a random game from about 1994 – the last season of the old Kop. I used to stand on the Kop with my brother, dad and uncles.

One game a gang of about five lads from Yorkshire were standing next to us and had obviously had a few pints before the game. They looked a bit sloshed and were talking rubbish and being a bit aggressive. One of the blokes started to lean on my brother's back for support and was becoming an increasing annoyance but it was the foul racist abuse that he was shouting that really sickened those around us.

My dad is not one to tolerate that kind of stuff and during a lull, tapped the guy who was leaning on my brother on the shoulder and said: "We on the Kop don't tolerate language of that kind, I don't know where you're from, but you can shut up or get out!"

Well, I nearly fell off the bar! I was only 16 and thought he was going to get a proper pasting! But before the neanderthals could retaliate, about 15 fellow Kopites turned around and showed their support. It was pure class to see those muppets shutting up and then leaving at half time!

It made me realise the how important it is to speak up and not to be intimidated. Self-policing is very important among football fans, it develops the bond between us and creates an unwritten code of what is and isn't acceptable.

I've seen things like this many times since on European travels – newcomers being told what they are doing isn't going to be tolerated because it drags the name of LFC and the city through the mud. It's what separates us from other groups of fans and ensures there isn't trouble when we go abroad.

Different to the rest
– Joe Hickey, Kopite

My favourite Kop memory was when we played Stoke City in the third round of the then Coca-Cola Cup. We went on to win the game 2-1 with a certain Ian Rush scoring both goals I think.

But what was special about that game happened prior to kick-off. Before the game, Brian Clough, in his infinite wisdom, declared that Liverpool fans were to blame for the Hillsborough disaster. What was more poignant about that statement was that Brian's son Nigel was a Liverpool player at the time.

Nigel and the press were concerned that Liverpool fans would turn on him in protest at his father's comment. Prior to kick-off at the Stoke game, the Liverpool side came out to warm up at the Kop end as usual and Nigel Clough joined them.

The whole of the Kop rose to their feet and chanted: 'He's red, he's white, he's fucking dynamite, Nigel Clough, Nigel Clough.' And in that moment I realised what made the Kop and Liverpool Football Club different to all of the rest.

It left me a bit emotional
– Paul Walsh, former Liverpool player

I settled in very quickly at Liverpool and the fans were absolutely brilliant with me. I remember coming back to Anfield with Tottenham in 1988, the day Liverpool won the league. I didn't come out for a warm-up but when we came out onto the pitch I got a fantastic reception from the Kop. They were singing my name and it left me a bit emotional I've got to say. I will never forget that.

Wacker, The Spirit of Scouse
– Excerpt from Panorama, BBC, April 1964

The gladiators enter the arena, the field of praise. Saturday's weather perfect for an historic Scouse occasion. Liverpool, in red shirts, were playing before their own spectators for the last time this season. The desire to win was an agonised one. They would be the champions of England and they wanted their own people to see them become so. They care so much about football.

This season over two million people on Merseyside have watched Liverpool or their neighbours Everton, last year's champions. But they don't behave like any other football crowd, especially not at one end of Anfield ground – on the Kop.

The music the crowd sings is the music that Liverpool has sent echoing around the world. It used to be thought that Welsh international rugby crowds were the most musical and passionate in the world. But I've never seen anything like this Liverpool crowd. On the field here the gay and inventive ferocity they show is quite stunning. The Duke of Wellington, before the battle of Waterloo, said of his own troops 'I don't know what they do to the enemy but by God they frighten me'.

And I'm sure some of the players here in this match this afternoon must be feeling the same way. An anthropologist studying this Kop crowd would be introduced into as rich and mystifying a popular culture as in any South Sea island. Their rhythmic swaying is an elaborate and organised ritual. The 28,000 people on the Kop itself begin singing together. They seem to know, intuitively, when to begin.

Throughout the match they invent new words, usually within the framework of old Liverpool songs, to express adulatory, cruel or bawdy comments about the players or the police. But even then they begin singing these new words with one immediate, huge voice. They seem, mysteriously, to be in touch with one another, with Wacker, the spirit of Scouse.

The spirit is good humoured and generous when they're winning, but not necessarily when they're losing. On Saturday they were certainly winning. In an hour, Liverpool scored five goals and could have scored more. Their poor, sacrificial victims were Arsenal. Southerners. On Merseyside, football is the consuming passion. It's hard to persuade people to talk about anything else, except perhaps the beat groups which the Kop crowd do a lot to explain.

'Thank you very much for paying our Giros'
– Ian Gibbs, Daily Mirror, 1989

The most famous chants in the game began on the Kop – and they stretched far beyond the bounds of football.

Who could forget the terrible time when Britain's unemployment figure hit three million with few areas worse affected than Merseyside?

The Kop were not only unbeaten but unbowed. They roared back – to the time-honoured tune by '60s group The Scaffold – "Thank you very much for paying our Giros!"

The Kop's greatest tribute came from the man who made them famous, the legendary Bill Shankly.

He described them as: "The only professional spectators in the game. They have made it an art of supporting a team and by doing so they have played a big part in the success of this club."

The Kop could be so cruel – and so kind. There was never a more instant victim than the one-time Leeds international goalkeeper Gary Sprake, who mistimed a throw-out and hurled the ball in his own net. Within seconds, the Kop opened their throats with a rendition of 'Careless Hands'.

But they loved their own and a Kopite came up with an ingenious answer to a poster outside a church: 'What will you do if the Lord comes down?' 'Move St John to inside left!' was the written answer underneath.

Tony Hateley was a particular hero who was once wooed with the love song: 'Have we told you Hateley that we love you?'

The Kop could even come up with a clever line when the opposition came from Petrolul in the Ploesti oilfields of Romania. The Romanians ran on to the Anfield pitch with 'The Esso sign means happy motoring' ringing in their ears.

Another Kop classic came on one of those many occasions when the fans believed they were as much a part of the team as the players. Roger Hunt got hold of the ball on a muddy pitch, no goals and not much time left. He ploughed on past two defenders to the edge of the area. A Kopite's hoarse voice just about managed to be heard: "You have to do it on your own now Roger, I'm finished".

Of course, Roger obliged and Liverpool won.

Only the Kop could come up with the ingenious nickname of 'Tarmac' for their England star John Barnes – the black Heighway, after their former winger Steve.

Manchester City came in for so much stick when they were a big success in the 1970s, that England striker Francis Lee – in exasperation – grabbed a zoom lens off a startled photographer – and pretended to shoot the Kop with it.

20,000 comics
– Stan Boardman, comedian

I learned my trade standing among natural comics on the Kop – all 20,000 of them. I had my own bit of concrete, always with the same dozen fellas around me. My spot was just beyond the right-hand goalpost. I chose it because I loved seeing Peter Thompson coming down that wing.

Conducting the Kop's last stand
– Mike Langley, Daily Mirror, May, 1994

The Kop's amazingly swift unanimity inspired the Liverpool Echo's resident humourist to invent 'Sir Malcolm', football's version of the former Liverpool Philharmonic conductor, Sir Malcolm Sargent.

Balancing on a barrier, flourishing his baton to call up more allegro and less moderato, 'Sir Malcolm' flicked and switched England's largest choir to a repertoire embracing everything from Rodgers and Hammerstein on to the Beatles and back to 'Yes We Have No Bananas'.

For Big Jack Charlton, they would turn into massed Al Jolsons parodying Mammy into 'Charlton, Charlton … we'd walk a million miles to the end of your neck, oh Charlton'.

Like Sherlock Holmes and other fictional inspirations, 'Sir Malcolm' turned into real life. People swore they'd seen him at matches. I probably saw him myself while Liverpool were losing 1-0 to Norwich. Was he the one beating time on a drum? Or the conductor using an East German banner complete with hammer and sickle? Or the one with a dummy slumped round his shoulders? Perhaps the one with the white topper, or the one with a giant inflatable Frankenstein wearing a hard hat splashed with pretend blood? Wherever he was, the orchestrator of the Kop swung his 16,000 voices though the Dam Busters, Yellow Submarine, Scouser Tommy, Those Were The Days and endless renditions of You'll Never Walk Alone.

Right at the finish, when once more reaching that beautiful line about the 'sweet silver song of a lark', two birds swooped out of the sun and flew together across the ground. Larks? A Pair of Lime Street pigeons which, unlike Liverpool's poorest side for nearly 40 years, refrained from causing a nuisance on the pitch.

The Kop applauded Norwich for their victory and raised a loyal but ritual 'There's Only One Roy Evans' for their own new manager. Contrary to legend, I left the Kop with my pockets neither picked nor peed in. It had been an afternoon of company and colour that would have been a crime to miss. An hour later, while tying scarves to the barriers, they were still chanting and I could hear them clearly 400 yards away in a car park.

What were they saying? One word over and over. "DALGLISH!"

Hitting the Kop wall
– The late Emlyn Hughes, former Liverpool captain

I remember when I chased a ball to the Kop wall, stumbled and crashed into it, cracking a finger.

Bob Paisley was physio at the time and could see immediately that a ring I was wearing must come off before the swelling got too bad. Bob said: 'Just have a look up at the Kop and don't think about it'.

To this day, I reckon the Kop must have thought I was a big softie, screaming out in pain as Bob yanked the ring off. But I had a great relationship with the Kop.

Carra: The heart and soul of the new Kop
– Oliver Holt, Daily Mirror, 2005

The loudspeaker system started off with a few dirges. The Smiths, that kind of thing. As if they were mourning Anfield's lost years.

But as the kick-off (to the Champions League semi-final second leg against Chelsea) grew nearer and the players came out to warm up, the giant flag bearing the club's crest rippled over the heads of the fans in the Kop and the noise grew louder. Twenty minutes before kick-off, you couldn't hear the loudspeaker any more. 'We Shall Not Be Moved' they roared. Then it was 'When The Reds Go Marching In.'

As the Liverpool players trotted back to their dressing room for their final preparations, a great roar went around this grand old ground that made the hairs on the back of your neck stand on end.

And when Anfield stood as one and 42,000 supporters held their scarves up and belted out the most rousing rendition of 'You'll Never Walk Alone' some of us have ever heard, it felt humbling to be in the presence of such passion.

One of the great sights in world football right there in front of you, reawakened by this magnificently unlikely attempt to stir the ghosts of the past.

Up on one of the top tiers, a banner spelled out a simple message. 'Respect for Your Elders Gives You Character,' it said. It was illustrated with the likenesses of four European Cups.

In the press box, Tommy Smith, Alan Kennedy, David Fairclough and Phil Neal and many more of the heroes of yesteryear, felt the emotion swell. Out there in the middle of it all, Jamie Carragher, the heart and the soul of this new Liverpool side finally knew he was a part of the great Liverpool tradition.

He saw Chelsea wilt as the walls of noise bombarded the players from the stands. Even this wonderful Chelsea side had never experienced anything like this intensity before.

Before four minutes had elapsed, Carragher saw the Kop suck a weakly-dinked chip from Luis Garcia over the goalline in front of them just as legend says that they can on nights like this.

They dragged it and dredged it over that line with the fury of their desire and they were ahead before William Gallas booted it clear. Carragher, born a few miles up the road in Bootle and brought up through the Liverpool ranks, must have thought in those moments of joyful pandemonium of Bill Shankly's claim that the Kop was worth an extra man on European nights.

He must have thought of how St Etienne were overrun here on the way to that first European Cup triumph in 1977.

And he must have begun to dream that Chelsea would be swept aside just like Borussia Moenchengladbach and Juventus have been in other famous Liverpool victories here. He has given more to the Liverpool cause than anyone this season. Only he has played in every single Premiership game, his form never seeming to falter.

His friends are still friends from this city, even if he has moved a few miles north of Bootle to Blundellsands. His values are still theirs. A couple of weeks ago, he recounted a story about how they had poked fun at him mercilessly for acquiring a wallet. It was seen by them as an affectation halfway to wearing a sarong. Carragher played like he was playing for all of them, throwing himself into every tackle, every header, never giving Didier Drogba a sniff.

His reading of the game was faultless, too. Time and again, he stifled danger with a smart interception to the point where Chelsea's frustration began to grow.

Over the two legs, Carragher's contribution more than any other helped to bridge the 33-point chasm that separates these two sides in the Premiership. He knew that this might be his best shot at playing in a European Cup final. He knew it might be his only shot. And he responded accordingly.

When the Kop sang 'You'll Never Walk Alone' again to welcome the players back after the interval, it suddenly seemed clear that if Liverpool were to win, this would be a collective triumph, shared between 42,000 people. A triumph of the will. So Carragher was far from alone. The rest of the Liverpool defence were superb as well. Jerzy Dudek produced one outstanding save from a Frank Lampard free-kick, Steve Finnan was meticulous. Djimi Traore was uncharacteristically and whole-heartedly brilliant, Sami Hyypia was commanding.

Infused by the spirit of the evening, they responded to ghosts of Shankly and Bob Paisley and the lingering spirit of Dalglish and Keegan, Hansen and Lawrenson. On other nights that might sound trite and wide-eyed but how else can you explain what happened here last night? How else can you explain it other than to say that Carragher and company are heading to Istanbul, transported there by the greatness that this ground still holds in its pores.

Justice for the 96
– Luke Traynor, Liverpool Echo, 2009

Nearly 30,000 people flocked to Anfield for the best-attended Hillsborough memorial service ever seen.

In a day of high emotion, fans packed all sides of Liverpool's famous ground on yesterday's 20th anniversary to honour the 96 football fans who lost their lives.

As feelings ran high, Secretary of State for Culture, Media and Sport Andy Burnham had to temporarily halt his speech as passionate chants of 'Justice For The 96' rang down from the Kop.

The numbers who flooded into Anfield were staggering, beating all estimations and dwarfing the previous best memorial service attendance of 10,000.

Twenty minutes before the service began, representatives from Celtic FC lay a huge You'll Never Walk Alone green banner on the field to tumultuous applause.

It was followed by ovations for the Hillsborough families who took their seats in the middle of the Kop.

Minutes later, they were followed by the Liverpool FC players, manager Rafa Benitez and staff, led out by goalkeeper Pepe Reina, after Tuesday night's heroic exit to Chelsea in the Champions League quarter-final.

The Bishop of Liverpool, the Rt Rev James Jones, told the crowd the Queen had sent a message and her thoughts and prayers were with them. He said the tragedy "broke the heart but not the spirit" of the Liverpool community.

At around 3pm, each of the 96 names were read out, accompanied by a peal of a bell and the lighting of a candle for each victim.

It was followed by an impeccably-observed two minute silence, as the bells of the city's cathedrals, churches and civil buildings could be heard ringing across Liverpool.

A host of former players and well-known city figures attended the service including John Barnes, Kenny Dalglish, Everton manager David Moyes, former FA chief executive and Reds fan Brian Barwick, and past players including Alan Kennedy, Gerry Byrne,

David Fairclough and Ron Yeats.

Trevor Hicks, president of the Hillsborough Family Support Group, who lost his two teenage daughters, told the huge audience: "We've never seen a turnout like this before.

"If ever the government, past or present, needs proof of the need for justice, just look around the stadium today.

"We've people here from Merseyside, the rest of the UK, Sweden and messages of support from Greece, South Africa and a great big tapestry was delivered yesterday from Australia.

"We are all here today to remember the 96 men, women and children who did not come home from a game of football on a beautiful, sunny day in Sheffield.

"They were 96 real people, our kin, our flesh and blood, real people who did not come home from a football game.

"I would like to publicly salute you for the way we have borne that loss, often in the glare of hostile publicity, but here we are 20 years on, still together.

"Despite all the odds, we are still determined, still with dignity to ensure that truth will defeat the lies and propaganda."

It was also revealed that a small memorial service was currently being held "in the dark" in Natal, South Africa, on a hill called The Spion Kop, from which Liverpool's famous stand takes its name.

Liverpool Lord Mayor Cllr Steve Rotheram, who was at Hillsborough, told the Anfield crowd: "Local residents in Sheffield opened up their houses so people could phone loved ones back home.

"The families of the 96 never received that call.

"We will never forget what happened at Hillsborough 20 years ago, we salute the bravery of the Liverpool fans whose actions helped save lives while those charged with ensuring our safety stood idly by and watched.

"We will be eternally grateful to those people of Sheffield who helped us in our darkest hour.

"We will never forgive MacKenzie and the reporting of the Sun newspaper which besmirched our fans and city.

"We as a city will continue to fight for truth and justice. We will never forget the 96."

The crowd rose as Cllr Rotheram and Reds boss Rafa Benitez walked on to the pitch to symbolically lay a scarf.

They were followed by local Liverpool players Steven Gerrard and Jamie Carragher who presented a Freedom of the City scroll to Trevor Hicks, on behalf of all the families.

The service was ended with an emotional rendition of You'll Never Walk Alone by singer Gerry Marsden as 96 red and white balloons were released into the sky. An ovation was also afforded to former Hillsborough Family Support Group frontman Phil Hammond who was unable to attend the service. At the Hillsborough Memorial, on Anfield Road, a sea of flowers and football mementoes completely covered the pavement.

Scarves and shirts from clubs across the country adorned the tributes including mementoes from Everton, Bolton, Blackburn, Celtic, Barcelona, Huddersfield, Newcastle and Inverness Caledonian Thistle.

A verse left by Liverpool performer Bobby Parry read:

Sick twisted person that Kelvin MacKenzie
Creating a stink, a media frenzy
Earning his cash, spewing at dinners
The venom he speaks is only for sinners.

Outside the stadium, Dave Kirk, from Anfield, who attended the service with his young grandson Liam, said: "I was at Hillsborough and it was an awful day.

"I remember it clearly and the service was very moving. When I was sitting in the crowd, I had a tear in my eye, it's always there.

"I was a little unsure of the politics, but we do like to be heard and that's OK too."

Andy Reeve, from Norfolk, said: "We came up after stopping at Hillsborough to lay flowers.

"We've been overwhelmed by the support for the 96 and to see the stadium so full was wonderful.

"It's important to pay our respects to the people and families who still suffer. We have come through our love of Liverpool Football Club."

Historic link to the Kop moves closer
– Liverpool Echo, 2009

Liverpool could be twinned with the South African town where scores of Merseyside soldiers died during the historic battle of Spion Kop. Liverpool FC's Kop stand was named after the Boer War battleground in 1906, after a journalist reported how the newly-built steep terrace at Anfield reminded him of the Spion Kop hill.

Now a proposal is set to be put forward to Liverpool council for a permanent twinning with Ladysmith, where more than 300 men, many of them from Liverpool, died as the British army attempted to capture the strategic hilltop.

Opposition leader Joe Anderson is behind the proposal, along with the suggestion Liverpool FC also erect a plaque on the Kop to those who died during the battle.

There is already a plaque in memory of the 96 who died during the Hillsborough disaster at the original Spion Kop hill.

The Spion Kop End

You'll Never Walk Alone

When you walk through a storm,
Hold your head up high,
And don't be afraid of the dark.
At the end of the storm,
There's a golden sky,
And the sweet silver song of a lark.
Walk on through the wind,
Walk on through the rain,
Though your dreams be tossed and blown.
Walk on, walk on,
With hope in your heart,
And you'll never walk alone,
You'll never walk alone.
Walk on, walk on,
With hope in your heart,
And you'll never walk alone,
You'll never walk alone.

Richard Rogers and Oscar Hammerstein II wrote the original in 1945 for Broadway musical play Carousel.

It has since been covered by a whole host of artists all over the world including: Louis Armstrong, Chet Atkins, Shirley Bassey, Glen Campbell, Ray Charles, Perry Como, Michael Crawford, Placido Domingo, Aretha Franklin, Judy Garland, Marilyn Horne, Mahalia Jackson, Patti LaBelle, Cleo Laine, Mario Lanza, Darlene Love, Jim Nabors, Olivia Newton John, Pink Floyd, Elvis Presley, The Righteous Brothers, Nina Simone, Frank Sinatra, Kiri Te Kanawa, Conway Twitty and Dionne Warwick.

But it was version that Gerry and the Pacemakers released in October '63 that the Kop took as their own and subsequently became the anthem of Liverpool Football Club.

In 1985 a recording of the song by pop and rock stars was released to raise money for the victims of the Bradford City fire disaster when 56 supporters lost their lives and almost 300 were injured after a fire at Valley Parade.

The song stayed at number one in the charts for most of the summer and hundreds of thousands of pounds were raised.

The Fields of Anfield Road

Outside the Shankly Gates,
I heard a Kopite calling.
Shankly they have taken you away,
But you left a great eleven,
Before you went to heaven ,
Now it's glory 'round the Fields of Anfield Road.

All 'round the Fields of Anfield Road,
Where once we watched the King Kenny play (And could he play),
Stevie Heighway on the wing,
We had dreams and songs to sing,
Of the glory 'round the Fields of Anfield Road.

Outside the Paisley Gates,
I heard a Kopite calling,
Paisley they have taken you away,
You led the great eleven,
Back in Rome in '77,
And the Redmen they're still playing the same way.

A re-write of the Irish folk-song 'Fields of Athenry', Liverpool's most popular current song was written in the 1995/96 season.

Again, the original was slightly different from the version that is sung now.

The first line of the chorus was originally 'Oh Ohh the Field of Anfield Road' rather than the 'All 'round the fields of Anfield Road' that we all know and sing today.

The 'And could he play' shout at the end of the second line was only added later and was originally 'And he could play'.

'Stevie Heighway on the wing' is also sung by the vast majority now, although originally it was written as 'We had Heighway on the wing'.

There's also been a few subtle changes to the first verse over time while the second verse was only added at a later date.

* * *

It's the off-the-cuff chants, the funny one liners that have made the Kop stand out from other crowds over the years. The Kop's sense of humour is unique. The hilarious and often crude put-downs that have rolled down from the Kop during its hey-day wouldn't be found anywhere else.

It's not simply a case of the old 'every Scouser's a comedian' cliché. If that was true then there'd be the same tales to tell from Goodison Park. There aren't. Every ground has witnessed its funny moments but few like the Kop did.

Remember these?

Who's Up Mary Brown (to the tune of 'Knees Up Mother Brown' and sung to Tommy Docherty after it was revealed he was having an affair with the wife of a United physio, Mary Brown)

Don't Cry for Me Tina, Tina, (sung to Peter Shilton after an encounter with a woman called Tina)

There's only one Blackpool Tower and What's the weather like up there? (sung to 6ft 7in striker Kevin Francis)

There's only one Freddie Boswell (sung to Liverpool chairman David Moores as he opened the Centenary Stand in 1992)

Denis Law, Denis Law is it true what Shankly says, you're sixty-four? (sung to a laughing Denis Law shortly before he retired)

Binman, binman, what's the score? (sung to former Llandudno binman Neville Southall when Liverpool were winning on derby day)

Are you City in disguise? (sung in ironic fashion, as it was originally their chant, to Man United fans during a 3-1 defeat at Anfield in 2001)

Elvis, Elvis, give us a song (sung to Fulham's Elvis Hammond in 2003)

Oh Charlton, Charlton, I'd walk a million miles to the end of your neck, oh Charlton (sung, to the tune of Al Johnson's 'My Mammy', to Jack Charlton when he played at Anfield for Leeds)

Go back to Italee, go back to Italee and Ee-aye-addio, Mussolini's dead (both sung during Inter Milan '65)

Are you watching Mrs Wark? (after John Wark had been struck in the groin during a match)

One Kevin Scully, there's only one Kevin Scully (sung during the filming of 'Scully' at half-time in front of the Kop)

*Freddie Laker, Freddie Laker, Bruce is better in the air
(sung when Bruce Grobbelaar caught a shot in a game
shortly after Freddie Laker's Laker Airways went bust
owing £270 million in 1982)*

*Where did you get them boots? (sung to Tommy Smith when he
appeared in white boots)*

*Thank you very much for paying a million, thank you very much,
thank you very, very much (sung during Ronnie Whelan's
testimonial against Newcastle after Kevin Keegan had paid
£1 million for Liverpool keeper Mike Hooper)*

*The Esso sign means happy motoring... (a famous TV advert in
the '60s, it was sung when Petrolul Ploesti, a team from the
Romanian oil country, walked out on to the Anfield pitch in 1966)*

*What a waste of money (sung to inspirational free transfer
signing Gary McAllister during his last game for Liverpool)*

*Stayed on the telly, you should've stayed on the telly... (sung to
new Newcastle manager Alan Shearer when his team lost at
Anfield before being relegated at the end of the 2008-09 season)*

*Taxed in the morning, you're getting taxed in the morning... (sung
to Spurs manager Harry Redknapp in January 2010 after he was
charged with tax evasion)*

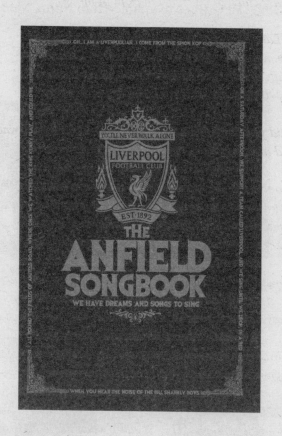

THE ANFIELD SONGBOOK

*The official collection from Liverpool FC.
A complete compilation of songs and chants from the best
football fans in the world. Published by TM Sport Media*

*On sale July, 2010, priced £9.99
To order, call 0845 143 0001 or www.merseyshop.com*

Other LFC titles available from Sport Media:

£16.99

The special relationship
between LFC and Ireland

£14.99

Revisiting the unsung life
and diary of Liverpool's
greatest scout

£9.99

Gerrard's unique insight into being
Liverpool captain – paperback

£14.99

Learn to play like your
Liverpool heroes

To buy any of these titles, or for a great range of Shankly and LFC books,
photographs and more, visit www.merseyshop.com or call 0845 143 0001

Sport Media

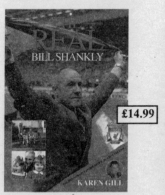

£14.99

Story of Bill Shankly as
told by his family.
Paperback edition only

£3.99

Glossy magazine special
celebrating 50th anniversary of
Shankly's arrival at Anfield

£20

The players' stories behind
the pictures

£20

Story of Bob Paisley as
told by his family

To buy any of these titles, or for a great range of Shankly and LFC books,
photographs and more, visit www.merseyshop.com or call 0845 143 0001